Great Flicks

Great Flicks

Scientific Studies of Cinematic
Creativity and Aesthetics

Dean Keith Simonton

UNIVERSITY PRESS

2011

OXFORD

UNIVERSITY PRESS

Oxford University Press, Inc., publishes works that further
Oxford University's objective of excellence in
research, scholarship, and education.

Oxford New York
Auckland   Cape Town   Dar es Salaam   Hong Kong   Karachi
Kuala Lumpur   Madrid   Melbourne   Mexico City   Nairobi
New Delhi   Shanghai   Taipei   Toronto

With offices in
Argentina   Austria   Brazil   Chile   Czech Republic   France   Greece
Guatemala   Hungary   Italy   Japan   Poland   Portugal   Singapore
South Korea   Switzerland   Thailand   Turkey   Ukraine   Vietnam

Published by Oxford University Press, Inc.
198 Madison Avenue, New York, New York 10016

www.oup.com

Oxford is a registered trademark of Oxford University Press, Inc.

Library of Congress Cataloging-in-Publication Data
Simonton, Dean Keith.
Great flicks : scientific studies of cinematic creativity and aesthetics / by Dean Keith Simonton.
p. cm.
Includes bibliographical references and index.
ISBN 978-0-19-975203-4
1. Motion pictures. 2. Motion pictures—Aesthetics. 3. Creation (Literary, artistic, etc.) I. Title.
PN1995.S498 2010
791.4301—dc22   2010009152

9 8 7 6 5 4 3 2 1
Printed in the United States of America
on acid-free paper

**To Kazie,
my film companion**

Preface

This book came about as the result of a serendipitous event. Since 1975 I've been churning out hundreds of publications on genius, creativity, and aesthetics. Over those years, I would study outstanding creators and creations in science, psychology, philosophy, fiction, drama, poetry, painting, sculpture, classical music, and even opera—but absolutely nothing about cinema. Moreover, since 1990 I've been teaching a popular course on "Genius, Creativity, and Leadership." Yet not once did I ever discuss cinematic creativity or aesthetics. And then one day a student asked, in quest of a term paper topic, "What about film?" Indeed, what about film? After all, isn't it a form of creativity? Can't there be a cinematic genius? Doesn't cinema deserve its own empirical aesthetics? At once I realized that the question was a good one. I also recognized that I could not give an equally good answer. Surely I had done no research on the matter. Nor was I familiar with much relevant research. Published studies could be counted on the fingers of one hand. So bad was the ignorance that the poor student had to change to another topic for his term paper. He wanted to write a review and critique of the research, but there wasn't enough published in scientific journals that was worth reviewing and critiquing.

Hence, I set to work, methodically compiling a huge database on literally thousands of films. The earliest films dated from the late 1920s and about 200 new ones were added annually. For each film, I recorded tons of information, at least to the extent that the data were available. In 2002 the first analysis of this database was published, and many other investigations were published since then. These articles appeared in such scientific journals as *Psychology of Aesthetics, Creativity and the Arts*, the *Journal of Creative Behavior*, the *Creativity Research Journal*, *Empirical Studies of the Arts*, and even *Sex Roles*, the *Journal of Applied Social Psychology*, *Psychology and Marketing*, and the *Journal of the Royal Statistical Society*. I also began to present my findings at professional meetings in North America and Europe.

In addition, I did everything in my power to read every pertinent scientific study, no matter what the discipline. So I've poured through journals in sociology, economics, management, marketing, communications, journalism, broadcasting, history, musicology, statistics, and, naturally, psychology. I cast a wide net because the subject has a broad interest. The only restriction on the scope was that the study had to be *scientific* and that it had to have some relevance to the question of *cinematic creativity and aesthetics*. By "creativity" I mean the processes that yield creative cinema, and by "aesthetics" I mean the processes that lead us to judge a film to be creative. A film is deemed "creative" if it claims both novelty and impact. It's new and it works.

These restrictions aside, I hope that this book can reach the broadest possible audience. Judging from theater attendance and DVD rentals, a respectable number of people are interested in film. And many of these moviegoers have probably asked themselves, "What makes a great flick?" This volume should provide some answers.

Contents

Great Flicks

Chapter 1

Prologue: Scientist as Cinema Connoisseur?

Cinema began as means of inexpensive diversion in the late 19th century. This embryonic era of silent shorts is perhaps epitomized by the nickelodeon theaters of the early 20th century, where this newfangled amusement literally cost a nickel. Yet, within a couple of decades the medium had progressed into a major form of artistic expression. This elevation in cultural status was already apparent in 1929 when the Motion Picture Academy of Arts and Sciences initiated the annual "Oscar" ceremonies in California's Hollywood. This occasion was followed three years later by the first Venice Film Festival, the oldest such event still to take place. And in 1936 the New York Film Critics Circle bestowed their first awards—more than a decade before the first Tony Awards were created to honor excellence in American theatre. The medium had evolved from brief diversions to serious feature-length creations. Film had become the "seventh art," after painting, sculpture, architecture, music, dance, and poetry.

Eventually, too, film became the legitimate subject of scholarship. Over time, universities became well stocked with courses in film studies and even whole film schools. Moreover, numerous professional journals and organizations emerged that were specifically devoted to the topic. The phenomenon also came to inspire an ample output of scholarly books treating various aspects of cinematic creativity and aesthetics. As a psychologist I cannot resist pointing out that members of my own discipline were quick to make noteworthy contributions to the growing literature. For example, in 1916 Hugo Münsterberg published *The Photoplay: A Psychological Study*, and in the 1930s Rudolf Arnheim began a series of articles that were later compiled into the volume *Film as Art*. The former book is often considered the first attempt at film theory, and the latter is considered a classic in the field of cinema aesthetics.

In due course the informed judgment of cinema connoisseurs led to the promulgation of various enumerations of the all-time masterworks in the form. A case in point is the American Film Institute's list of the "top 100 American movies of the last 100 years." AFI's ranking begins with *Citizen Kane* (1941), then *Casablanca* (1942), *The Godfather* (1972), and *Gone with the Wind* (1939), and ends with *Bringing Up Baby* (1938), *Unforgiven* (1992), *Guess Who's Coming to Dinner* (1967), and then, in the 100th spot, *Yankee Doodle Dandy* (1942). Such films are presumed to represent a canon comparable to "top plays," "best novels," "classic paintings," or "greatest operas." In this view, *Citizen Kane*'s artistic standing parallels that of Shakespeare's *Hamlet*, Tolstoy's *War and Peace*, Picasso's *Guernica*, or Wagner's *The Ring of the Nibelungen*—all masterpieces in a specific mode of artistic creativity.

Notwithstanding the gradual attainment of this lofty position, the movies still offer a prominent vehicle for mass entertainment. Just as select pieces of popular music ascend to the top of the billboard charts, attaining gold or platinum status, so certain movies attain the position of blockbusters—some even breaking all previous box-office records. It is this aspect of the form that renders it a most financially lucrative form of artistic expression: A highly successful movie can earn a few hundred million in US dollars. For example, *Titanic* (1997) grossed over $600 million in the United States alone, and it took in over a billion dollars abroad. In all, *Titanic* earned one seventh of the total world box office received by more than 600 movies released the same year. Such exorbitant profits provide hefty incomes for those who are directly involved in filmmaking, especially the producer moguls and the hottest movie stars. By the beginning of the 21st century an A-list actor could earn $20 million or more per film—an amount exceeding the total production costs for many medium-budget movies.

The movie business obviously supports many peripheral beneficiaries, such as the innumerable journalists reporting on the private lives of the industry's rich and famous. Examples include the writers who contributed to *Photoplay*, a fan magazine that debuted in 1911 and that eventually included the writings of such notables as Hedda Hopper, Dorothy Kilgallen, Louella Parsons, Adela Rogers St. Johns, and Walter Winchell. But more substantial from this book's perspective are the film critics who review the latest releases. In the United States alone this role is fulfilled by several dozen reviewers. Some of these critics even attain fame in their own right. The most conspicuous example is Roger Ebert, the reviewer for the *Chicago Sun-Times* and co-host of a long-running television show featuring thumbnail critiques and thumbs-up/thumbs-down verdicts. In 1975 he became the first to win a Pulitzer Prize for Criticism, and 30 years later he became the first film critic to receive a star on the Hollywood Walk of Fame.

Not surprisingly, given its widespread impact and popularity, the movies have made permanent contributions to modern culture. People distributed all across the globe will likely recognize the line "Go ahead. Make my day" from *Dirty Harry* (1971), the shark's theme from *Jaws* (1975), the voice of Darth Vader from *Star Wars* (1977), or the visage of Marlon Brando in the title role of *The Godfather* (1972). Certainly uncountable are all the film posters that decorate bars, restaurants, and bedrooms with classic Hollywood images. Moreover, with the arrival of the World Wide Web, thousands of Web sites proliferated that are devoted to various aspects of film and those involved in filmmaking. Perhaps the most well-known example is the massive Internet Movie Database located at www.imdb.com—a treasure chest of facts both substantial and trivial.

Many of those involved in movies—whether filmmakers or aficionados, journalists or critics—operate according an implicit or explicit assumption: It is possible to identify something that might be called a "great flick." Some films are really bad, others passable, still others reasonably good, and a privileged few are unquestionably great. Thus, the Oscar for best picture sets the winning film above its fellow nominees, just as nomination for that honor distinguishes the latter films from the dozens nominated for more specialized awards in the same year. Likewise, critics will usually assign stars to their reviews, stars that indicate relative magnitude of cinematic success. A five-star film may count among the best ever, while a "turkey" or "bomb" might be allotted no star at all. Even box-office performance in some loose manner reflects how potential moviegoers judge what movies are worth seeing more than once versus what are not worth seeing at all. Yet regardless of the particular assessment, it is pertinent ask: What separates superb cinema from the mediocre, and the mediocre from the dreadful?

Oddly, with the exception of box-office success, comparatively little scientific research has been dedicated to addressing this issue. In drawing this unfortunate conclusion I must emphasize the adjective *scientific*. So before we can continue, it is first necessary to describe what I mean by this term.

Science

Most of the research in film studies originates in the humanities. The contributions consist of insightful essays that examine a diversity of questions. Far less common are investigations that can be considered scientific in a strict sense. By "scientific" I mean a study that is abstract, systematic, objective, and quantitative. To illustrate, suppose that an investigator wanted to learn whether a film's critical acclaim was related to its box-office success. The specific hypothesis might be that the two are negatively correlated—that the critics pan the Hollywood blockbusters while heaping praise on foreign films that earn a pittance on the art house circuit. The first step would be to gather a sample of representative movies. For example, the sample might consist of all feature-length, narrative films released between 2000 and 2006 that were reviewed by all critics writing for wide-circulation newspapers and magazines in the United States. The critics' separate evaluations could then be averaged to produce an overall assessment of critical acclaim, and box-office performance could be assessed in terms of gross US returns. The two numbers could then be correlated. If that correlation is negative, the hypothesis would be confirmed. If not, then it would have to be rejected.

Scientific research has other assets to provide an objective thumbs-up-versus-thumbs-down answer. For instance, another advantage is that these methods allow us to determine the magnitude of the relation. Is the negative association between box office and critical acclaim so strong that no exceptions are allowed? Or, is the correlation weak enough that the critics can occasionally heap high praise on some big-studio blockbusters while categorically condemning some low-budget indie films? At various places in this book we will encounter other distinctive virtues of taking a scientific approach to film studies. These virtues provide a key justification for devoting a whole volume to just these kinds of studies.

But right now we should turn to the substantive issues addressed by the research reviewed in this book.

Issues

In this volume I will examine several interrelated topics. Chapter 2 begins the discussion by looking at whether various movie awards and critical evaluations concur on the relative merits of feature films. For example, do the Oscars agree or disagree with the judgments represented by the Golden Globes, the New York Film Critics Circle Awards, the awards bestowed by the British Association of Film and Television Arts, and the diverse honors conferred by numerous guild organizations? Chapter 3 then uses movie awards to determine the cinematic components that most contribute to a film's success. To what degree is a film's greatness contingent on its dramatic, visual, technical, and musical assets? Chapter 4 introduces two additional factors into the analysis: production budgets and box-office performance. Does money make the movie? And does a well-made movie make money?

The next four chapters concentrate on specific aspects of the cinematic product: the screenplay (Chapter 5), the direction (Chapter 6), the acting (Chapter 7), and the music (Chapter 8). Can we identify attributes of the script that predict cinematic success? To what extent does the director influence the quality of the final product? Does the impact of the actors depend on whether they are male or female? Do cinematic masterpieces contain masterful music?

Chapter 9 then switches to the question of whether the factors that predict a film's success also can be used to predict a film's failure. Are motion pictures that receive Golden Raspberry Awards—the infamous "Razzies"—the inverse image of those that receive the much-coveted Oscars? Does a bad movie do everything wrong that a good movie does right?

Chapter 10 then wraps everything up by detailing the strengths and weaknesses of a science of cinema.

Caveat

Before we begin our survey of the research findings, I should specify a major restriction on the scope of the forthcoming inquiries. Cinema is a highly diversified medium of artistic expression. Some films are feature length, running two or three hours and even more; others are shorts with running times far less than an hour, and even less than ten minutes. Some are documentaries that attempt to convey information or images; others are narratives that try to tell a story with a beginning, middle, and end (even if disassembled and rearranged, as in the 2000 *Memento*). Some use live action, others animation. And some are delivered in the English language while others are spoken in any of a large number of the world's languages, even including dead languages like Latin and Aramaic, as in Mel Gibson's 2004 *The Passion of the Christ*. Then, if you generate all possible permutations of these forms, the multiplicity of types becomes overwhelming.

Clearly, if the goal is to determine the recipe for cinematic greatness, a heterogeneous sample will not work. A short will not be judged by the same criteria as a feature, nor will a documentary be evaluated by the same standards as a narrative film. And animated characters cannot be assessed by the same rules as real flesh-and-blood actors on the silver screen. Although in theory language should not make any difference, in practice it has to. Seeing a film in your native tongue will always be a different aesthetic experience than seeing the same film in a foreign tongue either dubbed or subtitled. Indeed, most major award organizations draw a sharp distinction between native- and foreign-language films, assigning many more awards in the former case. This is as true of the Oscars and Golden Globes in the United States as it is true of the César Awards in France or the Goya Awards in Spain.

As a consequence, the scientific studies reported in this book will concentrate on English-language, live-action, feature-length narrative films. It is this specific type of film that currently dominates the worldwide market. This restricted category has also attracted by far the most scientific research. Admittedly, this restriction leaves out a large number of truly great films, including many of my own personal favorites like *Les Parapluies de Cherbourg* (1964), *Fantasia* (1940), and *Koyaanisqatsi* (1982), just to name a few. But to adopt more inclusive samples would render any findings meaningless. There are actually several kinds of great film. It is for this reason that many critical and professional organizations retain separate award categories for shorts, documentaries, animations, and foreign-language films. And as we will learn in later chapters, what remains after excluding these categories still represents a rich array of cinematic products.

Chapter 2

Oscars, Golden Globes, and Critics: Consensus or Dissension?

When the first Academy Awards were bestowed in 1929, it was an amazingly small affair: a private banquet held in the Blossom Room of the Hollywood Roosevelt Hotel, hosted by actor Douglas Fairbanks and producer William Cecil de Mille. The brief ceremony—just 15 minutes!—was devoid of suspense. The award winners had already been announced three months earlier. Moreover, by today's standards the number of awards and nominations was very small. But in subsequent years the ceremony underwent a striking expansion in scope and splendor, becoming a major media event broadcast across the globe. The number of awards and nominations has appreciably grown as well, rendering it a more finely differentiated indicator of cinematic achievements. The thrill of the occasion has also been heightened considerably, the victors kept super-secret until some celebrity opens the fateful envelope on Oscar night. As a result of this dramatic transformation, it is likely that anyone reading this book has seen at least one televised ceremony.

Frills and hype aside, these awards and nominations should have considerable prima facie merit. After all, the Academy of Motion Picture Arts and Sciences boasts a membership consisting of some of the most outstanding figures in the movie business. Furthermore, the selection criteria and voting procedures are now conducted under a strict set of rules that are available for anyone to see on the Internet. Certainly it can be said that winning an Oscar or procuring a nomination confers considerable status upon the recipient. This status often translates directly into higher pay on future films as well as the opportunity to work on better film projects. How many workers in the film industry would omit an Academy nod or Oscar win on their job résumé?

Yet according to unofficial histories, the Oscar allotments are often subject to behind-the-scenes political maneuverings, advertising campaigns, and other arbitrary events. As a result, film fans and experts alike have often felt obliged to second guess the Academy's decisions. In fact, the New York Film Critics Circle (NYFCC) awards began in 1935 precisely as an antidote to the Academy awards, which the New York City critics thought were distorted by studio intrigues and Hollywood provincial tastes. In their inaugural set of awards, these NYC critics selected RKO's *The Informer* for best picture, in contrast to the Academy's choice of MGM's *Mutiny on the Bounty*. Although they agreed on best director—John Ford for *The Informer*—they disagreed on the acting awards. For best female lead, the Oscar went to Bette Davis in *Dangerous*, but the NYFCC Award to Greta Garbo in *Anna Karenina*. And for best male lead, Victor McLaglen received the Academy Award for his performance in *The Informer* but Charles Laughton received the critics' award for his performance in *Mutiny on the Bounty*. In a way, the male acting awards were switched with the picture awards.

Nor are the critics the only ones offering competing awards. In 1944 the Hollywood Foreign Press Association launched its own annual awards— the Golden Globes—to interject a more international perspective on the year's cinematic honors. Just a handful of years later, the British Film Academy of Film began bestowing the awards that eventually became known as the BAFTAs (for British Academy of Film and Television Arts). A medley of additional awards was also offered by guilds and societies organized by more specialized professions. For example, in 1949 the Directors Guild of America offered its first award for outstanding direction in a designated motion picture—an award granted to Joseph L. Mankiewicz for *A Letter to Three Wives*. With the passage of time these more restricted honors would extend to every major award category covered by the Academy.

The proliferation of alternative awards raises a crucial question: Are these rival honors complementary to the Oscars? Or do they seriously undercut Academy credibility? Do the diverse awards exhibit a clear consensus or do they diverge so much as to display dissenting opinions? Happily, scientific research has been conducted on this question. I cannot say more—no spoilers allowed!

Oscar Quality

In 2004 I published an empirical investigation designed to address four related questions. First, do all of the award categories exhibit a conspicuous consensus across major organizations that bestow awards comparable to the Academy's? If so, do the Oscars provide the best single indicator of that overall consensus? Second, do the awards and nominations given by general organizations correlate with more specialized awards granted by professional guilds and societies? If so, do the Oscars usually display the tightest congruence with those more narrowly conceived honors? Third, do the Oscar awards have meaningful predictive value about cinematic achievement beyond that provided by Oscar nominations alone? Do we really have to pay attention to the outcome of Oscar night or do the nominations announced much earlier say it all? Fourth, are the awards and nominations handed out by broad-based organizations congruent with the evaluations of critics? If so, do the Oscars show the highest correspondence?

These questions were addressed using a sample of movies that met four conditions: First, the film had to receive a nomination or an award in at least one of the following 17 categories: picture, directing, screenplay or writing (whether original or adapted script), male lead actor, female lead actor, male supporting actor, female supporting actor, cinematography (or photography), art direction (and perhaps set decoration), costume design, makeup (with or without hair), film editing, score, song, visual effects, sound effects editing, and sound (or sound mixing). These categories accommodate all of the major contributions germane to the evaluation of most films. In contrast, the study ignored such ephemeral or overly-specialized categories as first film, independent picture, experimental film, specialized film, motion picture promoting international understanding, most promising newcomer, break-through performance by a male or female actor, juvenile performance, and so forth. By definition, these awards have no relevance to judging most films. For better or worse, few films display a break-through performance, and fewer still make any attempt to promote international understanding.

Second, the nomination or award had to be conferred by one of the following seven organizations:

1. The Academy of Motion Picture Arts and Sciences (AMPAS)—founded in 1927, with membership now exceeding 6,500 artists and experts; bestows what have become known (both popularly and officially) as the "Oscars."
2. The Hollywood Foreign Press Association (HFPA)—founded in 1943 (with television added in 1956); current membership includes over 80 movie journalists representing almost 50 nations; bestows the "Golden Globes."
3. The British Academy of Film and Television Arts (BAFTA)—founded in 1947 (adding television in 1958); has over 5,000 individuals actively involved in either film or television production; awards sometimes called the "BAFTAs."

4. The New York Film Critics Circle (NYFCC)—founded in 1935; strictly print-only film critics who write for such NYC-based publications as *Newsweek*, *Time*, *The New Yorker*, the *New York Times*, *Entertainment Weekly*, and *Rolling Stone*.
5. The National Board of Review (NBR)—founded in 1909, with awards beginning in 1932; membership consists of teachers, actors, writers, and workers in film production; publishes the magazine *Films in Review*.
6. The National Society of Film Critics (NSFC)—founded in 1966, awards began in 1967; 55 leading critics from major US publications and media outlets.
7. The Los Angeles Film Critics Association (LAFCA)—founded in 1975; over 50 critics in the L.A. area who review movies for newspapers, magazines, television, and online media.

At the time of the investigation, the above seven organizations had been in existence for at least a quarter century and had consistently granted annual awards in most if not all of the major categories. The seven also focus on widely-distributed motion pictures and represent a range of judgments on cinematic contributions and achievements.

Third, for reasons expressed at the end of Chapter 1, the sample was further confined to English-language, live-action, feature-length narrative films. That criterion deleted all animations, all shorts, all documentaries, and all films in a language other than English. The latter condition even excludes US, British, or Australianfilms that use a non-English tongue as the primary vehicle for dialogue and narration. Thus, Mel Gibson's 2004 *The Passion of the Christ* and 2006 *Apocalypto* would not be allowed in the sample, even were these admitted by the next standard.

Fourth, all films had to have been released between 1975 and 2002. The sample began with the 1975 release date because that was when the Los Angeles Film Critics Association began presenting its awards. The closing date was simply the latest date that could accommodate data collection and analysis for an investigation published in 2004. Hence, the sample began with the year that saw *One Flew Over the Cuckoo's Nest, Nashville,* and *Barry Lyndon,* and ended with the year that witnessed *The Hours, Chicago,* and *The Pianist.*

The preceding four restrictions did not produce a small sample. On the contrary, fully 1,132 films qualified for inclusion in the study. That is a larger sample than usually seen in psychology and kindred behavioral sciences. It's even larger than many other studies of cinematic creativity and aesthetics. This gives us more "elbow room" for addressing the four questions raised earlier.

Agreements and Alternatives

To address the first issue, we need quantitative measures of nominations and awards received in each category and for each organization. Here, and in many other places in this book, we will adopt a very simple measurement rule. A film will get 2 points if it receives an award, 1 point if it only receives a nomination, and 0 points if it receives neither an award nor a nomination. For instance, at the 1997 Academy Award ceremony, the Oscar for best picture went to *The English Patient*, with best picture nominations going to *Fargo*, *Jerry Maguire*, *Secrets & Lies*, and *Shine*. Therefore, the variable "best picture Oscar" equals 2 for the first film, equals 1 for the four other nominated films, while all other films in the sample from that same award year get a 0 for this specific variable. Expressed differently, a film gets 1 point for a nomination and 1 extra point if the nomination leads to an outright award. No points if neither.

This coding scheme is extremely crude. In essence, it assumes that getting an award distinguishes a film from getting a nomination by the same magnitude as getting a nomination distinguishes a film from not getting any nomination in that particular category. Given that most films will not receive any nomination at all, it is easily argued that getting a nomination is much more difficult than getting an award. However, this measurement procedure was adopted for three reasons.

First, and most obviously, it is very easy to apply. Quantification using integers is always easier than quantification using decimal fractions. Scaling is reduced to counting distinct events, to wit, nominations and awards.

Second, when this scheme is applied to highly select samples such as this one—films nominated for at least one award from a major organization—it provides a reasonable approximation to a regular measure. About 200 English-language, live-action, feature-length narrative films enjoy fairly wide distribution in US movie theaters, but fewer than half of these obtain a nod for some major award category from an important organization. For this elite set, a 0-1-2 coding usually yields higher correlations with other pertinent variables than does any other integer alternative (e.g., 0-1-1 or 0-2-3). Stated differently, the consequence of going from a nomination to a win is about the same as getting the nomination in the first place.

Third and last, a commonplace principle of measurement in the social sciences is that "it don't make no nevermind." That is, a wide range of measurement schemes will pretty much yield the same general conclusions. Indeed, this principle is often witnessed in everyday affairs. When one takes a test of any kind (e.g., to procure a driver's license), all questions are given equal weight regardless of importance (e.g., a question about driving under the influence counts the same as a more trivial question about parallel parking). Similarly, the inferences drawn here and elsewhere in this volume are not at the mercy of this particular coding scheme. The rough-and-ready indicator does about as well as a more fussy measure.

Given the foregoing measures, we can then create *composite measures* for each of the award categories. For example, the composite measure for best picture award would consist of the sum of the scores received from the seven organizations. Such a measure could range from 0 (no best picture nominations or awards from any of the organizations) to 14 (an award in that category from all seven organizations). This range applied to not just best picture honors, but also to the directing award and the four acting awards (male and female lead, male and female supporting). Other award categories were not recognized by all seven organizations. In particular, screenplay had only six; cinematography, five; score, four; and song, three. The remaining award categories were recognized by two or less (viz., film editing, art direction, costume design, makeup, visual effects, sound effects editing, and sound mixing). Because the statistical analysis of consensus and dissension required that an honor be bestowed by at least three organizations, these latter awards and nominations were not used in this part of the investigation.

The next task was to assess the degree of consensus among the 10 award indicators with at least three participating organizations. The appropriate statistic to use in this case is the internal-consistency reliability coefficient (sometimes called Cronbach's alpha or α). Preferably, the reliability should be .70 or higher. When this statistic is calculated for the 10 award categories under view, we obtain the results reported in the first column of decimal fractions in Table 2.1.

The most immediate inference is that a substantial consensus exists for virtually all of these measures. For those six award categories recognized by all seven organizations, the reliabilities range from .74 to .78. This degree of reliability is comparable to those seen in the best personality tests used by psychologists. Consider, for example, the reliabilities for the following personality measures: Openness to Experience .73, Agreeableness .75, and Extroversion .78. Even screenplay honors, which is based on six indicators, has a reliability of .73, and song honors, based on only three, has a reliability of .86—the highest of all. In comparison, the consensus is only .66 for cinematography and merely .59 for score. Although these statistics are less impressive, they remain in the same league of many other measures in the behavioral sciences. For instance, the reliability coefficient for assessing the spontaneous emergence of leadership in groups is .62, a figure almost exactly between .59 and .66.

Another way to appreciate the consensus indicated by these reliabilities is based on the fact that the square root of the coefficient provides an estimate

TABLE 2.1   Reliabilities for Composite Measure and Reliabilities When Single Measures Deleted

Award Category	Composite	O	G	B	N	R	S	L
Picture	.76	**.67**	.71	.71	.73	.74	.76	.75
Directing	.78	**.71**	.72	.77	.77	.77	.77	.76
Male lead	.76	**.67**	.73	.73	.73	.76	.75	.72
Female lead	.77	**.69**	.75	.75	.74	.75	.76	.74
Male supporting	.74	**.66**	**.66**	.73	.70	.73	.72	.72
Female supporting	.74	**.65**	.68	.73	.72	.74	.71	.69
Screenplay	.73	**.66**	.67	.71	.70	–	.72	.70
Cinematography	.66	.58	–	**.57**	.64	–	.67	**.57**
Score	.59	.47	**.41**	.49	–	–	–	.63
Song	.86	**.72**	.75	.91	–	–	–	–

Note. Composite measure consists of a count of awards and nominations from all seven organizations. O = Academy of Motion Picture Arts and Sciences (Oscars), G = Hollywood Foreign Press Association (Golden Globes), B = British Academy of Film and Television Arts (BAFTAs), N = New York Film Critics Circle, R = National Board of Review, S = National Society of Film Critics, and L = Los Angeles Film Critics Association. Dashes (–) indicate that an award was not offered by that organization for that particular category of creativity or achievement. Boldface indicates the biggest decline in reliability once that particular indicator is deleted.

of the composite measure's correlation with the *true score*. The latter is the hypothetical score that would be received if there was no measurement error whatsoever (i.e., the actual merit of that particular cinematic achievement). The square root of .59 is .77, which indicates a reasonable degree of correspondence for even the smallest reliability among those calculated. The first column of Table 2.1 provides conclusive confirmation that the consensus among the movie awards is quite substantial. This consensus is especially prominent in the case of the award categories recognized by all seven organizations.

But how do the Oscars fit in with this consensus? I answered this question by seeing what happens when the awards and nominations of a particular organization are deleted from the composite measure. If a given organization displays a strong agreement with the overall consensus, then the reliability coefficient will drop substantially. But if the agreement is much smaller, then deleting the contribution of that organization will have less of an effect—and the reliability might actually increase. This analytical criterion is shown in the remaining columns of Table 2.1. Each column indicates what would happen when that organization's awards and nominations are deleted from the composite score. The reliability coefficients showing the biggest decline are indicated in boldface.

Judging from these results, the awards and nominations bestowed by the Academy of Motion Picture Arts and Sciences are closest to the overall consensus with respect to most categories of cinematic achievement. With the exception of cinematography and score, deleting the Oscars causes the largest drop in the internal-consistency index of reliability. Even in the case of cinematography, the decrement is close to that of the other organizations that exhibit a stronger consensus (BAFTAs and LAFCA). In addition, in not one single category does the omission of the Oscar judgments actually enhance the reliability of the residual composite. That embarrassing fate is reserved for some of the other organizations—most notably the BAFTA's poor showing with respect to best song. Perhaps the Brits have different tastes! (I'm married to one, so I should say "probably" rather than "perhaps.")

The upshot is twofold: First, the consensus among the seven organizations is impressively strong—particularly in the most prestigious categories of cinematic achievement. Second, the Academy Awards most often provide the single best indicator of that consensus. Oscars should be listed on the top of any filmmaker's résumé.

General and Guild Awards

Rather than pit the seven organizations against each other, we can contrast them against a more specialized but still highly prestigious set of awards. In particular, the general awards and nominations can be compared with those of the Directors Guild of America (directing), the Writers Guild of America (screenplay), the Screen Actors Guild (male and female lead, and male and female supporting), the American Society of Cinematographers (cinematography), the Art Directors Guild (art direction), the Costume Designers Guild (costume design), the American Cinema Editors (film editing), and the Grammy Awards (film score and song). The variables were constructed according to the same coding used for the seven major organizations: 2 = an award recipient, 1 = a nomination recipient, and 0 = neither an award nor a nomination recipient. Table 2.2 shows the correlations between the two sets of variables.

In this case, the boldface indicates the largest correlations in each row. The Oscar awards and nominations measures have a patent edge over the other six organizations. They boast the highest correlation in 8 out of the 12 categories, and are tied for first place in one of the categories (female supporting actor). In the remaining three award categories, the Oscars' correlations with the guild honors are not far behind (i.e., a difference of between .01 and .03 decimal points). Finally, it must be pointed out that the correlations between the Oscar measure and the corresponding specialized award are usually fairly large, especially for the six award categories deemed of sufficient significance to be bestowed by all seven general organizations. Moreover, the correlations for the two lead acting awards

TABLE 2.2   Correlations Between Specific Honors And Corresponding Honors In Seven Organization

Specific award	O	G	B	N	R	S	L
Directing (DGA)	**.68**	.57	.39	.09	.22	.15	.31
Screenplay (WGA)	**.71**	.50	.40	.25	.05	.20	.25
Male lead (SAG)	**.82**	.53	.44	.40	.30	.27	.40
Female lead (SAG)	**.87**	.58	.57	.10	.41	.04	.33
Male supporting (SAG)	**.73**	.52	.18	.11	.09	.14	.20
Female supporting (SAG)	.62	**.62**	.41	.22	.09	.27	.20
Cinematography (ASC)	**.74**	–	.41	.11	–	.06	.24
Art direction (ADG)	**.58**	–	.47	–	.16	–	.31
Costume design (CDG)	.18	–	**.19**	–	–	–	–
Film editing (ACE)	**.73**	–	.53	–	–	–	–
Score (Grammy)	.31	.32	**.34**	–	–	–	–
Song (Grammy)	.46	**.48**	–	–	–	–	–

Note. Abbreviations O, G, B, N, R, S, and L defined as in Table 2.1. Dashes (–) indicate that an award was not offered by that organization for that particular category of creativity or achievement. Boldface indicates the highest correlation in each row. DGA = Directors Guild of America, WGA = Writers Guild of America, SAG = Screen Actors Guild, ASC = American Society of Cinematographers, ADG = Art Directors Guild, CDG = Costume Designers Guild, and ACE = American Cinema Editors.

actually exceed the reliability coefficients shown in Table 2.1 for the same cinematic categories.

In any event, it should be apparent that the results presented in Table 2.2 offer additional evidence on behalf of Oscar quality. Not only are the Oscars most representative of the general consensus, at least in the major award categories, but also the Oscars usually correspond more closely to the more specialized honors the films receive from the diverse guild organizations.

Oscar Wins and Nods

Although the Oscars perform quite well relative to other awards, both general and specific, the above two analyses were predicated on the make-shift 0-1-2 scale (i.e., no nomination, just nomination, and outright award). It is conceivable that this scale obscures the fact that most of the Academy success might occur at the nomination phase, whereas receipt of the actual award on Oscar night could be meaningless. This conjecture ensues from the less-than-optimal nomination and voting procedures adopted by the Academy. On the one hand, nominations in most categories are confined to a specific branch of the Academy. For instance, members of the acting branch are solely responsible for nominating candidates in the four acting categories. Hence, the nominations are more comparable to the recognition granted by the guilds. On the other hand, when it comes to voting for the actual winner, the votes are cast by the entire membership regardless of branch. Thus, cinematographers are allowed to vote on best music. Because professional expertise is much less relevant in this decision, the final award may be given for reasons that have less to do the actual quality of a particular cinematic contribution. As an example, those nominated for films that are also up for the best picture award may get an extra boost through some kind of *positive contagion* or *halo effect*. That is, the exalted status of being an overall great film rubs off on the more specialized awards, giving credit where credit is not due. If so, then the awards would have appreciably less validity than the nominations.

To test this conjecture, the nominations and awards were split into two dichotomous 0-1 measures: (a) award = 1 if Oscar, but award = 0 if otherwise and (b) nomination = 1 if nominated, but nomination = 0 if otherwise ("dichotomous" just means that a variable can only have two values, in this case 0 and 1). In addition, a new award composite for each award category was constructed that excluded the Oscar awards and nominations. This composite was based on the honors the film got from the remaining six organizations. The correlations are shown in Table 2.3.

One general inference should be obvious at once: A measure that combines awards and nominations into a single 0-1-2 scale (A+N) is uniformly

TABLE 2.3   Correlations of Oscar Total (A+N), Awards (A), and Nominations (N) with Composite Measures Based on the Remaining Six Award Series

Award category	A+N	A	N
Picture	.71	.48	.68
Directing	.68	.44	.66
Screenplay	.60	.51	.51
Male lead	.72	.54	.15
Female lead	.71	.55	.66
Male supporting	.65	.46	.61
Female supporting	.63	.49	.57
Film editing	.56	.41	.52
Cinematography	.48	.45	.41
Art direction	.53	.40	.49
Costume design	.44	.36	.39
Makeup	.44	.43	.37
Visual effects	.52	.45	.48
Sound	.47	.42	.40
Score	.44	.37	.38
Song	.70	.58	.62

superior to separate indicators of awards (A) and nomination (N) using 0-1 scales. There is not a single exception, albeit sometimes the superiority is somewhat small. Furthermore, although the nomination correlations are more often larger than the award correlations, in five instances the award correlation is equal to or larger than the nomination correlation.

This second finding is remarkable given that the statistical odds are stacked against the award measures. Why do I say that? The 0-1 award measure pits one Oscar-winning film against all other sampled films in the same award year, while the 0-1 nomination measure pits up to five nominated films against the rest. This means that the former has less variation than the latter, which lowers the expected size of the correlations. Correlations shrink, or are attenuated, if the variation is truncated on one or both variables. Correlations gauge covariation, and that means that variables must have variation to covary. More variation, more covariation, more correlation.

The end result of these analyses is clear: Winning an Oscar in a given award category provides almost as much information about the quality of a film as does receiving a nomination in that category. Even though the entire Academy is voting on these awards, its membership is nearly as discriminating as when it picks the nominees from the confines of the more specialized branches.

Movie Awards and Critic Evaluations

All of the previously reported analyses might be subjected to the same complaint: Awards and nominations are being compared to awards and nominations. Making matters worse, the various honors are not completely independent. For instance, an unknown proportion of the membership in the Screen Actors Guild also belongs to the Academy of Motion Picture Arts and Sciences. Perhaps some part of Oscar's good showing can be attributed to this overlap. As a consequence, it would behoove us to introduce a different standard; namely, the evaluations of film critics. It is possible that the Oscars would do less well when judged by this criterion. Indeed, the awards bestowed by the critic organizations—namely the New York Critic Circle, the National Society of Film Critics, and the Los Angeles Film Critics Association—would then seem to enjoy the advantage in such comparisons. But how are we to gauge the assessments of film critics?

The solution in my 2004 study was to use *movie guide ratings*. These are provided by the books that people buy to help them decide what DVD to rent or what TV showing to watch. Previous investigations have shown not only that movie guides agree very highly with each other, but also that these guides agree reasonably well with how films are evaluated by consumers or audiences (see Chapter 4 for more on this point). Here, critical evaluations were assessed using the ratings received in five popular movie/video/DVD guides. In these guides professional movie critics provided some rating system, most often using "stars" (but one using "bones" where zero bones gets a "woof!"). To illustrate, Leonard Matlin's bestselling movie guide assigns 1-4 stars, including half stars, with the exception that a 1-star film is simply identified as an out-and-out "BOMB"—the score rightfully assigned to the 1995 *Showgirls*.

The five ratings were transformed into a quantitative measure by the following procedure. To begin with, whenever necessary, each rating was converted into a 5-point scale in which 1 = "turkey" or "bomb" and 5 = "masterpiece" or "classic" (e.g., if the guide assigned between 0 and 4 stars, then 1 star was added). The five assessments were next averaged to yield a combined measure that also could range from 1 to 5. The average number of stars received was 3.4 (i.e., 3 stars plus two fifths of a star). This indicates that, as a whole, the sampled films are somewhat better than average, where 3 stars would indicate a film in the middle of the pack. This outcome is expected given the sampling criteria. These aren't entirely run-of-the-mill movies.

Yet the full range of scores is still represented. At the top of the scale, with 5 stars, are films like *Annie Hall, One Flew Over the Cuckoo's Nest, Tootsie,* and *E.T. the Extra-Terrestrial.* At the bottom, with only 1 star, are movies like *36 Chowringhee Lane, Jacqueline Susann's Once Is Not Enough, The Other Side of Midnight,* and *The Swarm.* And the latter are movies that earned a nod for *some* cinematic accomplishment from *somebody* important! To give an example, *The Swarm* got an Oscar nod for best costume design. The movie was not only panned by the critics but also flopped at the box office, earning only half of what it cost to make!

Two statistics show that the resulting indicator of movie guide ratings provides an excellent measure of the critics' judgments.

First, the five-item measure of movie guide ratings has an internal-consistency reliability coefficient of .82. Thus, this particular reliability is rather respectable. In fact, it is higher than all of the reliabilities given in Table 2.1, with the exception of that for the song category. It is also higher than the reliability coefficients received by most psychometric instruments, with the exception of general intelligence (which is usually in the .90s). Critics show consensus.

Second, the movie guide ratings correlate .74 with the score that the more recent films received at Metacritic.com. This website summarizes the evaluations of dozens of film critics into a single 100-point scale. Yet unlike the movie guide ratings, which are published after the film comes out in video or DVD, the Metacritic score is based on reviews published during the period of the film's theatrical run. This correlation is quite good—especially when we consider that we are dealing with a select sample. Unfortunately, these scores are only available for films released from 1999 on, and therefore were not suitable for the current investigation, which started with films released in 1975. Even so, because we will exploit the Metacritic summary ratings in later chapters, keep them in mind.

Table 2.4 exhibits the correlation coefficients between these movie guide ratings and the award and nominations granted by the seven general organizations. Boldface is again used to pinpoint the highest correlations in each row. Looking at these highlighted correlations should lead to one overall inference: These statistics are somewhat lower than seen in earlier tables. This reduction is to be expected because the size of the correlation is affected by the frequency distributions of the two variables. The correlation tends to be higher when the distributions are very similar and lower when the distributions are very different. The latter situation holds in this analysis.

On the one hand, in previous analyses we were comparing award-nomination measures, all of which will have highly skewed distributions: Only a small number of films receive nominations or awards in any category. In concrete terms, out of about 40 films in each year, relatively few get

TABLE 2.4   Correlations between Movie Guide Ratings and Award Measures from Seven Organizations

Award category	O	G	B	N	R	S	L
Picture	**.43**	.41	.40	.26	.22	.23	.26
Directing	**.44**	.39	.37	.24	.20	.24	.22
Screenplay	**.49**	.40	.41	.20	.18	.18	.23
Male lead	.29	.24	**.31**	.17	.15	.14	.17
Female lead	.22	.09	**.25**	.11	.11	.11	.10
Male supporting	**.30**	.22	.26	.15	.13	.12	.13
Female supporting	**.24**	.14	.18	.11	.10	.14	.17
Cinematography	.24	–	**.26**	.14	–	.11	.17
Art direction	**.21**	–	.20	–	.03	–	.08
Costume design	.12	–	**.15**	–	–	–	–
Makeup	.03	–	**.19**	–	–	–	–
Score	.18	.09	**.26**	–	–	–	–
Song	−.10	−.21	–	–	–	–	–
Film editing	**.36**	–	.35	–	–	–	–
Visual effects	.04	–	**.09**	–	–	–	–
Sound	.20	–	**.26**	–	–	–	–

Note. Abbreviations O, G, B, N, R, S, and L defined as in Tables 2.1 and 2.2. Dashes (–) indicate that an award was not offered by that organization for that particular category of creativity or achievement. Boldface indicates the highest correlation in each row.

a 1 (for a nomination), and about 3-5 times fewer get a 2 (for an award), while the vast majority receives a score of 0 (neither award nor nomination). To give a specific illustration, consider the 32 films in the current sample that were featured at the 2000 Academy Awards ceremony. Only one received the Oscar for best picture (*American Beauty*), and another four received a nomination for this honor (*The Cider House Rules*, *The Green Mile*, *The Insider*, and *The Sixth Sense*), while the remaining 26 had been nominated for some other category than best picture, and thus received a 0 on this measure.

On the other hand, the movie guide ratings are quite different. Most films are average, a few very good, and a few very bad. Masterpieces and bombs are much rarer. To be specific, the distribution of stars assigned by the film critics closely approximates the "bell-shaped" or normal curve. This empirical fact is evident in Figure 2.1, which presents the frequency distribution. Instead, of the overwhelming majority of films receiving just one star, most rate about 3 1/2 stars. The only departure from a nice symmetric distribution is that the peak has been shifted to the right by about a half star, a shift reflecting the sampling criteria. Every film had to stand out by at least one cinematic criterion. In any case, the difference between the almost symmetric movie guide ratings and the highly skewed award measures partly

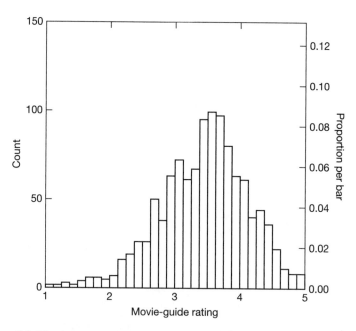

Figure 2.1 The frequency distribution of stars received by 1,132 films, where the number of stars was averaged across five separate movie guides.

accounts for the attenuation of the observed correlations. Where film critics try to distinguish the full range of merit, award bestowers are only engaged in separating out the best from the better.

This technical point aside, it should be evident that the Oscar measures perform well across most of the categories of cinematic achievement. The Academy measures exhibit the highest correlations in the categories of picture, directing, screenplay, male and female supporting, art direction, and film editing. Interestingly, the Academy's closest rival is the British Academy of Film and Television Arts, a very similar organization. The BAFTA's honors even come out on top in the case of male and female lead, cinematography, costume design, makeup, music score, visual effects, and sound mixing. To be sure, whenever the BAFTAs surpass the Oscars by a given criterion, the superiority is never substantial. Yet, because most of the movie guides were published in the US rather than in the UK, it's likely that contrasts between the two academies would be more conspicuous were movie guide representation more equal. This study probably stacked the cards in favor of the US Academy.

The awards and nominations given by the remaining five organizations do a noticeably inferior job in comparison to the two academies. Of the five, the Hollywood Foreign Press Association does the best. Its movie guide correlations are second highest for picture and directing, and third for screenplay and male supporting, but beyond that the Golden Globes do not seem to rise above the level seen for the New York Film Critics Circle, the National Board of Review, the National Society of Film Critics, and the Los Angeles Film Critics Association. Given that the movie guide ratings represent the evaluations of critics, it is especially surprising that the three critic organizations did so poorly. The concordances are highest for the major award categories of picture, directing, and screenplay, and thereafter drop off appreciably. So, if you wanted to predict critic evaluations as recorded in movie guides, you are better off using the Oscars and BAFTAs than using critics' awards and nominations!

An observant reader will have noticed a conspicuous pattern in Table 2.4: Not only do the correlations vary within any given row, but also they vary within any given column—and in a fairly consistent pattern. The correlations tend to be highest for picture, directing, writing, and film editing, somewhat less high for the four acting awards and cinematography, and generally lower for the rest of the categories. This pattern suggests that the diverse categories of cinematic achievement have variable connections to the quality of the final product. This suggestion will be followed up in the next chapter. Not every member of the cast and crew contribute equally to a film's cinematic glory. But first we have to finish discussion of the issues that motivate the current chapter.

Oscar Qualified

The foregoing results provide substantial support for the following four conclusions. First, almost all award categories exhibited a conspicuous consensus across all seven organizations, but the Oscars usually provide the best indicators of that consensus. Second, awards bestowed by the seven organizations corresponded with more specialized awards granted by guilds and societies, with the Oscars more often than not providing the best correspondence with guild assessments. Third, Oscar awards provided meaningful information about cinematic accomplishments beyond that provided by Oscar nominations alone. So it is not just a matter of the Academy getting the nominations right but the awards wrong. Fourth, awards and nominations correlated positively with critics' evaluations—as gauged by standard five movie guides—the correlations being especially large in the categories of picture, direction, screenplay, and acting. But in this case the decisions of Hollywood's Academy were rivaled by those of its British counterpart.

I hasten to add that my 2004 investigation is not the only one germane to this topic. Other studies have corroborated or extended its specific findings. For instance, in a 2007 inquiry to be discussed in Chapter 8, I looked at the consensus across the 17 cinematic categories using a different mix of awards and nominations. Specifically, the composite measures were based on honors received from the Academy of Motion Picture Arts and Sciences, the Hollywood Foreign Press Association, the British Academy of Film and Television Arts, the Los Angeles Film Critics Association, the Chicago Film Critics Association, the Broadcast Film Critics Association, and the Online Film Critics Society (the last three replacing the National Board of Review and the National Society of Film Critics), plus the more specialized honors bestowed by the Producers Guild of America, Directors Guild of America, the Writers Guild of America, the Screen Actors Guild, the American Cinema Editors, the American Society of Cinematographers, the Society of Motion Picture and Television Art Directors, the Costume Designers Guild, the Motion Picture Sound Editors, and the Grammy Awards.

The resulting composite measures had the following reliability coefficients: picture .85, directing .90, lead male .89, lead female .89, supporting male .81, supporting female .87, screenplay .86, cinematography .88, score .80, and song .81. If we ignore the last, these reliabilities are uniformly higher than what is shown in the first column of Table 2.1. The study also calculated reliabilities for seven award categories not shown in that table. The result was as follows: film editing .79, art direction .79, costume design .58, makeup .78, visual effects .72, sound effects editing .40, and sound mixing .75. With the exception of costume design and sound effects editing, these are impressive statistics. Fifteen out of 17 categories manifest a strong consensus on the winners, also-rans, and losers in cinematic accomplishments.

At the same time, other researchers have endorsed the conclusion that the Oscars provide the best indicators of this overall consensus. As an example, Victor Ginsburgh compared best picture awards against three lists of top-100 movies—like the AFI list noted in Chapter 1. About two-thirds of the movies appearing on at least one list had received that Oscar, and 26% of those appearing on all three lists received that honor. The best picture awards bestowed by other organizations—the Hollywood Foreign Press Association, the New York Film Critic Circle, and the National Board of Review—do noticeably worse. Fewer than 10% of the Golden Globe recipients appear on all three top-100 lists, and the corresponding hit rates for the remaining two organizations are 14% and 7%, respectively. So in this comparison the Oscars have nearly twice the success rate as their nearest rival. Although top-100 movie lists are far more selective than movie guide ratings, Ginsburgh's main inference was the same, namely that the "Academy does much better in terms of choosing high-quality movies than do other organizations."

That author's conclusion does not mean that the garlands are not sometimes heaped on the wrong film. In 1953, the Oscar for best picture was conferred on *The Greatest Show on Earth*. Yet that Cecil B. DeMille extravaganza was no where close to being the greatest film released that year! It won over such distinguished nominees as *High Noon*, *Moulin Rouge*, and *The Quiet Man*. Worse yet, the eligible *Singin' in the Rain* was not even nominated in this category—just for best female supporting actor and best music! Even so, *Singin' in the Rain* was ranked 10th in AFI's top-100 list, while *High Noon* came in 33rd; the remaining best picture nominees for that year not making the cut. The five-item movie guide ratings defined in the 2004 inquiry reinforce the mismatch indicated by the AFI list. The best picture Oscar went to a film that got 3.5 stars—about middle of the pack for award-nominated films. In contrast, *Singin' in the Rain* earned the maximum of 5 stars, *The Quiet Man* 4.8 stars, and even *Moulin Rouge* 4.1 stars. The remaining best picture nominee, *Ivanhoe*, is the only film that scored as low as the Oscar winner. In 1953, the Academy voters really goofed. Too bad this was the first award ceremony to be telecasted nationwide!

These discrepancies indicate that assessments of cinematic merit are subject to errors of measurement. Such measurement errors can adopt two forms: random and systematic.

Random Errors of Judgment

The reliability coefficients calculated in this chapter can be derived from so-called "classical test theory." According to this theory, the observed score on a given variable is a function of that variable's true score plus a random error. This contaminating factor represents all those extraneous events that operate to raise or lower the observed values relative to the genuine values. The contamination yields the *fallible score* instead of the true score. Applying this logic to the 1953 Oscar ceremony, we would assume that the random error was positive for *The Greatest Show on Earth* but negative for *Singin' in the Rain*. Sometimes, just by chance, the A student gets a B+ on a particular test while a B student gets an A- on the same test.

The events that prevented *Citizen Kane* from winning the best picture award at the 1942 Oscars might be considered of this nature. If Orson Welles had decided to target anyone else besides William Randolph Hearst, or had used a bit more subtlety in his representation—especially with respect to Hearst's lover Marion Davies—it might have won over *How Green Was My Valley*. After all, according to movie guide ratings, *Citizen Kane* gets 5 stars to the winner's 4.8 stars. When the competition is that close, the tiniest incident can tip the balance in one direction or another. Hearst's aggressive campaigning against the picture might have provided just such an event.

Systematic Errors of Judgment

Alas! The assumption that the error is random is not always valid. On occasion, there is method to the madness. That is, certain errors are systematic. In the early days of the Academy awards, for example, it was obvious that the big studios exerted a lot of clout. As already noted, that is one reason why the New York Film Critic Circle initiated their opposing award series. Below, I want to discuss two scientific inquiries that help us comprehend the potential sources of these orderly biases: vote clustering and past history.

Vote Clustering

According to classical test theory, the error in the assessment of one variable is independent of the error in the assessment of another variable. In less abstract terms, any errors committed by the Academy voters in deciding the best picture in a given year will be uncorrelated with the errors involved in deciding the best director in that same year. But is that assumption necessarily valid? Might not the two decisions be correlated? For example, most of the films that have won the Oscars for best picture have also earned Oscars for their directors. Could it be that if the error is positive for best picture it will often be positive for best directing? If so, how?

Earlier, I mentioned the possibility that votes might be contaminated by a halo effect or positive contagion. Perhaps a great motion picture manages to sweep many other nominees into the victory column simply because of their association with that film. The 2003 *Lord of the Rings: The Return of the King* was honored with 11 Oscar nominations and took home 11 statuettes—the record for the most nominations without a single loss. Yet how many of those Oscars were stolen from more meritorious nominees who had the misfortune to have their cinematic contributions appear in lesser films?

In 2006, Alan Collins and Chris Hand attempted to address this question by looking at the frequency distributions of awards and nominations in the Oscar ceremonies. They argued that if the nominations and awards are allotted independently of each other, then the result should be something known as the *Poisson distribution*. Such a distribution would make it very unlikely that a motion picture could receive as many awards and nominations as did *Lord of the Rings*. In contrast, such sweeps are actually fairly common. The 1959 *Ben-Hur* also received 11 Oscars from 12 nominations while the 1997 *Titanic* received 11 Oscars from 14 nominations. Such occurrences imply that success breeds success. If so, then we would expect the frequencies to be closely approximated by what is known as the *Yule distribution*. The latter applies to situations in which "the rich get richer" owing to an "accumulative advantage" process.

Collins and Hand tested this prediction by scrutinizing the award and nomination distributions for both Oscars and Golden Globes given between 1983 and 2000. The data led to a forthright rejection of the Poisson distribution and a reasonable confirmation of the Yule distribution. With the sole exception of films receiving seven nominations, the Yule's fit is almost perfect. This result implies that votes may be assigned to films owing to some positive contagion or halo effect. If you've made contributions to a great motion picture, you're likely to accrue honors beyond those you're due.

Although these results are very suggestive of systematic error, that is not the only possible inference. Conceivably, some portion of this vote clustering can be ascribed to a different sort of contagion process. Rather than taking place at the aesthetic perception end—the judgment of cinematic products—the contagion could occur at the creative production end—the initial generation of those products. For instance, a superior screenplay might inspire the film's various contributors to a level of performance that rises well above mediocrity. Or the director's enthusiasm, competence, and vision may provide the necessary inspiration. I will return to this issue in Chapters 3 and 6, but for now we need to examine a less ambiguous illustration of systematic error.

Past History

One could argue that the general superiority of the Academy voters is deceptive. The Oscars may offer the best overall indicator of the consensus because, in a sense, the Academy members cheat. Oscar night is now the last major event in the annual award cycle. Consequently, the voters already know the nominees and often even the winners from earlier events in the cycle. A case in point is the Golden Globe ceremony, which now takes place about a month before the polls close on the Oscar vote. The Academy membership can then take advantage of whatever expertise or wisdom was displayed by members of the Hollywood Foreign Press Association. Under this scenario the Oscars best represent the consensus because they are the cumulative outcome of that consensus. Those who have the most hindsight will have the most foresight.

In 2005, Ian Pardoe published an investigation demonstrating that such across-award influences might take place. His specific goal was to predict the Oscar winners in the major categories of picture, directing, male lead, and female lead. The sample consisted of all films nominated in those categories from 1938 to 2004. The predictions were not only very accurate, but in addition the success rates tended to increase over time, reaching levels of 93% for best directing and 77% for best picture, best male lead, and best female lead. Among the predictors was taking home the Golden Globe for best picture in either drama or musical/comedy. This award predicted not only the Oscar for best picture, but also the Oscars for best lead actors. Guild awards provided predictors as well. Specifically, awards from the Producers Guild of America predicted the Oscars for best picture, awards from the Directors Guild of America predicted the Oscars for best directing, and awards from the Screen Actors Guild predicted the Oscars in the two acting categories.

Hence, to some extent these predictions may represent influences from one award ceremony to another. That inference is especially strong in the case of the Golden Globes. Unlike the guilds, which share some voting members with the Academy, the voting membership of the Hollywood Foreign Press Association does not overlap that of the Academy. To be sure, we could also interpret the congruence between Oscars and Globes as reflecting an underlying consensus on the relative merits of the achievements in the four categories. Even so, we cannot deny the possibility that the Academy voters have the Golden Globe ceremony in mind when they cast their ballots for the Oscars. Some of the voters may have even been in the audience as nominees.

Pardoe identified some other predictors that are even more disconcerting: the past history of awards and nominations. Ideally, the Oscars should be granted based on the merit exclusively demonstrated in a nominated film. Yet this doesn't always happen. In 2007, Martin Scorsese obtained the best directing award for *The Departed*. This was his first directing Oscar, but his sixth nomination, the previous five received for the 1980 *Raging Bull*, the 1988 *The Last Temptation of Christ*, the 1990 *Goodfellas*, the 2002 *Gangs of New York*, and the 2004 *The Aviator*. We would like to believe that the preceding five unsuccessful nominations had nothing to do with his eventual win. But that seems unlikely. According to Pardoe's analysis, the number of previous nominations does increase the probability of getting the award in this category of cinematic achievement. Hence, these past failures may have tipped the balance in his favor relative to his fellow nominees, namely, Alejandro González Iñárritu, Paul Greengrass, Stephen Frears, and Clint Eastwood. Iñárritu and Greengrass had never before earned an Oscar nod, and Frears had earned just one, for the 1990 *The Grifters*. Even Eastwood had only been nominated three times previously for this particular honor—for the 1992 *The Unforgiven*, the 2003 *Mystic River*, and the 2004 *Million Dollar Baby*—plus he had already picked up the statuette for the first and last of these achievements. So it was beyond doubt Marty's turn. And he got it, handed to him personally by the equally legendary directors Francis Ford Coppola, George Lucas, and Steven Spielberg.

This prior-nomination bias also affects who wins the Oscar for best male lead—albeit this did not help poor Peter O'Toole who, also in 2007, was hoping to parlay his eight nominations into a long overdue Academy award. But this very effect may have helped Denzel Washington. Prior to his best lead acting award for the 2001 *Training Day*, he had already been nominated in the same category for the 1999 *The Hurricane* and the 1991 *Malcolm X*. Of the other nominees—Will Smith, Tom Wilkinson, Sean Penn, and Russell Crowe—only the last two had two previous nominations. But Crowe had received the best acting Oscar for *Gladiator* just the year before. So the choice was really between Penn and Washington, and the latter came out on top owing to an array of contingencies both random and systematic.

Crowe's weakened candidacy illustrates another critical Pardoe empirical finding: Those who have already walked off the stage on Oscar night with a statuette for best lead acting will suffer a lowered likelihood of receiving another one. This one-per-customer bias affects both male and female categories. Evidently the Academy voters believe that it is better to spread the wealth around rather than allow some star to monopolize the laurels. Naturally, as is always the case, exceptions exist to any tendency. Katharine Hepburn walked away with a best lead acting award for *On Golden Pond* (1981), notwithstanding her winning Oscars in the same category for *The Lion in Winter* (1968), *Guess Who's Coming to Dinner* (1967), and, over three decades earlier, *Morning Glory* (1933). Nevertheless, this discrepancy is counterbalanced by the fact that she also had unsuccessful nods for best female lead in *Long Day's Journey Into Night* (1962), *Suddenly, Last Summer* (1959), *The Rainmaker* (1956), *Summertime* (1955),

The African Queen (1951), *Woman of the Year* (1942), *The Philadelphia Story* (1940), and *Alice Adams* (1935). So the bias against multiple Oscars was overwhelmed by the bias in favor of accumulated unsuccessful nominations. And, of course, the Academy voters may have simply been giving credit where credit was due.

Pardoe's study has identified some of the systematic errors that to some degree undermine the integrity of the Academy awards handed out in four major categories. It would be hard to believe that comparable biases do not contaminate the other award categories as well. Nonetheless, Pardoe has gone beyond just spotting voter partialities. On the basis of his predication equations he has been able to determine when the Academy voters truly departed from their favored modus operandi. A salient instance is Peter O'Toole in the 1969 awards. Earning a nomination for his lead performance opposite Hepburn in *The Lion in Winter*, his probability of a victory was the highest ever during the course of his career—fully .89! Given that there are five nominees for the honor, the baseline probability would have been .20. So it seems like a sure bet that he would have been invited up to the stage— particularly when you consider that he had already endured failed nominations for leads in *Becket* (1964) and *Lawrence of Arabia* (1962). Yet the Oscar went to Cliff Robertson for his title role in *Charley*. This happened despite Robertson's probability of success standing at virtually zero, well below the baseline. And Robertson never received a major acting honor before or since. So, I guess that sometimes random error can override systematic bias!

Wrap Up

The English historian Thomas Carlyle once observed, "Fame, we may understand, is no sure test of merit, but only a probability of such." This statement certainly applies to the fame anyone gains when handed an Oscar, Golden Globe, BAFTA, or other shiny trophy on some gala occasion. The voter's decision to pick this or that winner is the complex product of actual merit and errors both random and systematic. To be fair, we must acknowledge that these professionals, journalists, and critics are being asked to do the near impossible: To make fine distinctions among similarly high achievements.

Consider the best picture Oscar. According to the five-item movie guide measure, pictures nominated in any of the 17 major categories average 3.5 stars. That subset nominated for best picture averages 4.1 stars while those that actually win average 4.4 stars. More exactly, the disparity between a nominee and a winner is 27/100ths of a star. That is really asking the Academy to split hairs with an axe. To give a specific illustration, according to Pardoe's prediction equations the movie *Reds* (1981) had a .87 probability of getting the best picture Oscar, whereas *Chariots of Fire* (1981) had a probability of only .01. So it may seem a travesty that it was the latter picture that received the laurel wreath. Yet the difference in their movie guide ratings is very small, 4.4 versus 4.5 stars respectively. The two films were a tenth of a star apart in cinematic merit. In a horse race, that's practically a photo finish!

It is a well-known principle in psychometrics that the reliability of a measure is contingent on the range of scores in the sample. When we claim, for instance, that an IQ test has a reliability of .90, this coefficient only applies when the test is applied to individuals representing the full variation in general intelligence. The reliability would be much lower if the test were administered to members of Mensa, an organization confined to people with IQs in the upper two percent of the population. The instrument would then have to distinguish persons who are all intellectually gifted, and that is a much more troublesome task. The measurement error increases proportionately. In this context, it is impressive that the reliabilities seen in Table 2.1 are as high as they are. The award organizations seem to do a commendable job distinguishing the very best from the best notwithstanding the difficulties involved.

Another psychometric principle will have immense utility throughout the remainder of this book: The whole is greater than the sum of its parts. Or, expressed more specifically, a multi-item composite measure is always more reliable than the individual items that make it up. Hence, the five-item movie guide ratings measure has less error than any of separate guides on which it is based. This improvement occurs because the random errors in any one measure will tend to cancel out when the scores are summed across all measures. If a positive error is added to a negative error you obtain a smaller aggregate error. Moreover, the larger the number of items composing the measure, the higher the odds that the sum of the errors will become zero. That is why a 50-item test is better than a 5-item test. That is also why in Table 2.1 the reliability coefficient almost always decreased when an award was deleted.

Admittedly, systematic errors cannot be obliterated in this fashion. If all measures have the same bias, that bias will not vanish when they are all put together in a composite measure. Even so, the impact of systematic errors will be reduced if the measures do not share the same biases. A critic's review might be biased by the film's genre, but if critics vary in their favorite genres, then summing across the evaluations of many critics helps lessen the bias. One critic's preference for dramas will be offset by another critic's preference for comedies.

As a consequence, many of the empirical findings to be reported in later chapters will use multiple-item measures whenever possible. Rather than rely on the judgment of a single organization or individual, the indicators will incorporate the assessments of many organizations or individuals. The resulting composite measures will represent the cinematic consensus far better than any single evaluation. That is another way to make the inquiries more scientific.

Chapter 3

Story, Sights, Tricks, and Song: What Really Counts?

Cinema displays amazing diversity. The genre categories alone include drama, comedy, romance, musical, adventure, action, thriller, war, crime, western, fantasy, sci-fi, mystery, horror, or film-noir—plus all of the diverse combinations of these genres. In more concrete terms, ponder the variety illustrated by the following films: *12 Angry Men* (1957), *Monty Python and the Holy Grail* (1975), *Vertigo* (1958), *Sweeney Todd: The Demon Barber of Fleet Street* (2007), *Lawrence of Arabia* (1962), *Fight Club* (1999), *Memento* (2000), *Casablanca* (1942), *Taxi Driver* (1976), *The Treasure of the Sierra Madre* (1948), *Star Wars* (1977), *Blade Runner* (1982), *Alien* (1979), and *M* (1931). Pretty disparate, and this disparity appears despite the fact that they're all English-language, feature-length, live-action narrative films.

Yet no matter what the variety, almost every film you ever see ends exactly the same way: with the final credits. Line after line of name and job title comes and goes. Often starting with the complete cast list—the producers, directors, and headliners already having appeared at the film's onset—the credits work down to more obscure contributors such as the camera operator, production sound recordist, scenario assistant, copyist, stunt double, chief animal trainer, unit nurse, transportation manager, rushes timer, catering supervisor, unit publicist, construction accountant, grip operator, foley artist, property master, rigger, etc. Sometimes hundreds of names will scroll by before the film terminates with perhaps a few thank you's and a dedication or two. So much information rolls by that the film's composer will often write special music to maintain the mood during the factual onslaught. And what appears on the screen does not include the dozens upon dozens of cast and crew members whose efforts went uncredited. The complete count of credited and uncredited contributors to the 2000 *Gladiator* exceeds 800 people—from the (credited) director Ridley Scott to the (uncredited) prosthetic assistant Michelle Wraight.

Although the credits make it manifest that film constitutes a collaborative artistic product, they also raise the issue of what contributions have the biggest impact on a film's aesthetic impact. Certainly not all job titles are of equal influence. In fact, the order of presentation partly reflects judged importance — so much so that many filmgoers will be leaving the theater before the credits are complete. Even if Michelle Wraight had been credited, how many people who watched *Gladiator* would have waited until her name scrolled by? But where exactly is the dividing line between the artist and technician, between creativity and expertise? Is it the casting director? The camera crew?

Fortunately, the movie awards treated at length in the previous chapter gives a clue. Presumably, the tasks most essential to a film's greatness will be singled out for special recognition. And on this basis, just 17 categories of cinematic achievement receive honors from two or more organizations. These are picture, directing, screenplay, male lead actor, female lead actor, male supporting actor, female supporting actor, cinematography, art direction (and set decoration), costume design, makeup, film editing, score, song, visual effects, sound effects editing, and sound (or sound mixing). In truth, the first of these, best picture, is better considered a global criterion of artistic accomplishment, leaving us with 16 major types of contributions. So which of these 16 are most crucial? If you're a producer who had to decide between paying for the best cinematographer or the best film editor, who would you pick?

Actually, some hint of an answer was given earlier in Chapter 2. There, Table 2.4 gave the correlations between movie guide ratings and the awards and nominations bestowed by the seven major organizations. In the case of the Oscars, for example, the directing and screenplay appear to be the most valuable, whereas makeup, song, and visual effects appear to be the least, with other contributions falling somewhere between. A similar pattern seems to hold for the remaining six organizations. It is telling that there is some correspondence between the size of the correlation and whether or not an organization offers recognition for the achievement. In particular, all seven bestow awards for directing, screenplay, and the four acting categories, but two ignore cinematography, three overlook art direction, four pay no attention to score, and the remaining categories are honored by only two organizations apiece.

Naturally, the number of stars earned in movie guides is not the sole available criterion of aesthetic success. A choice that's just as natural is best picture honors. As should be apparent in Table 2.4, this measure is not identical to the critics' evaluations. Indeed, its correlations with the movie guide ratings are about the same as those for directing and screenplay. Even so, the two criteria may still have similar correlates. For instance, one investigation found that the Oscar for best picture was most strongly associated with directing, screenplay, and film editing. However, this inquiry suffered from two major limitations. First, it used measures derived from but one award series, that of the Academy of Motion Picture Arts and Sciences. As pointed out at the end of the last chapter, a composite indicator consisting of multiple measures is superior to any single-item measure. We would rather avoid putting all of our evaluative eggs in a single basket. Second, the study disregarded the fact that some of the award categories are very highly correlated. For example, the best directing and best screenplay honors very often go to the same films, just as best costume honors are often linked with best art direction honors. Hence, before scrutinizing the predictors of cinematic impact, we first must deal with what I've called *creative clusters*. These clusters will be discussed in several chapters besides this one, so pay close attention to what follows!

Creative Clusters

In the preceding chapter, I discussed the phenomenon of vote clustering. Awards and nominations tend to concentrate in a relatively small number of films. This concentration has been attributed to a contagion process during the nomination and award process. Yet I indicated that this contagion could occur at the production rather than perception end. Cinematic creativity may entail mutual inspiration. After all, the various contributors do not collaborate in isolation but rather are often engaged in face-to-face interaction. At the same time, certain collaborations involve more direct exchanges than do others. The director will spend much more time working with the actors than with the composer. As a result, the various contributions may cluster into more specialized groups. Those individuals who collaborate most intensively together will form a given cluster. If the final product of their particular collaboration attains a high level of cinematic merit, they become more likely to receive nominations and awards together. Accordingly, the distribution of honors could reflect the structure of these potentially synergistic relationships.

In 2004 I published an article devoted to teasing out this possibility. With the exception of the time interval, the sampling criterion was identical to that of the main study of Chapter 2: English-language, feature-length, live-action narrative films released between 1968 and 1999 that had received one or more nominations or awards from seven organizations. The resulting sample consisted of 1,327 films. These films were then assessed on 16 composite measures regarding achievement in the following categories: directing, screenplay, male lead, female lead, male supporting, female supporting, film editing, cinematography, art direction, costume design, makeup, visual effects, sound effects editing, sound, score, and song. These measures were then subjected to an exploratory factor analysis to determine which variables tend to highly correlate with each other and which tend to be more or less uncorrelated. The resultant factor matrix is shown in Table 3.1. Because the factor loadings indicate how much variable loads on a factor, the highest loading in each row has been put in boldface font.

It should be obvious from these boldface numbers that the 16 award categories fall into four distinct clusters:

1. The *dramatic* cluster consists of awards and nominations for directing, screenplay, acting (male and female leads and supporting), and film editing. It includes all those elements of the film that are most immediately engaged in the presentation of the story and its characters. With the exception of film editing, it's the part of the film most strongly associated with the essence of theater, especially as portrayed

TABLE 3.1   Factor Matrix for 1,327 Films Assessed on 16 Award Categories

Contribution	Factors			
	Dramatic	Visual	Technical	Musical
Directing	**.81**	.14	.10	.07
Screenplay	**.84**	.00	−.02	−.07
Male lead	**.67**	−.18	.10	−.09
Female lead	**.37**	.13	−.25	−.06
Male supporting	**.48**	.04	−.04	.15
Female supporting	**.52**	−.02	−.17	−.15
Film editing	**.61**	.13	.36	.27
Cinematography	.27	**.54**	.04	.31
Art direction	.02	**.79**	.11	.08
Costume design	−.08	**.90**	−.16	−.08
Makeup	−.03	**.52**	.20	−.36
Visual effects	−.10	.07	**.73**	−.10
Sound effects editing	−.02	−.07	**.76**	−.09
Sound	.30	.21	**.58**	.31
Score	.11	.43	.03	**.51**
Song	−.16	−.11	−.06	**.71**

Note. The largest factor loading in each row is indicated by boldface type. Factor loadings represent the correlation between each individual contribution and each of the four factors.

in barebones dramas like Thornton Wilder's *Our Town* or Samuel Beckett's *Waiting for Godot.*

2. The *visual* cluster consists of awards and nominations for cinematography, art direction (and set decoration), costume design, and makeup. This cluster entails everything about the film's "look"—what's left when you can only flip through stills taken from the film. If cinematography can be said to be akin to lighting design, then these contributions also have parallels in the theater.

3. The *technical cluster* consists of awards and nominations for visual effects, sound effects editing, and sound (or sound mixing). Unlike the previous two clusters, these contributions are usually added to the film in post-production. These aspects are also more distinctively cinematic rather than generally theatrical. These technical contributions help make the film experience so strikingly different from what we encounter on the stage.

4. The *musical* cluster consists of awards and nominations for score and song. The contributions in this cluster may be made anytime during production or post-production, and often include a separate composer and songwriter. Because of the nature of most awards, this cluster is almost always confined to original music. In fact, when Nino Rota's score for *The Godfather* (1972) was found to have reused his music for the much earlier *Fortunella* (1958) his nomination had to be withdrawn, obliging him to wait four years when he finally won for his original contribution to *The Godfather: Part II* (1974).

To some extent these four creative clusters represent well-defined collaborative groups. This conclusion is especially evident in the case of the dramatic cluster. Quite commonly the directors, actors, and writers will work together, refining the interpretation or even revising the script. The film editor often collaborates with the director, and sometimes also with certain screenwriters and actors (i.e., at least those with the power to ensure that they do not "end up on the cutting-room floor"). Indeed, when that working relationship breaks down between the editor and other members of this group, the film often suffers as a result. A classic case is Orson Welles' 1942 *The Magnificent Ambersons*, the editing of which was taken over by the studio, which proceeded to ruin the final product. Some directors, such as Stephen Spielberg, will even shoot in such a manner that it would be possible for an unaided editor to make heads or tails of the film rolled up in the can.

The personnel belonging to the other clusters are most frequently involved at other phases of the filmmaking process. The visual features of the film will often be worked out prior to shooting whereas the technical and musical features will usually be contributed after the shooting is complete. Even when the contributions are concurrent, the interactions between clusters will normally be less frequent than interactions within clusters. The one principal exception to this generalization is that the director often maintains contact with almost everyone during the filmmaking process. This enables him or her to maintain "artistic control." As will be seen in Chapter 6, this comprehensive supervision may contribute greatly to the film's ultimate merit.

But now to the really important question: How well do these four creative clusters predict cinematic success? Do some have a bigger wallop than others?

Cinematic Success

To address the above issue we will use two composite measures of success, namely, the seven-item best picture honors and the five-item movie guide ratings. These were the same measures introduced in the prior chapter. Composite measures (factor scores) were also generated for each of the four creative clusters. These scores were simply the sum of the measures that had the highest loadings on a given factor (as indicated by boldface in Table 3.1). To illustrate, the dramatic cluster was defined as the sum of the following measures: directing, screenplay, male and female lead acting, male and female supporting acting, and film editing. Again, these composite measures were based on the awards and nominations from 7 distinct organizations, where awards counted 2 points and nominations 1 point. The resulting scores for the four clusters had the following reliabilities: dramatic .88, visual .83, technical .73, and musical .55. With the exception of the last, a film's score on the clusters can be measured with relatively little error. In explaining the poor showing of the fourth creative cluster we have to make allowance for the fact it that consists of only two items: score and song (but see Chapter 8 for added problems).

Given the above variables, I conducted two types of statistical analyses: correlation and prediction.

Correlation: What Goes With What?

The correlations between the two cinematic success measures and the four creative clusters are shown in Table 3.2. The first column of decimal fractions shows the coefficients for best picture honors. All four clusters are correlated with this criterion, albeit the dramatic cluster boasts a correlation more than twice as large as the visual cluster and about four times

TABLE 3.2 Correlation and Regression Coefficients for Two Criteria of Aesthetic Impact and Factor Scores on Four Creative Clusters

	Correlation		Regression	
Creative Cluster	Best picture	Movie guides	Best picture	Movie guides
Dramatic	.85***	.55***	.80***	.52***
Visual	.42***	.25***	.10***	.06*
Technical	.23***	.20***	.02	.08**
Musical	.20***	.02	.04**	−.06*

Note. Sample size for best-picture results is 1,326; for the movie-guide results 1,322. The regression analysis includes controls for the film's release date, runtime, genre, and the MPAA rating. The regression coefficients are all standardized ("betas").

*p < .05. **p < .01. ***p < .001.

larger than either the technical or the musical clusters, with the last cluster having the smallest association. Judging from nominations and awards for best picture, directing, screenplay, acting, and film editing have the biggest say regarding what makes a great film. In fact, the correlation between the dramatic cluster and best picture honors is so high that the two measures are practically equivalent. *One Flew Over the Cuckoo's Nest* (1975) and *The Silence of the Lambs* (1991) are exemplars: Both won Oscars for picture, writing, directing, male and female lead, plus nominations for film editing. It's hard to imagine a great flick not involving great direction, writing, acting, and editing. To be sure, the very first Oscar for best picture went to *Wings* (1927) even though it got not a single nod in any of the dramatic categories. But it only rates 3.2 stars in the movie guides. Have you seen it?

The correlations in the second numerical column pertain to the movie guide ratings. Once more, the dramatic cluster has over twice the impact as the next most influential cluster, which is again the visual cluster. Although these two correlations are noticeably smaller than those in the first column, some decrease would be expected for reasons expressed in the previous chapter: Whereas best picture honors have the same skewed distribution as the four cluster scores—which are also based on awards and nominations coming from the same seven organizations—movie guide ratings have a more or less normal distribution. Given this expected reduction, it is a bit more surprising that the technical cluster has about the same effect as before. But even more surprising is the impression made by the musical cluster, which shrunk substantially. Indeed, it is only one-tenth as small.

To better appreciate the magnitude of this diminution I have added asterisks to these correlation coefficients to indicate their levels of statistical significance. Every correlation but one is significant at the .001 level.

So the probability is less than one out of a thousand that the correlations are the upshot of some random quirk in the sample. The lone exception therefore becomes all the more remarkable; this one alone is not statistically significant at even the lowest conventional level (i.e., $p < .05$). Because we cannot reject the hypothesis that the true correlation in the general population is actually zero, the relation between critical evaluations and great scores and songs may be truly zip.

Notwithstanding my including the asterisks, I believe that significance tests have limited value for most of the investigations discussed in this book. The sampled films in these studies are not randomly selected from some indefinite population. Instead, the films are systematically selected according to precise selection criteria. Any researcher who collects a sample of films employing the specified criteria will obtain the exact same films! In this sense, the samples are equivalent to the population. No films are left out that fit the sampling criteria. Furthermore, these samples are not arbitrary but rather they represent an inventory of motion pictures that have inherent worth: English-language, feature-length, live-action narrative films that have received at least one nomination from a major professional or critical organization—aren't these the great flicks whose workings we would most want to understand?

Consequently, the correlations reported in Table 3.2 and in other tables throughout this book will have descriptive import apart from whether they can be said to apply to all films ever released since the advent of the art form. A case in point is the correlation of .55 between movie guide ratings and the dramatic cluster. This coefficient is *exactly true* for the 1,327 films that satisfied the given sampling criteria. In this context, it makes no sense whether this result was obtained "just by chance" or whether it can generalize to some hypothetical population of films. What is far more noteworthy is this correlation's effect size: It's large. By the same token, the correlation between movie guide ratings and music cluster for this set of films is only .02. That's a useful contrast regardless of significance level. We can claim with absolute certainty that the dramatic cluster has 28 times the impact of the musical cluster on the ratings these 1,327 films earn in five major movie guides.

Prediction: What Predicts What?

Unfortunately, these correlations cannot be taken on face value. A lot of variables may influence both the measures of cinematic success and the indicators of the four creative clusters. As a consequence, the correlation between the two might be spurious. Take film genre as an example. Some genres may be favored in movie awards, creating an inflated correlation between best picture honors and some creative clusters. In particular, if dramas are favored by the Academy voters, then that might raise the correlation between best picture and the dramatic cluster, which has an intrinsic link with drama. Dramas provide a superior showcase for directors and actors in particular.

Yet it can also happen that some variable contaminates the association so that it is smaller than it should be. For instance, movie guides might be biased against the genre of musicals, a bias that may account for the almost zero correlation between that measure and the music cluster. It is therefore conceivable that adjusting or controlling for genre might increase the relation between movie guide ratings and the music cluster. When a measure of association gets bigger rather than smaller in this way, psychometricians call it *suppression*. In a sense, suppression is the opposite of spuriousness. In suppression the correlation is too small; in spuriousness it is too large—once allowance is made for the artifacts introduced by other variables.

Fortunately, we can use multiple regression analysis to estimate the relationship between two variables holding all of the other variables constant. All that is necessary to implement this method is to define a set of appropriate *control variables*—the factors that are going to be held constant or equalized. In this specific study controls were introduced for (a) the film's *release date*, (b) its *runtime* (or duration in minutes), (c) the four genres of *dramas*, *comedies*, *romances*, and *musicals* (which represent the most common categories for these films), and (d) the ratings assigned by the Motion Picture Association of America (MPAA); namely *G* (general admission), *PG* (parental guidance advised), *PG-13* (parents strongly cautioned because some material may be inappropriate for children under 13), *R* (Restricted, children under 17 would not be admitted without an accompanying parent or adult guardian), *NC-17* (no one 17 and under admitted), and *Not Rated* (rarely used in films of the kind sampled). The last two columns of Table 3.2 indicate the outcome of implementing this more sophisticated analysis.

The first inference to be drawn from the table is that the standardized regression coefficients (or "betas") are visibly smaller than the correlation coefficients. The difference between the two sets is smallest for the dramatic cluster but largest for the technical cluster. Indeed, in the case of best picture honors the association with the technical cluster was reduced tenfold, from .23 to .02, which is no longer statistically significant. This suggests that the .23 correlation was completely spurious. In contrast, the impact of the visual cluster was not so drastically reduced. The two regression coefficients are about one-fourth the size of the corresponding correlation coefficients.

The outcome for the musical cluster is perhaps the most curious. On the one hand, the relation with best picture honors was reduced by one-fifth, much like what happened to the visual cluster. On the other hand, the relation with movie guide ratings went from almost zero (.02) to a statistically significant *negative* relationship (−.06). From the standpoint of the critics that compile these evaluations, films that receive recognition for best score and best song are actually somewhat inferior to those that do not. This negative association is so unexpected that it will be revisited in Chapter 8.

Despite the divergence between the correlation and regression coefficients, two conclusions replicate across both sets of statistics. First, the single most critical cluster is the dramatic. In fact, the difference between the two sets of coefficients is negligible. Second, the visual cluster remains consistently important, but has about one-eighth the impact of the dramatic cluster. Judging from these results, the best films feature great directing, writing, acting, and film editing, with a smaller contribution from great cinematography, art direction, costume design, and makeup. By comparison, the effects of the technical and musical clusters are negligible or inconsistent. In later chapters we will tease out the reason for the disparity. There is indeed cinematic method in this movie madness.

Besides providing a means for implementing statistical control, the multiple regression analysis also offers an overall estimate of the joint predictive power of a set of variables. In the present study, 73% of the variation (or *variance*) in scores on best picture honors was accounted for using the four creative clusters (or 75% including the control variables). In the case of movie guide ratings, this figure reduces to 33% (or 35% with the control variables). Yet to account for a third of the variation in these critics' evaluations is no mean achievement. In one respect, the 73% is less impressive than the 33%. In the former case movie awards are being used to predict movie awards. Because the same voters often cast ballots on the four creative clusters and best picture honors, some portion of the prediction precision reflects what is known as *shared method variance*. All five variables are measured the same way by largely the same people. In contrast, the movie guide assessments are much less plagued by this extraneous influence. The critics who compile these guides cannot be voting members of all seven organizations, and can seldom even vote in one.

The multiple regression analysis can accomplish yet another task: detecting whether any *interaction effects* take place. Does the effect of one variable on the criterion moderate the effect of another variable on the same criterion? The answer is yes. The four creative clusters do indeed exhibit some interaction effects. Moreover, in every single instance it is the dramatic cluster that serves as the moderator. For example, with respect to best picture honors, the dramatic cluster intensifies the impact of both visual and technical clusters. Expressed differently, the visual and technical contributions to making an award-winning film are rendered more influential when those contributions occur in the context of a great drama. So not only does the dramatic cluster have the largest main effect on cinematic greatness, but it also shapes how the other clusters contribute to the film's positive impact. In other words, these interactions imply some kind of synergistic relation among the creative clusters.

Happily, the consequences of these interaction effects are far smaller than the main effects. To be specific, the former only increase our explanatory power by about 1%. As a result, it is possible to concentrate on just the main effects. That's fortunate because it's much easier to contemplate additive effects than multiplicative effects. Nonetheless, we should always keep in the back of our mind the fact that the dramatic cluster is doubly important. It makes the biggest contribution to cinematic success and it moderates the contributions of all the other creative clusters. When it comes to great flicks, drama is indispensable.

Collaborative Creativity

It seems that we have made some headway toward answering the question framed by this chapter's title. Great flicks are mostly great stories told by means of writers, directors, actors, and film editors. This main course is slightly seasoned by some great visuals contributed by cinematographers, art directors, costume designers, and makeup artists. Yet special visual effects, sound effects editing, and sound as well as the music, whether score or song, seem less potent or consistent in impact. This ordering of priorities is fairly consistent with what consumers tend to report: characters, storyline, and acting are far more critical than scenery, costumes, or music.

I will explore in later chapters some of the reasons for the differential repercussions of the four creative clusters. Right now I'd like to address another question: What predicts the predictors? Why do some films score higher than others on the four creative clusters? Or, what is tantamount to the same issue, what factors support exceptional achievement in the award categories that define each cluster? With respect to the dramatic cluster, for instance, what are the predictors of awards and honors received for directing, writing, acting, and film editing?

One route to answering this question may be to look at the impact of special collaborative relationships that each individual has with others involved in making the same film. Some features of the collaborations may enhance the individual achievements recognized at the award ceremonies. The best illustration of this approach is the research carried out by Gino Cattani and Simone Ferriani. The investigators focused on seven major contributors to the final film product, namely, the producer, director, scriptwriter, film editor, cinematographer, production designer, and composer. In particular, the investigators examined 11,974 crewmembers who worked on one or more of 2,137 films that were (a) released in the United States between 1992 and 2003 and (b) distributed by Universal, Paramount, Warner Bros., Columbia-Tristar, Disney, 20th Century Fox, Metro-Goldwyn-Mayer, Dreamworks, Miramax, or New Line. On the average, each team consisted of about a dozen members.

Each crewmember's creative performance on a particular film was then assessed by counting the number of awards and nominations he or she received from 10 professional societies: (a) the Academy of Motion Picture Arts and Sciences, (b) the Hollywood Foreign Press Association, (c) the National Board of Review, (d) the New York Film Critics Circle, (e) the Los Angeles Film Critics Association, (f) the Producers Guild of America, (g) the Directors Guild of America, (h) the Writers Guild of America, (i) the American Society of Cinematographers, and (j) the American Cinema Editors. These organizations should be already familiar to the reader. Studies discussed earlier have often relied on honors bestowed by the same organizations. The difference is that the awards and nominations are here being used to assess the achievements of individual crewmembers rather than the merit of entire films.

The investigators then used regression analysis to identify the predictors of a crewmember's creative performance. These predictors fall into two general categories of effects: linear and curvilinear.

Linear Effects: More is Better

Cattani and Ferriani discovered that two variables had a positive linear relation with the criterion. One such predictor was *individual creative freedom*, a measure of the average number of distinct roles each individual carried out in the film projects on which he or she worked in a given year. For instance, Robert Rodriguez was producer, director, writer, cinematographer, and editor for the 1992 *El Mariachi* and producer, director, writer, production designer, cinematographer, editor, and composer for the 2003 *Once Upon a Time in Mexico*. Not only was creative freedom a positive predictor of individual performance, but it had a very large effect. Admittedly, a filmmaker who occupies many different roles in a given year may not necessarily perform those roles in the same film. On occasion a crew member might work on more than one film in a single year. Yet even in this exceptional case someone who has served multiple roles on different films brings something distinctive into the collaboration. A director who has recently served as screenwriter will work differently with both directors and screenwriters.

Another predictor variable was *team quality*. This variable was defined as the average number of awards and nominations earned by other team members in the preceding two years. Hence, a crewmember does gain by working with recently successful collaborators. At least, it enhances your prospects for recognition if you collaborate with others who have earned recent honors. This variable had about half the impact of creative freedom.

Interestingly, the investigators also tested the impact of *individual quality*, but found no significant effect. This was a measure of the number of awards and nominations that a given crewmember had received in the prior two years. It is striking that this variable did not predict achievement whereas team quality did. The contrast underlines the collaborative nature of filmmaking. Who you know (and work with) is often more crucial than who you are. Even so, the positive contribution of creative freedom implies a limit on this collaborative emphasis. Sometimes it works better when a crewmember collaborates with himself or herself, occupying two or more filmmaking roles. I shall return to this finding when we discuss Auteur theory in Chapter 6.

Curvilinear Effects: Neither Too Much nor Too Little

Cattani and Ferriani hypothesized that the crewmember's creative performance—as judged by awards and nominations—would be contingent on two additional variables: coreness and repeated ties.

Coreness involves whether the crewmember worked near the core or the periphery of the social network of artists and experts engaged in filmmaking. Someone at the core collaborates with many others who are frequent collaborators on top film projects—with big names like Steven Spielberg, Martin Scorsese, Woody Allen, Thelma Schoonmaker, Conrad L. Hall, and John Williams. In contrast, someone at the periphery lacks "connections" with key players in the industry. The latter are the outsiders who have so far only teamed up with wannabes still hoping for their cinematic breakthrough. In terms of working on the same films, those in the core can always be said to be within "six degrees of Kevin Bacon" whereas those in the periphery are seldom anywhere near that close.

Repeated ties concerns how often a crewmember had prior experience working with other crewmembers defined by the seven categories. At one extreme, the target individual might never have joined forces with any of the other collaborators on a previous film. At the other extreme, the person might have had a long working relationship with one or more of the principal collaborators. A classic example is the collaboration between director Alfred Hitchcock and composer Bernard Hermann—including such masterworks as *The Man Who Knew Too Much* (1956), *Vertigo* (1958), *North by*

Northwest (1959), and *Psycho* (1960). A more recent example is the collaboration between director Steven Spielberg and editor Michael Kahn, a collaboration that has included every Spielberg feature between *Close Encounters of the Third Kind* (1977) and *Munich* (2005), with the lone exception of *E.T.: The Extra-Terrestrial* (1982). It is important to note that the investigators only considered recent collaborations in tabulating this measure—that is, collaborative ties in the last few years. They presumed that older experiences with coworkers on film projects would undergo a noticeable degree of decay.

Significantly, instead of a linear association, Cattani and Ferriani anticipated a *curvilinear* function. To be specific, they predicted an inverted-U relationship for both variables. This single-peaked curve is indicative of a tradeoff between the advantages and disadvantages of assuming extreme scores on either measure. At some middle range between the extremes appears the optimum level of coreness or repeated ties. As an example, if crewmembers are working together for the first time, unfamiliarity may undermine their effectiveness. Only by working on a few consecutive projects will they attain the necessary intuitive appreciation of their respective technical skills and aesthetic preferences. Once that appreciation matures, a degree of creative synergism may emerge. But should they work on too many projects together, that dynamic interaction may become stale and static—yielding predictable teamwork in which everyone is just going through the motions. In an analogous fashion, crewmembers too entangled in the center of the cinematic network may become too conventional and constrained; those out on the fringe of the periphery may veer toward the amateur or experimental. Like Goldilocks and the three bears, somewhere in the middle is "just right."

That's precisely what the researchers found. Single-peaked curvilinear functions appeared for both predictor variables. This conclusion is evident from Figure 3.1. For the first predictor, increases in a contributor's coreness at first increase the number of awards and nominations they are likely to receive. But almost two-thirds through the full range of the coreness measure a peak is reached, and thereafter the relationship becomes negative. Those who are most embedded in the core are less likely to receive such recognition than those who are a little more removed from the center of the filmmaking network. For the second predictor, the optimum appears earlier—almost one-third into the repeated ties indicator—and so the decline is more disastrous. The initial impact of acquiring experience with other crewmembers is positive, but very quickly it becomes negative. Soon it becomes time to move on, find another set of cinematic collaborators who can help revitalize one's creativity rather than doing more of the "same old, same old."

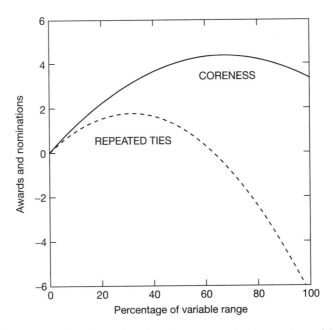

Figure 3.1 The number of awards and nominations received by members of the film's core crew as a function of two social network variables: coreness and repeated ties. To permit direct comparison, both have rescaled to a common intercept (= 0) and expressed as a percentage of their full range (0-100).

One might criticize these findings because the specific crewmembers do not all participate at the same stages of the filmmaking process. Producers and screenwriters are most likely to collaborate during the pre-production phase whereas the composers are most likely to get involved in the post-production phase. Only the director, cinematographer, film editor, and production designer collaborate during the production phase. Nevertheless, when the investigators repeated the data analysis using just these four crewmembers, the empirical outcome turned out the same. This is another illustration of the principle "it don't make no nevermind" first introduced in the previous chapter.

Teasers

This chapter began by identifying the four creative clusters of filmmaking; awards and nominations tend to cluster into the dramatic, visual, technical, and musical. The dramatic is defined by directing, screenplay, acting, and film editing; the visual by cinematography, art production, costume design, and makeup; the technical by visual effects, sound effects editing, and sound mixing; and the musical by score and song. These four clusters were then shown to predict cinematic success as gauged by best picture honors (awards and nominations) and critical evaluations (movie guide ratings). The dramatic cluster was especially important, followed by the visual cluster, the remaining clusters having weaker or inconsistent relationships with cinematic acclaim.

These predictions then led to the issue of what predicted the predictors. The creative clusters are defined by awards and nominations received by crewmembers (plus the actors in the case of the dramatic cluster), but what predicts the honors bestowed on the crewmembers? This question was answered by looking at the process of collaborative creativity in nine central crewmembers: producer, director, scriptwriter, film editor, cinematographer, production designer, and composer. A crewmember's performance was shown to be a positive linear function of team quality and creative freedom and a curvilinear single-peaked function of coreness within the social network and repeated ties with fellow crewmembers.

Needless to say, these four predictors do not exhaust the possibilities. So we will return to this issue in later chapters. Thus, Chapter 4 will look at whether the production budget is a critical determinant. To what extent can the film's producers buy the services necessary to ensure the exceptional dramatic contributions that win awards and nominations from major professional, journalistic, and critical organizations? Subsequent chapters will focus on some specific components of the dramatic cluster. Chapter 5 will concentrate on the characteristics of the script, Chapter 6 on the career course of the director, and Chapter 7 on the actors—most notably on the differences between men and women in lead and supporting roles. These chapters, in combination with Chapters 8 and 9, will also help us understand why among the four creative clusters, it is the dramatic cluster that really counts.

Chapter 4

Rave Reviews, Movie Awards, and Box Office Bucks: Which Doesn't Belong?

Any film aficionado should've noticed something fundamentally missing in the previous chapters: Nowhere did I address box office success! What about the blockbuster? How about those movies which fill up thousands of theaters week after week? The criteria that I have so far used have involved either movie awards or critical acclaim. Yet clearly most filmmakers also want to make money. By the beginning of the 2000s it cost, on average, more than 40 million in US dollars to produce a mainstream feature film. No one is going to plop that amount of cash down just to get an Oscar statuette or an extra star in a movie guide.

To be sure, it would be a nice treat to get that high-level recognition *and* earn megabucks. But if you were a producer and had to opt for just one or the other, which option would you pick? If to win an award or receive a five-star rating you knew that you'd gross a mere $10 million on a flick that cost $100 million to make, would you change your plans? And if you could earn $100 million by investing only $10 million in a film, but knew that it would be uniformly panned by the critics and utterly ignored in the award ceremonies, would you still chuckle all the way to the bank? Which is a more powerful set of goals, fame but bankruptcy or wealth but infamy?

Ponder Walt Disney's experience. Having made ample profits producing cartoon shorts with characters like Mickey Mouse and Donald Duck, Disney became decidedly more ambitious. He wanted to promote the animated film as a form of high art. So in 1940 he produced the revolutionary *Fantasia*, a vivid interpretation of eight works of classical music conducted by the illustrious Leopold Stokowski. Besides the highly imaginative visual choreography, compositions by J. S. Bach, Ludvig van Beethoven, Franz Schubert,

Pyotr Tchaikovsky, Modest Mussorgsky, Paul Dukas, Amilcare Ponchielli, and Igor Stravinsky were presented in an innovative multi-track recording system—the first stereophonic sound in a major film. *Fantasia* is now recognized as a bona fide classic, earning itself a secure place in the American Film Institute's Top 100. It was also acknowledged as a substantial cinematic achievement in its own time. At the 1942 Oscar ceremony David O. Selznick handed Disney the prestigious Thalberg Award. Yet the recipient broke down in tears during his acceptance speech. "Maybe I should have a medal for bravery," Disney said, "We all make mistakes. *Fantasia* was one but it was an honest one. I shall rededicate myself to my old ideas." Why did the cartoon genius play the crybaby? *Fantasia* may have been an incredible creative fantasy, but it was even more a fantastic financial flop. It cost him about $2,280,000 to make, and it made only $361,800 in the US during its regular theatrical release. That was a big loss in 1940s dollars. Indeed, Disney's closing remark before he returned unhappily to his seat suggests that he deeply regretted having embarked on a work of art.

Since I've never financed a flop but have often lamented buying a ticket to see a blockbuster not worth seeing, I don't think Disney needed to retrogress. I'm eternally grateful that filmmakers continue to make films for fun rather than profit. Life is short, so why waste our hours viewing movies forgettable rather than profound, entertaining but not inspiring, mind-numbing instead of thought-provoking? Besides, my lifelong program of scientific research has been consistently devoted to creativity and esthetics, and especially to geniuses and their masterworks. I'm a psychologist, not an economist or MBA. All that said, I must also concede the pragmatic reality that cinema is among the most expensive forms of artistic creativity. Perhaps only architecture has more severe budgetary requirements. For instance, Frank Gehry's 2003 Walt Disney Concert Hall built in downtown Los Angeles required about $274 million, a figure only exceeded by the 1963 *Cleopatra*—staring Elizabeth Taylor and Richard Burton—which cost over $286 million in comparable dollars. And Disney Hall is no skyscraper.

Moreover, money-making movies are often used to help finance the art films. This connection was particularly prevalent in the golden age of the Hollywood studios when the profits from cheap B-movies and pure entertainment products were used to underwrite an occasional prestige film designed for eventual submission for Oscar consideration. An analogous link appears today when a director or an actor with an impressive box office record can manage to get financial backing for a pet project, even if it may require some time to get all the ducks lined up in a row. The movie rights to *One Flew Over the Cuckoo's Nest* were held for many years by

Kirk Douglas, whose attempts to realize the project were finally brought into fruition by his son Michael Douglas.

But rather than speculate more on this question, why don't we look at some actual data? I start by summarizing a 2005 study that I conducted on the relations among production budgets, box office performance, major movie awards, and critical acclaim both during and after a film's theatrical run. I will then put these empirical findings in a larger context by comparing them with the results obtained by other investigators. Such comparisons will help overcome some of the limitations of my own investigation.

Film as Art versus Movies as Business

The study began with the collection of an appropriate sample. Sampling started using the same strategy described in the preceding chapters. First, all films had to receive a nomination in at least 1 of 17 award categories from at least 1 of 7 major organizations. As a reminder, the award categories were best picture, direction, screenplay, male and female lead, male and female supporting, film editing, cinematography, art direction, costume design, makeup, score, song, visual effects, sound effects editing, and sound mixing; and the organizations were the Academy of Motion Picture Arts and Sciences, the British Academy of Film and Television Arts, the Hollywood Foreign Press Association, the National Board of Review, the National Society of Film Critics, the New York Film Critics Circle, and the Los Angeles Film Critics Association. The sample was again confined to English-language, feature-length, live-action, narrative films. However, unlike in previous studies where I ended up with well over a thousand motion pictures, I had to confine the sample to films released between 1997 and 2001. This restriction was necessary in order to have readily available certain key variables, such as production budget (or what the industry refers to as a film's "negative cost"). Although the result was only 203 films, the sample included some critical test cases. Most notable was the participation of the big-budget *Titanic*. This cost about $200 million to make and then earned about three times that in the US box office alone.

Now let's turn to the assessments and the analyses.

Assessments

To the extent possible, the 203 films in the sample were assessed on production budget, two measures of box office success, five measures of movie awards, and two measures of critical acclaim. The first measure was simply the cost of the film expressed in millions of US dollars. I've already mentioned the most expensive movie in the sample, the 1997 *Titanic* (staring Leonardo DiCaprio and Kate Winslet). The cheapest, in contrast, was really, really cheap, namely, the 1999 *The Blair Witch Project*, which was made on a shoestring budget of well under a million (and thus stared nobody). The average budget for films in this sample was about $45 million. That's the cost of producing the 1997 *Liar, Liar* (staring Jim Carrey), the 1998 *Blade* (staring Wesley Snipes), and the 2000 *All the Pretty Horses* (starring Matt Damon).

Performance in the theaters was assessed two ways. First was how well the film did on the first weekend of release (again expressed in millions of US dollars). This variable ranged from 0 to 93 million, with an average of about 11 million bucks. If you're curious, the film that had the best first weekend earnings in this sample was the 1997 *The Lost World: Jurassic Park* (staring lots of scary dinosaurs). The second measure was the total domestic income, which had a minimum of 0 and a maximum of 601 million—the latter, the *Titanic* again. The mean or average box office gross was about 63 million, just shy of the amount gained by the 1997 *In & Out* (for which both Kevin Kline and Joan Cusack received Golden Globe nominations).

The movie award indicators should be very familiar by now, in light of what we learned in Chapters 2 and 3. First and foremost is the assessment of best picture honors using the nominations and awards bestowed by the seven organizations that defined the sample (on the same 0-1-2 scale already discussed and defended in Chapter 1). Next are the measures of how a film scores on the four creative clusters, that is, the dramatic (directing, screenplay, all four acting, film editing), the visual (cinematography, art direction, costume, makeup), the technical (visual effects, sound effects editing, and sound mixing), and the musical (score and song) clusters (again using a 0-1-2 scale summed across all organizations that bestow the award).

Last, but most likely foremost, are the two assessments of critical acclaim. One we have already encountered in previous chapters—the movie guide ratings. As you'll remember these are based on five different guides, yielding an overall measure with a high degree of reliability. In theory, the scores could range from one star (turkey or bomb) to five stars (masterpiece or classic). The actual range in this sample was from 1.9 stars to 4.9 stars, with an average of 3.5 stars (instead of 3 stars, the hypothetical middle score). In other words, because of the sampling criterion of at least one nomination, these 203 films are a bit better than the norm. There are no outright artistic disasters. The worst film has a little less than two stars out of five.

The second measure takes advantage of the ratings published by Metacritic.com, which summarizes the evaluations of dozens of major eminent critics on a 100-point scale. As noted in Chapter 2, these evaluations differ from the movie guide ratings in that the former appear during the films theatrical release whereas the latter appear after the film comes out on video or DVD. This means that the two critical assessments are separated by a year or more. Even so, the two still strongly correlate ($r = .75$). It is also worth pointing out that Metacritic scores have been shown to correlate very highly with other critical evaluations, such as those posted at RottenTomatoes.com ($r = .97$). In any case, in the current sample the Metacritic scores ranged from 19 to 95, with an average of 65.7. So again, the sample includes no genuine turkeys or bombs, and the typical film is in the upper range of the scale. I'll return to this point later in the chapter.

Analyses

Let's start the analysis by asking: What can money buy? If you have enough cash in hand, can you make a great flick by any reasonable criterion? The answer is shown in Table 4.1. The table presents the correlation coefficients (r's) plus the sample size (n's) for each correlation. Because production budget was not available for all 203 films, samples are no greater than 168, and in the case of the Metacritic ratings—which were not available until 1999—the sample was reduced to just 63 films. Anyhow, please note four points.

First, money can buy love, if you define love as lots of people loving your movie. The more you spend on your film, the more money it tends to earn on its opening weekend and during the course of its domestic theatrical release. These are both impressive effects.

TABLE 4.1   Correlations between Film Budget and Measures of Cinematic Success and Creative Clusters

	r	n
Box office earnings		
First weekend	.69***	166
Gross	.71***	167
Best picture honors	.03	168
Creative clusters		
Dramatic	–.09	168
Visual	.27***	168
Technical	.54***	168
Musical	.33***	168
Critics ratings		
Metacritic	–.36**	63
Movie guides	–.22**	139

*$p < .05$. **$p < .01$. ***$p < .001$.

Second, if you're the kind of filmmaker who defines love as winning all sorts of best picture awards and nominations, then tough luck. The correlation is practically zero.

Third, the same null effect is found for awards and nominations in the dramatic cluster. You cannot get honors for directing, screenwriting, acting, and editing simply by throwing buckets of dollar bills around the set. If anything, the association is slightly (even if not significantly) negative. Nonetheless, a handsome production budget can finance prestigious awards in the remaining three clusters: visual, technical, and musical. Just pay the sizable salaries of top-flight cinematographers, production designers, visual effects supervisors, sound editors and mixers, composers, song writers, etc. Are these crewmembers hired guns?

Fourth and last, if you want to get the approval of the film critics, then less is more. Huge budgets are more likely to provoke contempt than acclaim, probably because such expenditures result in flicks full of sound and fury but signifying nothing. The visual, technical, and musical fireworks only betray the emptiness of the dramatic center—a hollow shell, however brilliant.

The next step in the analysis was to perform a multiple regression analysis. In particular, film budget and the scores on the four creative clusters were used to predict the two indicators of box office earnings, best picture honors, and the two indicators of critical acclaim. In addition, control variables were introduced for the film's release date, runtime, genre, and the MPAA rating—the same controls used in calculating the results reported in Table 3.2. Hence, the conclusions cannot be contaminated by any of these very obvious factors.

Now I would like you to make the following three sets of observations from the findings presented in Table 4.2:

1. Nothing predicts first weekend earnings except for the film's budget. Box office gross is also most strongly related to production costs, but in this case honors in two creative clusters have a small but significant impact. These are the dramatic and technical clusters, with the latter having slightly more influence. Special visual and sound effects trump direction, script, acting, and editing!

2. The production budget, in stark contrast, again has no relevance to predicting best picture awards and nominations. The latter are instead predicted by two creative clusters, namely, the dramatic cluster and, to an appreciably lesser degree, the visual cluster. Consequently, directing, writing, acting, and editing *is* crucial to the making of a great picture by this standard. Photography, set, costume, and makeup add frosting to the cake.

TABLE 4.2   Regression Coefficients for Success Criteria as Function of Film Budget and Creative Clusters

	Box Office Earnings		Best Picture Honors	Critics Ratings	
	First weekend	Gross		Metacritic	Movie guides
Film Budget	.64***	.60***	−.03	−.46**	−.21**
Creative Clusters					
Dramatic	−.13	.13*	.71***	.45***	.67***
Visual	.13	.06	.16**	−.01	−.04
Technical	.08	.18**	.09	.23	.13
Musical	−.12	.04	.10	−.04	−.03
R^2	.49***	.59***	.76***	.40***	.51***
n	166	167	168	63	137

Note. The regression coefficients are all standardized ("betas").

*$p < .05$. **$p < .01$. ***$p < .001$.

3. The dramatic cluster remains the most potent predictor of the two critics' evaluations: the Metacritic and movie guide ratings. Indeed, in the latter case the standardized regression coefficient is about the same size as that for best picture honors. Nevertheless, the production budget also provides some predictive information, but in a *negative* direction. Reinforcing what we saw in Table 4.1, critics' evaluations are a negative function of the amount of money spent on making a film. Interestingly, production budget and the dramatic cluster have about equal impact on the Metacritic ratings (albeit of opposite sign), but by the time the movie guides come out a conspicuous differential appears—the dramatic cluster having over three times the influence as the production costs. In the end, what matters most is the "four 'ings'"—directing, writing, acting, and editing.

Table 4.2 also provides the squared multiple correlation, or R^2. Again, this statistic tells us the proportion of variation in the predicted variable that is explained by all of the predictor variables. Thus, 59% of the variance in gross domestic box office can be explained by the predictors in the regression equation (including the control variables). We do an even better job of predicting best picture honors—76%—but that is because the main predictors are other awards offered by the same organizations, which probably exaggerates the concordance. With respect to critical acclaim, between 40% and 51% of the variation is accounted for by the specified predictors. It should be apparent that these R^2s provide rough indices of the extent of our scientific knowledge. We know about half of what's involved in having good first weekend earnings, about two-fifths of what it takes to get good reviews during a film's theatrical release.

If you want the primary message from all this, it's probably the negative relation between the cost of making a film and its later standing with film critics. Table 4.3 provides a concrete illustration of this inverse relationship.

Here I picked films that were released in 2000 and 2001 that were in either the top 10 or bottom 10 in budget or in the top 10 or bottom 10 in Metacritic ratings. It's manifest that the two lists overlap very little, and when they do overlap, they do not do so in the same way. For example, *Pearl Harbor* was the most expensive movie ($140 million), but it's in the bottom 10 in critical evaluations. In comparison, *You Can Count on Me* was the least expensive film to produce ($1.2 million), but it scored in the top 10 in the critic ratings. Other films showing this inverse placement are *In the Bedroom* ($1.7 million), *Memento* ($5 million), *Hedwig and the Angry Inch* ($6 million), and *The Deep End* ($3 million). Absolutely no film is in the bottom 10 on both lists. Certainly no film was harmed in the critics' eyes because the filmmaker spent too little money. Finally, only one film is in the top 10 on both lists—*The Lord of the Rings: The Fellowship of the Ring* (which cost $93 million). That's not enough exceptions to negate

TABLE 4.3   Top 10 and Bottom 10 Movies in 2000-2001 According to Budget versus Metacritic Ratings

	Budget	Metacritic ratings
Top 10	Pearl Harbor	Almost Famous
	Harry Potter and the Sorcerer's Stone	Gosford Park
	How the Grinch Stole Christmas	Lord of the Rings (Part 1)
	The Perfect Storm	In the Bedroom
	The Patriot	You Can Count on Me
	Lord of the Rings (Part 1)	Traffic
	Ali	Hedwig and the Angry Inch
	Gladiator	Mulholland Dr.
	Planet of the Apes	Memento
	Black Hawk Down	The Deep End
Bottom 10	Best in Show	What Women Want
	Hedwig and the Angry Inch	Vanilla Sky
	Iris	Vertical Limit
	Billy Elliot	Pearl Harbor
	Memento	The Cell
	Requiem for a Dream	Miss Congeniality
	Monster's Ball	Vatel
	The Deep End	102 Dalmatians
	In the Bedroom	I Am Sam
	You Can Count on Me	Hollow Man

the negative association between financial costs and cinematic benefits. There are films that intend art and there are movies that mean business. Only very rarely is art good business.

Comparisons and Contrasts

I personally conducted the study just reviewed. But I would be the first to admit that the investigation contains many faults. Above all, I would have preferred to have had larger samples at my disposal. My earlier investigations would usually include well over a thousand films, so it was a letdown to settle sometimes for only 63 films. Another problem is that the sample was confined to films that had received one or more award nominations in one of 17 categories of cinematic achievement. Even granting that some of these categories are less important than others—like makeup artist—it remains true that none of these films could be said to have been scraped off the bottom of the barrel. There were no out-and-out turkeys or bombs in the sample. Even the 2000 *Hollow Man* in Table 4.3 got a Metacritic score of 24 and averaged 2.5 stars in the movie guides. Perhaps different results might have been obtained had the sample dipped a bit lower into the pool of available films. For instance, the sample did not include the 2000 *Battlefield Earth: A Saga of the Year 3000*, which received just a 9 from Metacritic and 1.1 stars from the movie guides—and yet cost $73 million to make. Would the negative correlation between production costs and critical acclaim become even more magnified were this Travolta travesty tossed into the sample?

So the results reported in Tables 4.1 and 4.2 must be considered tentative without additional empirical corroboration. We need to look more closely at budget, critics, and awards, their interrelationships, and their connections with box office. But before doing so, the reader needs a warning. The research on this topic is not always consistent. For a given pair of variables, one researcher may obtain a positive association, another researcher a zero correlation, and perhaps even another researcher a negative relationship. Sometimes the same investigator may obtain conflicting findings in successive studies. This inconsistency might lead one to infer that research in this area cannot be called scientific—at least not if science is expected to produce a cumulative body of knowledge. Yet that conclusion is unjustified. If you look at the studies more closely you'll always find that the investigations did not use identical methods.

First, studies may vary in the sampling criteria they use to select the films for the inquiry. Most noticeable are the differences in the time periods covered. Films produced in the halcyon days of the Hollywood studios are not comparable to those produced in the post-TV era. Some inquiries use samples confined to the films released in a single year! Other contrasts in sampling criteria are more subtle but no less serious. For example, where some investigators will confine the sample to films nominated for a major award or that received a threshold number of critical reviews or that featured specified movie stars, other investigators might choose just films that earned a specified absolute or relative amount in the box office, and still others might simply draw a random sample of all films—no matter how esoteric—that are released during a given period. These diverse sampling criteria cannot be expected to yield the same results. It would be like evaluating the best teaching technique using samples ranging from prep schools to reformatories. Moreover, researchers occasionally differ on whether or not to include foreign-language films, documentaries, and animations. A sample of 2004 films that includes the Spanish-language *Pan's Labyrinth (El laberinto del fauno)*, the documentary *An Inconvenient Truth*, and the animated feature *Happy Feet* might produce different empirical outcomes than one that excludes these and other films of the same type.

Second, research will often define certain key variables in contrasting ways. For example, what counts as a movie star? Where some researchers posit star status for anyone who has received an Oscar or comparable award for best female or male actor, other researchers may determine star status according to surveys of moviegoers. Or stardom might be gauged by the financial performance of an actor's most recent films, by the total number of prior films he or she has appeared in, or by industry determinations of the "top 10" or "top 100" most "powerful" or "bankable" stars, the actors with the highest "marquee value," or the "A" and "A+" list performers. Yet there's definitely no reason to suspect that these alternative definitions would correlate with other variables in the same fashion, such as box office or critical acclaim. Kathy Bates won an Oscar for her lead performance in the 1991 *Misery*, but this does not equate her with Jennifer Lopez, who earned a Razzie for Worst Actress in the 2003 *Gigli* despite earning $12 million to display her much more minimal acting skills. An award-winning woman actor is not the same as a bankable sexy starlet.

Third, even when the variables might be defined in the same manner, inquiries will seldom include exactly the same variables. Why is this so critical? As pointed out in the previous chapter, sometimes the relation between two factors can be spurious because both are a consequence of other factors. Introducing the latter factors as control variables in a multiple regression equation then removes the source of spuriousness. Alternatively, the correlation between two factors may be unjustly small because the association is contaminated by extraneous variables. So the latter can be put into the equation to act as suppressor variables (i.e., variables that suppress the influence of the contaminants). Yet if two studies do not have the same set of control variables, then it's not possible to directly compare the results with any certainty. To provide a clear-cut case, if one equation includes production budget and another does not, many of the findings will not be directly comparable. If one finds that stars have an effect on box office and another finds no effect, perhaps the contrast is a mere consequence of the presence or absence of budget as a variable in the equation. If production costs are held constant, then movie stars might have an impact, but if no adjustment is made for production costs, then stars might have no impact. You get the point. Multiple regression equations from two different studies are not really comparable unless they contain the same predictor variables.

Fourth and last, investigations will frequently employ rather distinct statistical methods. But on this last point I will impart the least. That's because the topic is very technical. Suffice it to say that there's more than one way to predict a criterion variable given a set of predictor variables, and that these different methods do not necessarily come up with identical results, even when the sample and all of the variables are absolutely identical. Although these alternative techniques can be distinguished with respect to sophistication, not all researchers use the most sophisticated techniques available. And, naturally, researchers whose work was published decades ago will not have had access to these more advanced methods.

In light of these complications, I focus discussion on those results that replicate most often. When findings don't replicate so well, then I stress the most recent results.

Budget

It's obvious to everyone that a film's budget must be a key factor in understanding cinematic creativity and aesthetics. Yet many scientific studies of box office performance ignore production costs. The reason isn't that scientists are lazy. The fact is this: Unlike box office data, the film's budget constitutes proprietary information that is frequently kept under wraps. The movie's cost might not even be known, as was often the case in the era of the big studios. Although occasionally rough estimates are available, these are often offered in very round figures, in contrast to box office stats. For example, the Internet Movie Database (imdb.com) says the following with respect to the 2001 *Harry Potter and the Sorcerer's Stone*: The budget was estimated at $130,000,000, but the film earned $90,294,621 on its first weekend in the United States (having opened on 3,672 screens on November 18th), and yielded a domestic gross of $317,557,891 (by May 19, 2002). Think about it! If you saw this movie and can remember what you paid for admission, you can calculate the exact percentage of the box office receipts that can be credited to your wallet or purse! But the budget itself is only known to the tens of millions of dollars!

In any event, a large body of empirical research supports a major point in Tables 4.1 and 4.2: Insofar as the data are available, a film's production budget is positively associated with box office performance. Expressed differently, it is rare for a blockbuster not to have been a big-budget production. However, this consistent and strong effect is not tantamount to asserting that expensive productions turn nice profits. If a film product does not bring in substantially more revenue than its costs, then it will count as a box-office flop. The 2004 *Alexander* provides a recent case in point. Made for about $155 million, its domestic gross was only slightly more than $34 million—a negative discrepancy amply exceeding $100 million. More amazing, that loss was incurred despite having the Oscar-winner Oliver Stone as both director and co-writer, and featuring a cast that included such stars as Anthony Hopkins, Angelina Jolie, Val Kilmer, Christopher Plummer, and Colin Farrell. How could a motion picture about such a momentous historical figure, and with such spectacular cinematic credentials, go so terribly wrong?

Making a Profit?

Because budget figures are so scarce, scientific investigations that concentrate on the determinants of profit are few and far between. Furthermore, the empirical findings are not very encouraging. One investigation of 2,015 movies released between 1984 and 1996 obtained a prediction equation with $R^2 = .118$. This means that only about 12% of the variation in profits can be accounted for. That proportion does not compare very favorably with the R^2s shown in Table 4.2. Other criteria of a film's success, whether box office, awards, or critical acclaim, can be much more successfully explained. Moreover, on the average, every buck spent on production only brings in less than half that much in revenue. We're not talking about a sure bet by any means. Sometimes good money is thrown after bad.

It's hard to conceive a more risky business than trying to produce a profitable film. Perhaps only the lottery has more risk, but then the stakes aren't nearly so high. If a few bucks don't make you a millionaire, so what! But if many million dollars invested don't make at least twice that, then why try? It is telling that Donald Trump, the billionaire entrepreneur and celebrity on the 2004-2008 reality-TV show "The Apprentice," had originally planned to become a movie producer but eventually switched to the real estate business when he realized that it would be much more reliably profitable. Filmmaking is not for the faint of heart.

Complicating the picture all the more, the relationship between budget and profits is not necessarily linear. More is not always better. For example, one study found that profits were a backward-J function of budget. That means it's the low-budget pictures that are most likely to make the most money. Costing the least to make, they don't have to bring in as much at the box office to earn a sizable return with respect to the investment. The extremely low-budget *Blair Witch Project* brought in $141 million in domestic gross. A more recent example is the 2003 *Open Water* that grossed about $31 million but cost only about $130,000 to make. By comparison, even when a big-budget film does make money, it's more likely to earn less relative to the cost. According to one analysis, more than a third of the big-budgeters will generate losses. But at least that's better than the poor expected return of middle-budget films.

Given these complexities, it should not surprise us that the typical film is unprofitable; "in fact, of any 10 major theatrical films produced, on the average, six or seven may be broadly characterized as unprofitable." As an example, between 1984 and 1996 a film had to reach the 78th percentile in gross returns before it even recouped its costs, and the median movie lost almost 4 million dollars. Given that a film must bring in more than twice its budget to count as truly profitable, films must fall into an even higher percentile to really make money. Fortunately, the upper tail of the distribution is so extended that about 80% of Hollywood's entire profit can be credited to just a little over 6% of the movies.

Thus, even though the typical mainstream movie loses money in the box office, the average amount of money earned by all such movies exceeds the average cost of making a film. Movies are profitable in the aggregate even if so few individual movies turn a profit. If it were otherwise, we would refer to the movie charity instead of the movie industry.

Reducing the Risk?

Obviously, some of the uncertainty involved in the budget-profit function might be alleviated if filmmakers knew what to spend money on. Judging from the results reported in Tables 4.1 and 4.2, cash doesn't always seem to be expended on the right things. On the one hand, as seen in Table 4.1, a lot of the money seems to be going to purchase the award-winning services of those responsible for the visual, technical, and musical clusters of cinematic creativity. On the other hand, as Table 4.2 indicates, the visual and musical components bear no connection with box office, and the technical cluster has only a small connection. Meanwhile, award-winning drama, which does relate to long-term box office, is uncorrelated with budget! So filmmakers seem too often to be investing in the wrong cinematic features.

Another inquiry into the profitability of over 2000 films corroborated this conclusion: "Heavy spending on special effects or 'production value' is the most risky strategy for making a movie a hit." So what is the *least* risky strategy?

The most obvious answer is to funnel the expenditures into the dramatic aspects of the film. Why not hire top-notch directors, screenwriters, actors, and film editors? Actually, the bulk of the scientific research concentrates on actors, so let's focus on those findings. I'll get back to directors and screenwriters in later chapters (and I know of no inquiries into film editors). Needless to say, when we speak of actors, what we really mean are *movie stars*. Producers often seek out the biggest stars of the moment to get a sure box office draw. There are many consumers out there who will head to the theater merely because the marquee blazons the name of Tom Hanks, Anthony Hopkins, Will Smith, Jackie Chan, Whoopi Goldberg, Julia Roberts, or some other celebrity. But do stars really sell a movie enough to ensure its profitability?

Here the answer is not simple. Some studies say that stars bring in the cash, and others say they don't. Some investigators have even found that stars can have a negative impact. Judging from these results, it would seem that their impact seems inconsistent and undependable. Part of the confusion may ensue from contrasts in how stardom is defined. As observed earlier, researchers vary in how they decide to measure the presence of stars in their sampled films. Even so, a certain consistency and dependability still pervades all of these results. Consider the following three conclusions:

1. Whatever impact stars have on profits is extremely uncertain. Because stars cost so much, they can increase the budget to a degree that cannot be recouped in the theaters. If you pay $20 million or more for a star, the breakeven point also rises by $20 million or more. "If a star is paid the expected increase in revenue associated with his or her performance in a movie then the movie will almost always lose money." This is the so-called "curse of the superstar." Hence, one of the best ways to take advantage of star power is to convince the celebrity to take a pay cut to contribute to a medium-budget but high-prestige project, with or without a percentage of the receipts.

2. There are "stars" and there are **STARS**. Not all, nor even most, putative big names on the silver screen display a sizable association with a film becoming a hit. A few may even become known as "box office poison," like what happened to Katherine Hepburn in the late-1930s. Ben Affleck may provide a more recent example, his name becoming associated with a series of flops, and reaching a nadir in 2003 when

he "won" the Worst Actor Razzie for *Daredevil*, *Paycheck*, and *Gigli*. Of course, like Hepburn, Affleck's career underwent a revival, which brings us to the next point.

3. A star's box office profitability is not stable over time. Not only can it change from one picture to the next, but also the specific trajectory may vary dramatically. To illustrate, one study of 1,687 films released between 1956 and 1988, which examined the market power of over 100 stars, identified: (a) linear increases for Marlon Brando, James Coburn, Tom Cruise, Clint Eastwood, Bette Midler, and Sylvester Stallone, (b) linear declines for Jessica Lange, Al Pacino, and John Travolta, (c) horizontal trend lines for Danny DeVito, Dustin Hoffman, Bill Murray, Burt Reynolds, and Barbara Streisand, (d) U- or J-shaped curves for Julie Andrews, Kevin Bacon, Robert De Niro, and Charlton Heston, and (e) inverted-U or inverted-J curves for Richard Dreyfuss, Harrison Ford, Tom Laughlin, Eddie Murphy, Paul Newman, and Robert Redford. Given these contradictory career trends, it stands to reason that exorbitant expenditures on headliners cannot guarantee a blockbuster. It may reduce slightly the uncertainty of the dice roll, but it's still not a sure thing.

Why are stars so unpredictable? A star's marketability is probably a very complex function of many diverse influences. Is the star doing the same old thing ad infinitum, merely intensifying mannerisms that were once so provocative or endearing? Has the star been terribly miscast into a role well outside his or her constricted sphere of acting expertise? Does the star have bad chemistry with co-stars on the set, extirpating the spark from love scenes or the tension from climatic showdowns? Is the star so uninspired by the role that he or she decides just to "phone in" the lines from the script? And has the star merely become a star because he or she was lucky enough to have a role of a lifetime, a role that was never granted before nor will ever be seen again? Stardom is not always snugly coupled with genuine talent. Film aficionados can come up with examples of each of these contingencies from their own cinematic experience. So I have no need to provide my personal list of talentless stars.

Critics

Table 4.1 showed that production budget correlates negatively with critic evaluations published both (a) at the time of theatrical release (Metacritic) and (b) after the films come out in video or DVD (movie guide ratings). Table 4.2 repeated this observation, and added that both critic judgments correlated positively with the dramatic creative clusters. So critics love modest-budget films that win recognition in the categories of best directing, screenplay, acting (male and female lead and supporting), and film editing. What is not shown in either table is the null finding of that investigation. Neither the earlier nor the later critic evaluation is associated with domestic gross, and first weekend earnings has a *negative* correlation with the earlier critical assessments ($r = -.25$). Also not displayed in the tables are the positive correlations that the critics' appraisals have with best picture awards and nominations. To be specific, best picture honors correlate .35 with the Metacritic score and .55 with movie guide ratings. Taken altogether, the judgments of film critics seem to be in accord with the most important movie awards, but rather out of sync with the box office, especially performance on the first weekend of release.

However, if you look more carefully at the overall findings, a curious discrepancy appears: Although the two sets of critic judgments correlate very highly—.76 for this study—they are by no means equivalent. Metacritic correlates negatively with first weekend earnings, but movie guide ratings do not, and the former do not correlate as highly with best picture honors as do the latter. Why the difference? Certainly some portion of the difference is that the two sets of critics are not always reviewing the same films. Passing judgment on a film viewed in a movie theater—with gigantic screen and luxurious sound—is not the same as rating the video or DVD version, even if played on a state-of-the-art home entertainment system. Indeed, the movie guides evaluations are sometimes based on the "director's cut" which are invariably longer than the theatrical release and thus contain more violence, more sex, and perchance even more plot and character development.

But another cause of the before-after contrasts is more interesting, namely, that one is predictive and the other retrospective. The film reviews going into the formula to compute the Metacritic scores were written early in a movie's theatrical run. In fact, many were written prior to the release, when the critics attended a special screening or preview. These critics have very little information at their disposal—just the marketing hype, the trailers, and the film itself. The critics who write the movie guides have much more to go on. After all, they know how the story turned out. They know the box office results, and they know the end result of the movie awards bestowed each year. Regarding the last point, it's no accident that the movie guide ratings correlate the highest with both best picture honors and recognition in the dramatic categories. These critics have hindsight on their side, whereas the Metacritic reviewers must be true prophets. And as they say, hindsight always has 20-20 vision.

I will have more to say about movie awards in the next section. Right now let me discuss some scientific studies that offer some insights into the nature of critical acclaim and its opposite—when a poor film is roasted by the critics. I'll start with critics who express their opinions at the time that the film is being exhibited in the theaters, and then turn to those who evaluate films after they've been available for rental and purchase by the general public.

Film Reviews during the Theatrical Run

Many older "baby-boomer" moviegoers may have fond memories of watching Gene Siskel and Robert Ebert in their weekly television program. Although the program changed names, sponsors, and personnel over the years, its basic format was the same. A film clip from some recent release, a three-level assessment—two thumbs up, one up and one down, or two thumbs down—and some explanations why, and some heated give and take when the two critics disagreed. Many viewers used the weekly program to guide their entertainment plans for the coming weekend. But did enough viewers do so for Siskel and Ebert to sway or prophesy the box office performance of the films they critiqued? Or, speaking in more general terms, is there any congruence between the judgments cast at the beginning a film's theatrical run and its eventual box office success?

Research results are all over the map. While most investigators have found that critical evaluations are positively associated with box office performance, others find either no relationship or even a negative relationship, just as I came across in my 2005 study that generated Tables 4.1-4.3. How could the outcomes be so contradictory? There are many answers, including the many method differences discussed earlier. One critical discrepancy has to do with the criterion of box office performance. Although the initial critical judgments usually predict gross returns accumulated by the end of a picture's theatrical run, they do not commonly predict early success, such as gauged by first weekend earnings. This striking incongruity in predictive timing has been expressed as a distinction between critics as "influencers" versus "predictors." The assumption is that a high association between critical praise and early box office would indicate that the critics are influencing consumers to purchase tickets, but if the association must wait much later then the critics are only assessing a film's quality and thereby forecasting its long-term financial earnings.

As if this differentiation were not complex enough, research has shown that the correspondence between critical acclaim and ticket sales, whenever measured during the theatrical release, is contingent on other considerations. One such factor is whether we are speaking of positive or negative reviews. Being branded as a turkey or bomb is not the same as being designated an outright masterpiece. And this difference has variable repercussions. In the first place, negative reviews tend to have a bigger impact than positive reviews, so critical disapproval has more adverse effects than critical approval has beneficial effects. Even so, the negative effects are of short duration in comparison to the positive effects. After a week or so moviegoers may ignore the bad reviews if word of mouth contradicts the critics. Although critics are influencers for pictures for which they turn their thumbs down, the critics are predictors with respect to pictures for which they give their thumbs up!

It gets worse: The connection between critic judgments and box office performance can be moderated by other factors. That is, the relationship might be large under certain conditions and small or nonexistent under other conditions. To offer two examples, the relation between critical assessments and box office performance is moderated by both the costs of production and the presence of stars. Alternatively, we can say that the critics' evaluations interact with budget and stars to determine how many consumers queue up at the box office. The critics' unfavorable opinions are most likely to depress the early financial returns for medium- or low-budget films with no movie stars in leading roles. But for films that feature big budgets and/or top stars, the critics become largely irrelevant. Moviegoers will then ignore the critics to see the magnificent special effects or their favorite performers. And a film that has already received critical acclaim will gain very little by its having sunk exceptional expenditures on production and stars.

I realize that all of this sounds very complicated. So let's just boil everything down to the gist: The relation between the judgments of the critics and the behavior of moviegoers is, well, very complicated. I know of no other aspect of cinematic success where the interactions are so convoluted.

Film Reviews after the Video/DVD Release

Sometimes consumers want to watch a movie some weekend but find that the local theaters are not showing anything they haven't already seen or want to see. In the days before Netflix and similar services, the solution to this problem was to take a trip to the local video store, Blockbuster or otherwise, and there rent out a few new releases or old classics. Although some customers would engage in impulse buying, others would be far more conscientious, consulting their favorite movie guide. As noted before, the ratings in these guides are most often compiled after a film's theatrical release, and are even based explicitly on the video cassette or DVD. As a result, these evaluations have a different foundation than those published at the onset of a film's projection on the big screen.

Although in my own investigation movie guide ratings were unrelated to financial performance, other studies find divergent outcomes. One 1994 inquiry found that such ratings were positively associated with box office gross, suggesting the possibility that those ratings might have been influenced by financial performance. Yet, a 1993 study identified a U-shaped relationship! The films that did the best in the box office were either identified as turkeys or bombs by the critics or else were considered masterpieces. According to the authors, "it appears that a bad movie has something to gain from being as trashy as possible" but for "a good movie, it apparently pays to strive for even greater excellence." Yet I should also note that the U-shaped curve implies that the *linear* relation between movie guide ratings and financial performance is zero, just as I found in my 2005 investigation. Hence, there's no general tendency across the full range of films for box office gross to increase with each star bestowed in a video/ DVD guide.

The upshot is that financial performance has a tenuous if not ambiguous connection with the critical evaluations published after the film's theatrical release. The picture is not all that different from that seen for the earlier evaluations, just much less complicated.

Awards

Although Table 4.2 showed that first-weekend earnings were uncorrelated with awards in any of the four creative clusters, it also showed that awards in the dramatic and technical categories are positively associated with final gross receipts, with the technical cluster having a slightly greater effect size. More specifically, awards for visual effects, sound effects editing, and sound mixing have the biggest impact, followed closely by awards for directing, screenplay, acting, and film editing. Unfortunately, it's impossible to find other scientific studies that validate these results. And the reason is simple: Researchers tend to concentrate on the dramatic awards. Indeed, most published research focuses on awards for best picture and best lead acting! The directors, screenwriters, film editors, and supporting actors are frequently just ignored. There are occasional exceptions, but the exceptions usually occur in only one or another award category, and most often with respect to direction. Or, the awards or nominations from all categories might be mixed together in one gumbo pot. Hence, I cannot say that the findings reported in Table 4.2 have been completely replicated in other studies.

Furthermore, it is necessary to recognize a certain complexity in how movie awards might relate to financial success. As we've seen, the relation between critical evaluations and box office depends on the timing of the measures. The critical judgments that become public at the onset of a film's theatrical release must be distinguished from those that are published after the film has been released on video or DVD. The former critics must demonstrate foresight whereas the latter must only exhibit hindsight—a far easier judgmental task. In the case of movie awards, contrast occurs with respect to the timing of the film's release. The major film awards are bestowed at the very end of a given release year or at the very beginning of the following year. Accordingly, many films released early in the year but after the previous year's award season will have already completed their theatrical runs by the time the first nominations are announced, whereas those released toward the end of the year will still be in the theaters at the time the awards are presented. In the former case, movie awards can only help if the film is re-released; otherwise any relation between earnings and awards represents the influence of earnings on awards. In the latter case, movie awards can directly enhance box office performance. For example, an Oscar nomination in a major category of cinematic achievement will become a featured part of the advertisements used to attract moviegoers to the theater. Naturally, the film industry is aware of this relationship and will therefore often reserve the final months of the year for the release of cinematic products that are likely to be award contenders.

These fine points aside, it remains valid that professional honors are positively related with a film's financial performance. However, four sets of qualifications have to be placed on this statement.

1. The most influential awards are best picture, best directing, and best acting in the lead roles, with the first category, for obvious reasons, having the biggest effect. No regular moviegoer wants to admit that they haven't seen the top picture of the year!
2. Oscars in these primary categories are far more crucial than other awards, such as the Golden Globes and BAFTAs. This superiority may reflect the prestige associated with the Academy as well as to the giant audience for the Oscar gala event. In 1998, 55 million viewers turned on their TV sets to see *Titanic* receive its 11 golden statuettes.
3. The precise financial consequence is not stable over time but rather will fluctuate greatly from year to year and decade to decade. These fluctuations probably reveal the intrusion of other factors, such as critical judgments and star power. In addition, the box office repercussions of prestigious professional honors may be noticeably less for films released by major distributors than for films released by small, independent distributors, who need any boost they can get to compensate for their poorer promotion resources.
4. There's still some debate about whether winning an award adds to box office success over and above the contribution of the initial nomination. Some researchers say "yes" and others "no." Part of the problem is that moviegoers will often go to theaters to see films already nominated for major awards, but once the awards are announced, consumers do not normally return to the theaters to see a film already seen. Only those moviegoers who wait until the award announcements before

making their viewing choices will be strongly influenced by the outcomes of the Oscar ceremonies. These "wait-and-see" viewers are probably a minority. And how many of them probably just add the films to their *Netflix* cue rather than transport themselves to the local theater?

We can draw one definite conclusion: Cinema consumers do seem more likely to buy a ticket to see a motion picture that has received at least a nomination for best picture or best lead male/female actor from the Motion Picture Academy of the Arts and Sciences. Any departure from any of these stipulations weakens the correspondence between honors and returns.

The Big Problem with Box Office Performance

We have just examined how a film's financial performance relates to production budget, critical evaluations, and movie awards. Although box office gross has a strong connection with budget, its links with the critical acclaim and professional honors are far more tenuous. It doesn't help matters that the cost of making a film can have a negative association with critical acclaim and a zero correlation with major awards and nominations. In contrast, critical judgments and movie awards are consistently and positively associated with each other. In particular, awards and nominations for best picture and in the dramatic categories are closely connected with the critics' assessments. On the basis of these findings it would appear that box office is not necessarily the best indicator of cinematic greatness.

To provide some concrete illustrations, let me update the case made in Table 4.3. There I showed that many blockbusters are artistic duds. Specifically, the following were among the top grossing films released between 2002 and 2006 (inclusively): *The Longest Yard* (48), *50 First Dates* (48), *Failure to Launch* (47), *Bruce Almighty* (46), *The Break-Up* (45), *Click* (45), *The Village* (44), *Meet the Fockers* (41), *Bad Boys II* (38), *Bringing Down the House* (39), *2 Fast and 2 Furious* (38), *Van Helsing* (36), *The Pacifier* (30), and *Mr. Deeds* (24). In particular, these films took in between $52 million (*The Break-Up*) and $279 million (*Meet the Fockers*). They have two other things in common besides being box office hits.

The first commonality is indicated by the numbers given in parentheses. These numbers give the critics' ratings that the films received as compiled in Metacritic.com. Because these ratings are on a 100-point scale, all films scored below the halfway point. All were mediocre films or worse. Indeed, a few films scored in the turkey or bomb range.

The second commonality is that not a single one of these films received any major awards in any important category of cinematic achievement. No Oscars, no Golden Globes, nothing ... not even for sound effects editing! Yet that dearth of credits did not prevent these films from making lots of money.

Thus the worst of the group, the 2002 *Mr. Deeds*, grossed over $126 million! Yet the 2002 *The Hours* earned only about $42 million! Despite earning only one-third as much, the latter picture received a Metacritic score of 81, and won the best film award from the National Board of Review, an Oscar, a Golden Globe, and a BAFTA for Nicole Kidman's performance in a lead role, a Writers Guild of America award for David Hare's adapted screenplay, and a BAFTA for the score composed by Philip Glass!

Why this glaring disjunction? One obvious explanation is that critical acclaim is not equivalent to consumer preference. After all, the leading film critics buy very few tickets at the box office. Usually they're invited to preview screenings so that their reviews can help stimulate consumer turn-out (unless the distributors anticipate negative reviews). Even if the critics paid their way, there are so few critics relative to consumers that only the latter have the ability to leave an enormous impression on the box office stats. Hence, if consumers are using different criteria than critics in deciding what films to see and enjoy, then that incongruity could alone undermine the degree to which box office reflects artistic merit.

Morris Holbrook carried out an investigation that directly compared popular appeal with expert judgments for a sample of 1,000 movies. Popular appeal was based on viewers' responses to a survey conducted by Home Box Office, whereas expert judgments were based on six movie guides. These two judgments did not have an identical foundation. On the one hand, consumers tended to prefer more recent, domestically-produced, English-language, family-oriented films with lots of star power and gorgeous color cinematography, but expressed a dislike for films that had more exotic origins and that contained more offensive content (e.g., sex and aggression). On the other hand, critics favored older films, often in black and white, with more exotic origins and foreign-language dialogue and narration.

Yet popular appeal and expert judgments shared some criteria as well. For instance, both favored films that featured leading directors and that won major movie awards. In fact, the association between the two assessments was positive, with a correlation of .25. Hence, the two cinematic evaluations are not at odds. Also, this correlation was probably underestimated given the somewhat selective nature of the film sample (which truncates the variation on both ratings). Other studies using more inclusive samples actually obtain critic-consumer correlations ranging between .72 and .84!

Curiously, popular appeal may be less predictable than expert assessments. Where 53% of the variance in movie guide ratings could be explained given the set of predictors, only 38% of the variance in consumer opinions could be explained given the same predictors. Insofar as box office is mostly contingent on the likes and dislikes of moviegoers, this is a more difficult audience to target than the critics. In all likelihood, this difficulty is the repercussion of the audience being far more heterogeneous in the various factors that predict cinematic preferences. Such factors include the moviegoer's gender, age, ethnicity, educational level, occupation, marital status, the number and ages of children still living at home, and so on.

Yet when all is said and done, any disconnect between critic and box office cannot be simply blamed on moviegoers lacking a full appreciation for cinematic art. If anything, the consumers agree more with the critics than they do with the box office stats. That statement is not contradictory notwithstanding the fact that it is the consumers are buying the tickets. The divergence is easily explained: Too many other factors besides consumer preferences affect a film's performance in the theaters. Even if critics and moviegoers agreed perfectly, these additional influences would still undercut the nexus between money and merit. These contaminants can be assigned to three categories: distribution, promotion, and exhibition.

Distribution

In essence, a film's distribution comes between the film's completed production (i.e., the end of post-production) and its actual exhibition in the movie theaters. Scientific research on distributional factors has focused on the following four variables:

1. *Major distributor*—Some distributors have more market clout than others. Although the industry has changed dramatically over the years, the following big names have stood out at various times in film history: Columbia, Universal, 20th Century Fox, MGM, Warner Bros., Paramount, Disney, and Dreamworks. These stand in stark contrast to various independent distributors or second-string distributors who are often left picking up the crumbs with respect to the available theaters. Of course, one would like to believe that the majors became the majors because their companies know how to pick the big moneymakers. But it may also be the case of a self-fulfilling prophecy. They provide brand names that can be used to market films beyond their intrinsic merits. Besides, they are trying to select products that make handsome profits. Majors will pick up indie films for distribution if it looks like the movies will bring in heaps of cash. The major distributors are not non-profits devoted to the dissemination of cinematic art.

I should point out that the business effect of major distribution is not always consistent across time. Not only will the rival majors vary in box office success, but also their draw may differ for domestic and international markets. This instability and unreliability renders box office returns all the more capricious. A major cannot guarantee a hit, nor does distribution by an independent spell a financial fiasco.

2. *Seasonal market*—Another crucial factor is the film's timing of release. Certain times of the year, such as the summer months, bring in bigger box office than do other times of the year. After all, a colossal number of teenagers with money in their pockets are on vacation from school and are bored silly. The summer months are particularly suitable for pictures with abundant special effects, car chases, shootouts, and explosions. A secondary time slot is the Christmas season, which is especially suitable for family-oriented films. In any case, independent of a film's genuine cinematic merits, its earnings can be maximized by a judicious choice of the date of its opening weekend. Thus, the 2002 *2 Fast and 2 Furious* was smart to open in June and run all the way through September.

3. *Wide release*—Probably the single best way to make a loud splash in the box office is to have a film open on thousands of screens. For instance, the critical turkey *Mr. Deeds* opened on 3,231 screens, whereas the critically acclaimed *The Hours* had its debut on only 11 screens. This means that even a terrible movie can make tons of money in its first week before word gets around that it's not worth seeing. But an upper limit to box office receipts is intrinsic to any film that initiates its run in a dozen theaters or less. Thus, *Mr. Deeds* made $37,162,787 its first weekend, and never did so well again, earning about half that amount the next weekend, and about one quarter that amount in the third weekend. *The Hours*? It earned only $338,622 on its first weekend, but slowly gained an audience (and screens) thereafter, reaching a peak about a month later but never able to catch up with *Mr. Deeds*. Admittedly, occasionally a movie's box office trajectory can imitate the famous fable of the tortoise and the hare. A classic example is another film appearing in 2002: *My Big Fat Greek Wedding*. It opened on only 108 screens and earned only $597,362 that weekend, but slowly attracted an audience until it was playing on over two thousand screens and earning over $10 million a week—eventually grossing almost $100 million more than *Mr. Deeds*! Even so, *My Big Fat Greek Wedding* is the exception that proves the rule.

4. *Current competition*—Yet one cannot presume that a film will earn megabucks just because it opens on thousands of screens on a summer weekend. It will not be the only film in the theaters that weekend, nor

even the only one opening that weekend. So it may find itself losing to the competition, whether continuing runs or rival openings. As a consequence, a film might actually earn more if it hits the silver screen when the competition is less fierce. I once had the pleasure of touring the Pixar Animation Studios in Emeryville, California, just a hop, skip, and jump from my university. When someone in my entourage asked the guide "Who's your greatest competitor?" the guy responded "Whoever has a movie opening the same weekend as ours!"

Yet how does a potential distributor determine the best time slot on the calendar? For instance, if the decision is made to debut the cinematic product during one of the downtimes, such as the first couple of months of the year, it may still have to face competition from other products marketed during the same calendrical window. Because the timing of release is such a gamble, box office returns may reflect more the merits of competing films than the quality of the film itself.

This is one place where triumph in the box office departs dramatically from the acclamation of film critics. Because a moviegoer can't be watching two films at the same time, financial performance is to a very large extent a zero-sum game. On a particular outing, a consumer sees one movie rather than another. That means that what one film gains in ticket sales another film loses. In contrast, the critics do not have to observe any quota in the assignment of stars to the films that they review. If all of the films opening in a given weekend deserve five stars, then all can be bestowed five stars. This same freedom applies to the critical judgments published after the film enters the realm of video/DVD rentals. The authors of movie guide ratings can allot as many stars as they want to all the new films added to the next edition. This suggests that critics can more finely differentiate relative cinematic quality relative to box office criteria. A critical winner does not presuppose a critical loser.

Promotion

Somewhat overlapping the distribution and exhibition phases of a film's theatrical release, operates the often decisive influence of advertising. Except for the showing of the movies themselves, ads are probably as conspicuous a part of movies as business. We watch trailers on television or when we view our DVD rentals, we see attention-grabbling film posters displayed on the walls of theaters, and we read promotional material in magazines and newspapers—not even counting the popup advertisements and eye-catching videos that often intrude on our computer screen! And for good reason: Advertising works. The more money spent, the more money earned, at least in the short run.

Conversely, nothing will kill a film's box office prospects than to give it no promotion whatsoever. When newspaper baron William Randolph Hearst failed in buying and then destroying the negative for *Citizen Kane*—whose central figure was partly modeled after him—he forbade any of his papers to run any ads for the film or for any other movies released by the same studio (RKO). The film critics for Hearst newspapers were also kept silent despite the fact that *Citizen Kane* received rave reviews in non-Hearst papers. Because one in four Americans at that time read a Hearst daily, these actions undoubtedly undermined the film's financial success.

Finances aside, the question then becomes whether the amount of advertising a film receives corresponds to the film's quality. It turns out that the main predictors of advertising expenditures are (a) production costs, (b) the presence of a major movie star, (c) the receipt of an important Academy award, and (d) specific film genres, such as comedy and action flicks. Of these four predictors, only the Oscar has any intrinsic relation with a film's artistic merit, and announcement of this honor is only applicable to a very small percentage of films. All of the other predictors are either irrelevant or else negative indicators of cinematic quality (viz. production costs). Most significantly, critical evaluations are not predictive of marketing expenditures! The critics may heap praise upon a film, but that does not directly affect how much money will be relegated to promoting the film. Ironically, therefore, the more effective advertising is in getting the public to buy tickets, the less strong will be the relation between box office returns and authentic cinematic excellence.

The mismatch between movies as business and films as art is nowhere more apparent than in the so-called "high concept" product. A high concept movie can almost invariably be described in just a sentence or two, and often in just a handful of words. Consider the following examples: "Flash Gordon meets cowboy movie," "*Jaws* in a haunted house in space," "*Alien* as a war picture," "Bus with a bomb," "Cop and bad guy switch faces," "Serial killer bases murders on the seven deadly sins," and "Human adopted by elves seeks his roots." The corresponding movies are: *Star Wars*, *Alien*, *Aliens*, *Speed*, *Face/Off*, *Se7en*, and *Elf*. Very frequently a big-name star or celebrity is part of the high-concept package: "Jim Carrey as God," "Robin Williams in drag," "Arnold Schwarzenegger and Danny DeVito as fraternal twins," "Vin Diesel as a nanny," and "Shaquille O'Neal as a genie" yields *Bruce Almighty*, *Mrs. Doubtfire*, *Twins*, *The Pacifier*, and *Kazaam*. Combining the two forms, you can scream out "Keenen Ivory Wayans as a little person who poses as baby in order to retrieve a stolen diamond." And you get the absolutely dreadful *Little Man*!

It's easy to see why high concept movies get made. In the first place, they're easy to pitch to studio executives too busy to read scripts. Just give the concept in a sentence fragment, name the star, and your project gets the green light. Furthermore, because such movies appear to be sure-fire hits, the producers won't skimp on anything necessary to make a slick product. A-list technicians will ensure that the movie is polished and professional. At the same time, the producers do not even have to worry about hiring a good writer. The plot can be as thin as the pitch, and character development is often reduced to the stars just playing themselves—or sometimes perversely playing against themselves as in *The Pacifier*. Just as importantly, it's not hard to appreciate how high concept movies make everything much easier for the advertising department. Often the tagline was already written for the pitch, and there's nothing like a most-familiar face to make for great movie posters. At times, everything necessary becomes encapsulated in the title. Try *Alien vs. Predator* or *Freddy vs. Jason*. Additionally, the promotion can often include various tie-ins that sell the movie via soundtracks, music videos, computer games, t-shirts, collectables, websites, and tiny tacky action figure toys tossed into flimsy fast-food kiddie-meal boxes. The *Star Wars*, *Star Trek*, and *Harry Potter* franchises amply illustrate an ingenious phenomenon whereby promotion practically pays for itself. With high concept, you can make money making money.

There's no doubt that high concept works. According to empirical research, such movies bring in more box office cash, and these earnings are indeed augmented by tie-ins and merchandising. It's good business. But it's much less evident that high concept yields film as art. Critics often pan such movies as pure, unadulterated hokum, and award nominators and voters are seldom more generous—unless the Golden Raspberries are considered honorific. With superficial characters floating lazily over watery storylines, with only a star's visage and some special effects to keep eyes glued to the screen, high concept products are often the culprits behind the negative correlation between production budget and critical acclaim. Even more importantly, high concept movies contribute to the disconnection between cinematic masterpieces and money-making movies. This is not to say that high concept products can never be great products. Some films can rise above their origins. It's just that most works of art cannot be reduced to a half-dozen words that connote only a single word spelled M-O-N-E-Y.

Exhibition

But now let's talk about the movie actually showing in the theater near you. We must then acknowledge many moviegoers do not make their viewing decisions based on any of the preceding factors. Even a great trailer or theater poster or fast-food trinket will leave them cold. What many viewers trust most is whether they know someone personally who has seen the movie and who reports to them that it's well worth seeing. A "You've just got to see it!" or an "It's a total turkey!" from a close friend, relative, or coworker can overrule even the most celebrated critics and the most costly advertising campaigns. Consumer surveys show that such "word of mouth" (and, more recently, Internet "click of mouse") is more powerful than not just advertising but also critical reviews, awards, and star actors and directors. Furthermore, this powerful influence is enhanced all the more in that it's self-perpetuating, generating a positive feedback loop. You then see the recommended movie and relay the message to others that this is a "must see," and you pass on the condemned movie with the explanation that you heard from others that it was a total bomb. This "rumor mill" starts "snowballing" until films become sharply differentiated into the blockbusters and the flops. Propelled partly by hearsay—or "the buzz"—and partly by confirming experience, the rich get richer, and the poor get poorer.

In such cases, this word-of-mouth generates what is technically referred to as *information cascades*. These cascades may be either positive or negative, where "a positive information cascade will lead to a hit, and a negative information cascade will lead to a flop." This erratic phenomenon then undermines the connection between the box office figures and cinematic merit.

First of all, this effect helps produce the highly skewed distribution of financial returns. As noted earlier in this chapter, the vast majority of films lose money while only a small proportion earns megabucks. This elitist distribution bears almost no resemblance to the distribution of cinematic quality, which tends to be described by the normal or bell-shaped curve, as observed in Chapter 2. Figure 2.1 specifically illustrated this reality with respect to movie guide ratings. On a five-star scale, most films receive between three and four stars, whereas relatively few receive either one star or five stars. To be sure, that graph came from a relatively elite sample of films (viz. those that had received at least one nomination in a major award category). Yet even a less selective sample of films yields much the same distribution, the main difference being that the peak of the curve will be shifted to the left, in the 3-star region, so that the left-side tail of the distribution becomes more equal to the right-side tail. In such a case, really bad movies are about as rare as really good movies, and most movies fall in the middle of the pack. Mediocrity is the norm, just like in everything else in life.

Hence, if box office mirrored cinematic merit, most films would earn an average amount of money and flops would be as rare as blockbusters. The skewed distribution completely upsets this potential correspondence. If less than 50% of films receive below-average evaluations, but films below the top 80% or so lose money in the box office, then most films must display a minimal or no connection between merit granted and money bestowed. In other words, on a scale in which earnings are expressed in millions of dollars, the number of critical stars granted at the lower end of the distribution will translate into only tens of thousands of dollars. So box office cannot possibly discriminate cinematic merit at the lower end of the distribution. Turkeys, mediocre, and even some better-than-average films—the ones between the 50th and 80th percentile in the distribution—will all be lumped together as financial losers. Only at the upper end of the box office distribution is there sufficient latitude for critical acclaim to tightly differentiate box office performance.

Naturally, one could argue that the upper end of the box office distribution might still reflect actual quality, but that the correspondence would be merely exaggerated. The difference between a movie that gets four stars and one that gets five stars might translate into a $50 million increment in gross. Yet it's not so simple. Those films that earn more may not necessarily be better films than those that earn less. A film judged inferior by the critics can eclipse in ticket sales one judged far better by those same critics. Certainly, part of this distortion can be attributed to the fact that it is the consumers rather than the critics who decide a film's financial success. So, word of mouth operates to squish and stretch the consumers' tastes rather than the critics' judgments. But beyond that deviating factor are many others that intrude on the process; compelling information cascades to operate in some rather whimsical, even almost random ways. These intrusions disrupt the ordering, rendering blockbuster status all the more unpredictable.

The Take-Home Message

So far this chapter is the largest in this book. That's because it deals with the most difficult of all questions: How do we judge whether this or that film constitutes a cinematic masterpiece? We have devoted a considerable amount of attention to the three rival candidates, namely, rave reviews, movie awards, and box office bucks. If we combine the empirical findings reported in this chapter with those reviewed in the previous chapters, we can arrive at the following three conclusions.

First, the critics appear to do the best job differentiating the relative aesthetic merits of the films released each year. The critics strongly agree among themselves, even when one set of evaluations appear at the beginning of a film's theatrical release while another set do not emerge until after the video or DVD is made available for rental or purchase. The critics also offer sensible judgments. Judging from the stars (or equivalents) that they bestow in their reviews, most films are average, and only a small number are either terrible or terrific. This distribution seems reasonable because it's hard to believe that the majority of films offered to the moviegoers would be turkeys or bombs. To the contrary, the average movie should be average, on the average. It must be admitted that the critics do not have their fingers on the pulse of popular appeal. Yet that's okay. Most critics are judging film as art, not movies as entertainment.

Second, movie awards are almost as good as the critics in separating the wheat from the chaff, at least if we confine our attention to best picture, best directing, and best acting awards. Even so, movie awards have certain liabilities vis-à-vis critical evaluations. For one thing, various kinds of superfluous influences can throw off the nomination and award procedures, as discussed in Chapter 2. In addition, the awards mostly separate the great from the good, making no effort to distinguish the average from the bad or bad from the worst (with the exception of the Razzies, to be treated in Chapter 9). These deficiencies aside, a cumulative count of awards and nominations in major cinematic categories from major professional organizations and societies offers an index of greatness surpassed only by critical acclaim.

Third and last is the least: box office gross. Given all the distortions introduced by the influences discussed earlier, it's difficult to conjure up a more inferior indicator of cinematic merit. The only thing that we can say for sure about blockbusters is that they bring in abundant receipts. All too often a truly great film will languish in half-filled theaters while some mediocre film attracts long lines in front of the box office. Even after a cinematic masterpiece finally completes the lengthy and uncertain tour of the nation's art houses, its earnings may not come close to what a worse-than-mediocre film might make on its first weekend. So blockbusters and great flicks may not always mix. If the goal is to comprehend cinematic creativity and aesthetics, critical reviews and professional awards should be placed well above money as indicators of greatness.

Chapter 5

The Script: Does the Narrative's Nature Matter?

At the very moment that I wrote this sentence, on January 20, 2008, the Writers Guild of America (WGA) was more than 11 weeks into a strike. The writers' basic contract had expired on October 31, 2007, and on November 5th the picket lines began to form in front of major studios and production sites. The immediate impact was minimal. Given the tremendous lead time in most productions, the producers still had ample completed scripts in the conduit to keep the cameras running. So the first casualties were the late-night talk shows that rely heavily on up-to-date material. Hence the live Jay Leno, Conan O'Brien, and David Letterman were replaced with reruns. From the standpoint of the film industry, the most observable repercussion was inflicted on the award galas. The Golden Globe ceremony held on January 13th was reduced to a mere press conference in which the winners were announced—sans the glamorous celebrities and their tearful acceptance speeches.

Perhaps the most eye-catching aspect about the strike was the picket lines. And I don't just mean the bright red t-shirts and red and black signs. Rather, the picketers were prominent for the near absence of prominent faces. To be sure, from time to time some celebrity figure would show up in support of the strike. Supporters who made appearances included the Reverend Jesse Jackson, Senator John Edwards, singer Alicia Keys, and actors Sally Fields, Rob Lowe, Sandra Oh, and Minnie Driver. But often the cameras would just flash, the familiar visage would vanish, and the far more ordinary faces were left behind.

It's not that highly illustrious screenwriters didn't show up. It's merely that even the most successful writers seldom have recognizable faces.

Here's a list of three active strikers who also won the Oscar for best writing: Paul Haggis (for the 2004 *Crash*), Akiva Goldsman (for the 2001 *A Beautiful Mind*), and Robert Towne (for the 1974 *Chinatown*). Be honest! Could you pick their faces out of a crowd? Aren't they less recognizable than the actors who appeared in their films? Can you not better visualize head shots of Sandra Bullock, Terrence Howard, Don Cheadle, and Matt Dillon; Russell Crowe, Ed Harris, Jennifer Connelly, and Christopher Plummer; Jack Nicholson, Faye Dunaway, and John Huston?

Moreover, as the WGA emphasized on its website during the strike, it's not just celebrity status that writers lack. It's also income. The average writer earns $62,000 per year. Even worse, to paraphrase Rodney Dangerfield, writers too often get no respect. Some very popular video/DVD guides do not even bother to identify who wrote the films reviewed. Directors and actors, yes, but writers, no. And how often do you see the writer's name on the theater marquee? They seldom become headliners. Besides the writer-director-actor Woody Allen, I mean.

Yet think about it: Is it possible to produce a great flick without a great script? Just ponder the following screenwriters and their creations (with a representative line in parentheses): Sidney Howard's 1939 *Gone With the Wind* ("You should be kissed and often, and by someone who knows how"); Preston Sturges's 1941 *The Lady Eve* ("I need him like the ax needs the turkey"); Joseph L. Mankiewicz's 1950 *All About Eve* ("Fasten your seat belts. It's going to be a bumpy night"); Billy Wilder's 1959 *Some Like It Hot* ("Nobody's perfect"); Paddy Chayefsky's 1976 *Network* ("I'm as mad as hell, and I'm not going to take this anymore!"); Paul Schrader's 1976 *Taxi Driver* ("You talkin' to me?"); John Milius and Francis Coppola's 1979 *Apocalypse Now* ("The horror, the horror"); Woody Allen's 1986 *Hannah and Her Sisters* ("I had a great evening; it was like the Nuremberg Trials"); William Goldman's 1987 *The Princess Bride* ("My name is Inigo Montoya. You killed my father. Prepare to die!"); Nora Ephron's 1989 *When Harry Met Sally...* ("I'll have what she's having"); Callie Khouri's 1991 *Thelma & Louise* ("You get what you settle for"); Eric Roth's 1994 *Forrest Gump* ("Life is like a box of chocolates. You never know what you're going to get"); Cameron Crowe's 1996 *Jerry Maguire* ("Show me the money!"); M. Night Shyamalan's 1999 *The Sixth Sense* ("I see dead people"); and Charlie Kaufman's 1999 *Being John Malkovich* ("Do you know what a metaphysical can of worms this portal is?"). Where would these pictures be without their scripts' creators?

And it's not that a great flick must end with a great script but rather it must begin with a great script. It's the script that serves as virtual scripture for the guidance and instruction of the producer, director, the actors, the production designer, cinematographer, the composer, and all the rest of the core crew.

Admittedly, the script will almost invariably undergo sundry transformations during pre-production, production, and even post-production. But all the script doctors in the world cannot salvage a basically bad idea. On the contrary, most often the more stitches sewn in, the more scars left behind.

Why do I raise this issue? No, I'm not trying to marshal support for the WPA. The strike was settled by the time I completed the first draft of this chapter. I'm just making a point necessary to introduce this chapter and the following three. Each of these four chapters concentrate on more specific contributions to cinematic success: the writing, the directing, the acting, and the composing—in that order. My coverage of the first on the list begins with a review of the scientific research on the screenplay attributes that predict cinematic achievement. I close with a postscript regarding the screenwriters themselves.

Screenplay Attributes

Because of the extreme complexity of the published findings, I concentrate on those results that have received the most attention in scientific research. In particular, I scrutinize the following attributes: (a) the screenplay's genre or general story type, (b) its final running time on the silver screen, (c) its MPAA rating during its theatrical release, (d) the type and intensity of "adult content" depicted in the film, (e) whether the script has connections with prior films as either a sequel or remake, (f) whether it purports to tell a true story about a real event or person, and (g) whether it is an adaptation of previous narrative material that has been successful in another medium besides feature-length film. In the last case we'll also consider the specific nature of the adaptation and who carried it out.

Each of these script characteristics will be discussed with respect to three criteria: financial performance, movie awards, and critical evaluations. I'll also include production budget in the first criterion so as to shed additional light on the distinction between films as art and movies as business. As we'll see, there are really two major kinds of screenplays that help us comprehend the complexities reported in Chapter 4. Afterwards I'll discuss some unanswered questions that deserve additional attention in empirical research on the scripts that make for great flicks.

Genres

Consumers, critics, and award voters all agree on one thing: film genre is an important element of any screenplay. Because genre decides many other aspects of the script, it makes sense to examine that first.

Financial Performance

Consumers list story type as the single most influential factor in deciding whether to watch a movie—the only factor more important than word of mouth. For those moviegoers who hate horror flicks, it matters not one iota how much praise such a film receives from friends, family, or coworkers. And if consumers have a passion for sci-fi, then it will take a lot of negative press to block them from lining up at the box office. Of course, because some genres are more popular than others, broadly favored genres will recruit a bigger box office than genres that represent more specialized or acquired tastes. Not everybody likes mad-slasher films, but many more can go for a really great romantic comedy, such as a fantastic "date flick."

It's not surprising therefore that numerous researchers have shown how a film's financial performance is contingent on the film's genre. For example, some investigations have pointed to the popular appeal of comedies, romances, sci-fi, fantasy, and horror films. Many other genre categories appear to be largely irrelevant with respect to box office success. This apparent irrelevance holds for such specialized genres as the western, war, mystery, film noir, and crime. Evidently, people seldom decide to transport themselves to a movie theater just because a western is playing. More crucial to the decision is whether that western is a drama or a comedy. The 1969 *The Wild Bunch* occupies a very different consumer universe than the 1974 *Blazing Saddles*.

Unfortunately, it's difficult to specify the most money-making genres because cinematic fads and fashions change fairly quickly over time. Hollywood musicals of the Fred and Ginger variety were once a major draw, but now that genre has largely faded into the background—the 2002 *Chicago* and the 2006 *Dreamgirls* notwithstanding. Making matters worse, the success of the genre may be contingent on geography as much as history. As an example, comedies do not transport well across cultural boundaries. What's funny in Hollywood may not be funny in Hong Kong. Humor is highly particularistic.

Even so, researchers have pinpointed the one genre that's best to avoid if you're interested in substantial profits: drama. Most moviegoers want light entertainment, not weighty enlightenment. Laughs and thrills, not tears and deep sighs. This consumer bias against dramas is striking insofar as a large percentage of films released each year falls into the drama category, often close to half. When I say that dramas do not do well, I should be more specific. Dramas open on fewer screens, have much lower earnings on the first weekend, and have an appreciably lower gross at the end of their domestic run. These negatives are consistent with the fact that dramas do not constitute the preferred genre for most consumers.

These data must make one wonder why filmmakers produce any dramas at all. There are several possible answers that are not mutually exclusive. But one conceivable response is that dramas are cheap to make. There's actually a negative correlation between production costs and a script in this genre. A great dramatic screenplay only requires a competent director and a handful of excellent actors to make a profitable film. The 2004 *Crash* cost only $6.5 million but made almost $55 million. That's better than making a special-effects intensive movie that cost $55 million but brings in $6.5 million. Even though the film got a slow start, it turned into a money-maker in the end.

Movie Awards

The film *Crash* also won the Oscar for best picture. So the dramatic genre can secure top-notch honors as well. In fact, drama is the favored genre for best picture awards received from most major organizations. The genre is also the genre most strongly associated with awards and nominations in the dramatic cluster, namely, directing, writing, acting, and editing. So, prize-winning scripts are most likely to be dramas. Interestingly, films in this genre are less likely to receive awards and nominations in the technical cluster. Hence, don't see a drama if you want to experience great visual effects, sound effects editing, and sound mixing. But the absence of these features partially explains why dramas can cost noticeably less to produce: sense and sensibility rather than bells and whistles. A great drama can even be shot under minimalist conditions. Hitchcock's 1944 drama *Lifeboat* earned Oscar nods for best director and screenplay (as well as cinematography), and Tallulah Bankhead's lead performance earned her an award from the New York Film Critics Circle. Even so, practically the whole film takes place on a lifeboat!

What about other genres? What impact might they have on awards and nominations? There's a three-part answer. First, romances are also likely candidates for best picture honors as well as recognition in the dramatic cluster of honors—but nowhere to the same degree as dramas. Yet romances compensate for that deficiency by being more likely to earn nominations and awards in the visual and music clusters. A great love story invites lush cinematography, sets, costumes, makeup, and music, whether score or song. Think *Doctor Zhivago*, which won Oscars for Best Art Direction-Set Decoration, Best Cinematography (Color), Best Costume Design (Color), Best Music Score (Substantially Original), and Best Writing (Screenplay Based on Material from Another Medium).

By comparison, comedies are less likely to receive recognition in the visual, technical, and music clusters, nor do they have to. Their scripts rely on wit rather than the extra accoutrements of the medium. The 1934 *It Happened One Night* won Oscars for Best Picture, Best Actor in a Leading Role, Best Actress in a Leading Role, Best Director, and Best Writing (Adaptation), but not so much as a nomination in the visual, technical, and music clusters.

Finally, I should acknowledge the fading genre of musicals. Not surprisingly, films in this genre are the most likely to win awards and nominations in the music cluster—score and song. Musicals also have an advantage with respect to the visual honors. Top-flight musicals often have first-rate production values. The 1951 *An American in Paris* won Oscars in color Art Direction-Set Decoration, Cinematography, and Costume Design in addition to Best Music (Scoring of a Musical Picture). Musicals are designed to provide a total sensory rather than deep philosophical experience.

Critical Evaluations

Film critics like dramas, too. This positive association holds for both reviews appearing during the film's theatrical run and those not published until after the film enters the market in video or DVD format. The preference for the dramatic genre may reflect an age-old aesthetic bias toward serious dramatic products. Shakespeare's tragedies are more highly acclaimed than his comedies and romances, for example, *Hamlet*, *King Lear*, *Othello*, and *Macbeth* surpass in fame *Midsummer Night's Dream*, *Taming of the Shrew*, and *Twelfth Night*. This hierarchy even extends back to the beginning of drama in ancient Athens. Of the four great playwrights, Aeschylus, Sophocles, Euripides, and Aristophanes, the last, the author of comedies rather than tragedies, is considered the lesser. Great plays, like great films, must take on the numerous deep issues of life and treat them with the utmost seriousness. Where comedy makes us laugh at life, drama should make us cry. And tears are worth much more thought than a chuckle.

The Golden Globes offer two sets of awards in the best picture and best lead acting categories, one set for drama and the other for musical or comedy. The former set of awards is most likely to correspond to the Oscars in the same categories, the latter not. Accordingly, it's of interest that the critics, besides liking drama better than comedy, also tend to dislike musicals. At least the musical genre is negatively correlated with movie guide ratings. Perhaps films in this genre do not look or sound as good on most home entertainment systems. If so, this negative bias may disappear as more consumers upgrade their systems to high-definition high-fidelity. That would explain why the critical evaluations appearing during the theatrical run do not display the same dislike. Those earlier evaluations are based on state-of-the-art theater showings.

Runtime

Films can vary tremendously in length. One of the first narrative films, the 1903 *The Great Train Robbery*, lasted only a dozen minutes. Nowadays such a film would be labeled a short. For instance, a film running 40 minutes or less qualifies for the best short Oscar. In contrast, other films can endure for hours. The 1988 *Little Dorrit*, which received two Oscar nods (for best supporting actor and for best writing), ran for 6 hours (albeit in two parts). Naturally, most films fall between these extremes, with an average duration of just under two hours.

A film's runtime may appear a somewhat messy property of the script. There are two problems, one methodological and the other conceptual.

On the methodological side, a film can have alternate versions with contrary running times. A case in point is the increasingly popular—courtesy of DVDs—"director's cut." This is a new edition of the theatrically released version that has reinserted long stretches of film previously left on the cutting room floor. Perhaps they should be better called the "director's splice" since seldom is anything ever cut out. To illustrate, the 1979 *Apocalypse Now* was reissued in 2001 as *Apocalypse Now Redux* with an addition of almost 10 minutes. So which runtime should researchers use, 153 minutes or 202 minutes? The usual solution is to adopt the runtime for the theatrical release. After all, this is the version seen by most of the critics, the movie-goers who decide box office stats, and the voters who confer movie awards. In those cases of films that have different theatrical versions (most often because of edits necessary for exhibition in different countries), then the investigator can use the runtime for the United States release. That choice is consistent with the fact that most researchers concentrate on US box office, critics, and awards.

On the conceptual side, we must concede that a film's duration constitutes a somewhat crude indicator of a script's properties. Consider the film *Blade Runner*, which has a 117 minute theatrical release (1982), a 116 minute director's cut (1992), and a 117 minute final cut (2007). Notwithstanding the nearly identical lengths, the first version differs dramatically from the last two versions. I can't give all the details without being guilty of spoilers, but one immediately noticeable contrast is that the theatrical version has a voice over by Harrison Ford (who plays the protagonist Deckard) that was later deleted. A huge hunk of script was scrapped without any appreciable effect on the running time. The disjunction can work in the opposite direction besides. When Vincent Gallo's 2003 *The Brown Bunny* was shown at the Cannes Film Festival it opened with a scene of the protagonist racing his motorcycle around a track for almost 20 minutes. Yet when this scene was severely trimmed for its theatrical release, and the entire film cut by 26 minutes, the script itself was not substantially altered. It still opens with the same motorcycle race with everything else pretty much intact, including the controversial sex scene.

The second problem be what it may, it remains true that the shooting script for a long film will tend to differ from that for a short film. Long films can have more scenes and longer scenes that feature more characters, greater character development, more complex plots and subplots, and with fewer plot holes. In conjunction with other screenplay characteristics, it will give us some insight into the nature of the cinematic product. That's an understatement, for it turns out to be a very central attribute, as I show below (see also Chapter 9).

Financial Performance

Let us begin with the observation that the length of a film is strongly correlated with its production cost. Short films have small budgets, long films big budgets. So, long films need to do much better in the box office to recover the initial investment. Fortunately, consumers do seem to have a preference for longer films. Moviegoers may feel that they get more for the price of the ticket. In compliance with this consumer inclination, longer films are more likely to have a bigger take on the first weekend of release. And as frosting on the cake, longer movies will usually gross more at the end of their theatrical run. Because the average film runs a little under two hours, we can say that a one-hour film will earn less than a three-hour film. Whether the latter will turn a profit is a separate issue. Sometimes the box office returns do not bring in enough to compensate for the costs. So, sometimes short and sweet will mean profitable instead. *My Big Fat Greek Wedding* (2002) ran only 95 minutes, but cost only $5 million to make, and eventually grossed $241 million.

Movie Awards

The voters who settle on the nominees and award winners agree with the consumers: More is better. The longer the film, the higher the probability that it will receive best picture honors. The most recent Oscar winners in this category provide examples: *No Country for Old Men* (122 minutes), *The Departed* (151 minutes), *Crash* (113 minutes), *Million Dollar Baby* (132 minutes), *The Lord of the Rings: The Return of the King* (201 minutes), *Chicago* (113 minutes), *Gladiator* (155 minutes)—only *Crash* and *Chicago* are of average length, and there's no brief film in the lot. Nor is that all: The longer the runtime the better the chance that the film will receive recognition in the dramatic, visual, technical, and music clusters. Thus the longest of the films just listed, the third and last installment of *The Lord of the Rings*, took home 10 additional Oscars in the categories of writing, directing, editing, art production, costume design, makeup, visual effects, sound mixing, score, and song—signifying two or more honors in each of the four creative clusters. Needless to say, long films give everyone the opportunity to show their stuff. Short films, in contrast, leave talents and technicians cramped for breathing space. And much of their best work might not make it past the film editor.

Billy Crystal, the host for the Oscar ceremony in which *The Lord of the Rings* was honored, quipped that it had received 11 nominations, one for each ending. And, indeed, the film did seem to feature multiple endings. No sooner did one closing scene fade out than it was replaced with another closing scene. Yet this concluding sequence can almost be viewed as a series of curtain bows, the audience getting one last chance for the film-makers to show off the cinematic range and depth of this epic. Happily, the script writers gave them plenty of room to do so.

Critical Evaluations

The critics seem to concur with the award voters and moviegoers. Longer films surpass shorter films, on the average. At least this positive association applies to the movie guide ratings that are published post-theatrical release. For example, the 201 minute *The Lord of the Rings: The Return of the King* averaged 4.9 stars out of 5 in subsequent video/DVD guides, a half star or more higher than the films that were nominated for best picture Oscars in the same year: the 137 minute *Mystic River* 4.4 stars, the 138 minute *Master and Commander: The Far Side of the World* 4.4 stars, the 102 minute *Lost in Translation* 4.2 stars, and the 141 minute *Seabiscuit* 3.9 stars. The only oddity is why runtime is unrelated to the critics' judgments during the films theatrical run. Perhaps it's one thing to watch a very long film while you're sitting upright in a movie theater, quite another to be viewing the same film in the comfort of home, in your favorite lounge chair, with a pause button at your finger tips. In the latter case your bottom may never get sore.

MPAA Ratings

I mentioned earlier that alternate versions of the same film will sometimes vary in runtime. Very often the director's cut is longer than the theatrical release. And frequently these cuts were not driven by artistic motives but rather by a very economic one: to get the desired rating from the Motion Picture Association of America (MPAA). Since 1968, the MPAA has rated films on a scale ranging from accessible to all audiences to restricted to audiences who are 18 and older. Although the rating system has changed over the past four decades, the current version runs: G, PG, PG-13, R, and NC-17 (see Chapter 3 for their respective definitions). Hence, to avoid an NC-17 rating, which would greatly restrict the potential box office— especially since many distributors won't even pick up such a film—the producer may delete a scene or two of highly graphic sex, violence, or gore. Or the producer may have an R-rated film edited to PG-13 or PG so that teenagers or even whole families can join the audience. When the director is finally able to restore these omitted scenes in the director's cut, the video or DVD will often get a more restrictive rating, and even become unrated— the latter constituting a potent cinematic caveat emptor.

It should be obvious that this tinkering around with the MPAA rating almost invariably involves changes in the script. That's because the number of criteria that affect the rating is very large, such as tense situations, mature themes, language, profanity, violence, intense battle sequences, gore, frightening/violent/disturbing images, nudity, sensuality, sexual content, sexual references, crude sexual humor, simulated or graphic sex, alcohol abuse, drug abuse, teenage drinking, and even bad sportsmanship. Consequently, there's something of a tradeoff between the film faithfully telling a story and the film receiving the rating necessary to convey that story to the broadest possible audience. This tradeoff is manifest in the empirical research.

Financial Performance

Consumers prefer films with more clean-cut, less objectionable or offensive material. And this preference is reflected in the box office: The money-making films are most often found among the most accessible MPAA ratings, especially PG-13—the very rating received by the three films making up the *The Lord of the Rings*. In contrast, R-rated films have a much higher probability of becoming financial flops with respect to both short- and long-term performance. For the most part, R-rated films open on fewer screens, earn less on the first weekend, and have a smaller domestic gross. As one study estimates for films released in the early 2000s, an R rating may decrease gross earnings by more than $12 million.

This discrepancy raises a curious paradox: the highly accessible G rating is very rare, whereas the R rating is often the most common, followed closely by PG-13. In fact, about half of mainstream films often fall in the R category! Thus, this R-rated movie paradox parallels the drama-genre paradox introduced earlier. Filmmakers are most likely to make serious films with abundant sexual and aggressive content that make them ill-suited for large audiences! This is not to say that such films cannot make money. It's just that it's extremely hard to have an R-rated blockbuster. At best, the distributors will be counting receipts in millions of dollars instead of tens of millions.

Movie Awards

Perhaps the R-rated films can get a booster-shot during the award season. Adding a few Oscar awards to the advertisements may draw an attendance that might otherwise avoid the films. The problem with this scenario is that R-rated films are not more likely to earn best picture awards or nominations, and they are actually less likely to receive recognition in the visual, technical, and music clusters. That is, such films are less prone to earn honors for art direction, costume design, makeup, visual effects, sound effects editing, sound mixing, score, and song. So why make R-rated films at all? Evidently, like the genre of drama, they seem to be more artistic. Because they are associated with "prestige" productions, such films are more likely to receive nominations and awards in the dramatic cluster— writing, directing, acting, and editing. And as noted earlier, honors in this cluster are most conspicuously associated with critical acclaim.

In comparison, the other MPAA ratings are connected to the wrong creative clusters. G-rated films are more likely to receive recognition in the music cluster but less likely to earn honors in the dramatic cluster (e.g. kids' musicals). Films rated PG-13 are also less likely to win honors in the dramatic cluster but are more likely to receive kudos in the technical cluster (e.g., teen-oriented action flicks with lots of awesome special effects). And PG-rated films score highest in the visual and music clusters (e.g. many family-oriented films like *Mary Poppins*).

Critical Evaluations

The critics are somewhat equivocal. On the one hand, some empirical studies find that critics prefer R-rated cinema. This preference shows up both during the theatrical run and the later video/DVD release. Right now, as I wrote this sentence, the films still in release that enjoyed the greatest critical acclaim were *There Will Be Blood, Atonement, Sweeney Todd: The Demon Barber of Fleet Street, Michael Clayton,* and *Juno*—all with Metacritic ratings between 81 and 92. All but *Juno* are rated R, and the latter is rated PG-13. Although a PG-13 rating has no correlation, positive or negative, with critical judgments, G and PG ratings have negative correlations, especially with the movie guide evaluations. Not serious enough, I suppose.

On the other hand, other investigations find no association, positive or negative, between an R rating and critical acclaim. Why the discrepancy? In looking over the two sets of studies, it seems that those that support a positive relation use samples restricted to films that received major award nominations, whereas those that fail to support any relation use samples that are more representative of the larger population of theatrically-released films. In other words, an R-rating only appears useful in discriminating the critical evaluations of elite films. This restricted applicability must again pose the question: So why make R-rated films? There seems to be more to lose than to gain from such cinematic practice.

Sex and Violence

A cinema connoisseur can raise a primary objection to the results reported in the previous section on MPAA ratings: Any given rating may result for any of a number of distinct reasons. Take the five films that were nominated for the 2008 best picture Oscar. All five received an R rating. *Frost/Nixon* received it for "some language," *Milk* for "language, some sexual content and brief violence," *The Curious Case of Benjamin Button* for "brief war violence, sexual content, language and smoking," *The Reader* for "some scenes of sexuality and nudity," and *Slumdog Millionnaire*, the film that took home the statuette, for "some violence, disturbing images and language." Quite clearly, the rational for the R rating was far from uniform. Sex, violence, language, smoking, and disturbing images all played different roles in the decision to turn away any non-adult not accompanied by an adult at the entrance to the theater. Hence, it becomes imperative to inspect the impact of specific types of "adult," "mature," "objectionable," or even "exploitative" content.

Financial Performance

Everybody knows that "sex sells." After all, wasn't the 1997 *Titanic* the biggest all-time moneymaker? And didn't it have lots of steamy sex and nudity? In fact, it is so strongly assumed that sexual content boosts box office that the assumption became a key element of a film script. In Blake Edwards's 1981 *S.O.B.*, the producer decides to turn a family film that flopped into a box-office hit by adding scenes in which an actress known for her wholesome image appears nude on the screen. Edwards chose his own wife to do the dirty work. How many moviegoers went to the theaters just to see Julie Andrews, the former *Mary Poppins* and Maria in *The Sound of Music*, bare her breasts for the first time? Well, not many, for *S.O.B.* was not a big success!

It is imaginable that at one time sex did sell. Yet a lot has changed in the last few decades. Hardcore pornography has become the mainstay of the commercial Internet, shops renting and selling hardcore videos and other pornographic items have become ubiquitous, and attitudes about sex in everyday life have become far more relaxed—as witnessed by the love-making guides available at your local bookstore. Does anyone these days really want to sit in a theater with dozens of complete strangers to watch celebrities engage in simulated sex acts magnified umpteen times on the big screen?

The answer seems to be negative. Even after adjusting for the MPAA rating, the more sex, the less sales. On the average, sexual content, including nudity and sensuality, is inconsistent with good cinematic business sense. This adverse consequence holds not just for domestic gross—where it might be dismissed as residual US puritanical prudery—but also for the supposedly more liberal audience in the United Kingdom, as well as worldwide receipts. Although the data show that "sex is cheap" (in the sense that films with "mucho sexual gusto" tend to cost less to make), films with highly graphic sex are still less likely to turn a profit. Again, this negative effect appears after adjusting for the MPAA rating. It's not simply a matter of fewer persons being allowed to see the movie because of the ages shown on their drivers' licenses. It's the sex that's hurting business.

Nor are sex and nudity the only "mature" content that make audiences (perhaps literally) "shy away" from the movie theaters. Moviegoers are also turned off by alcohol and drugs as well as profanity and smoking. In contrast, if the filmmaker's goal really is to make money at the box office, violence is the way to go, especially if accompanied by guns and weapons, and frightening or nail-biting scenes with corresponding scary or tense music—with plenty of "jump scenes" for shock value. There's nothing like the sadistic villain unexpectedly appearing out of nowhere to get the adrenaline rush that sends some masochistic moviegoers back for more. There might even be some element of sadism if the moviegoers then invite friends who have not yet seen the shocker to join them in another viewing! Interestingly, although graphic sex and nudity do not help a film turn a profit, more modest PG-13 level sexuality, combined with conspicuous but not gory violence provides a more optimal formula for success. The James Bond flicks and other action-adventure-thrillers featuring virile heroes and sexy vixen offer prototypes.

But what about the *Titanic*? It constitutes a pure outlier. This unique status becomes particularly evident when its earnings are adjusted for inflation. Once that adjustment is made, *Titanic*'s financial performance is exceeded by *Gone with the Wind* (rated G by the MPAA on re-release), *Star Wars* (PG), *The Sound of Music* (G), *E.T. The Extraterrestrial* (PG), and *The Ten Commandments* (G). These are not the kind films to attract the prurient interests of anybody! *Titanic* is the exception that proves the rule. Or it might not be much of an exception: A scene of partial nudity, a nude drawing, and a steamed-over car window hardly puts *Titanic* in the same class as mainstream films with far more explicit R-rated sex, as any avid moviegoer can testify.

News flash! As *Great Flicks* went into production, James Cameron came out with a film that shattered the box office records set by his previous *Titanic*. The film was of course the 3-D *Avatar*—with rather innocent PG-13 level sex and violence! *Titanic*'s outlier status becomes even more salient.

Movie Awards

If sex doesn't sell, then it's logical to ask: Why is it there? One possibility is that sex and nudity help push a film over the top come award season. Wasn't *Titanic* nominated for 14 Academy Awards, bringing home 11 Oscars? And didn't Kate Winslet—whose erotic nudity constitutes a sensual highpoint of the film—get herself honored with an Oscar nod for Best Actress in a Leading Role? Yes, this is all true, but we must be cautioned against drawing inferences from a single case. *Titanic* may be an outlier by this second success criterion as well. As far as I can tell, only one empirical study explicitly addressed this issue with a large sample. The investigators counted Oscar and Golden Globe nominations and awards in the categories of best picture, director, screenplay, and male and female leads and supporting. The outcome was somewhat complex. Although strong sex and nudity were negatively associated with getting these major honors, sexual content, when coupled with profanity, smoking, drinking, and drug abuse, could augment the likelihood that a film receives Oscar and Golden Globe recognition. The researchers suspected that this combination may look "artsy" or "edgy" in a manner that apes the more daring cinematic fare that crosses the Atlantic from Europe. Nonetheless, if the goal is to win such kudos, a superior route may be to create films that address difficult topics and issues, especially those that might portray tense family scenes. Whether these areas of content can account for *Titanic*'s award prowess, I leave for the reader to decide.

Critical Evaluations

So, the only success criterion left is the film critics. Perhaps the sex and violence is put in the film to appease the tastes of those who make their living viewing hundreds of movies per year. Getting sated with mainstream imagery, perhaps critics get desperate for something really tantalizing or shocking. Nope, this explanation will also not work. In the main, the critics are not fond of sex and violence either. Indeed, highly graphic violence is even more of a turn off than highly graphic sex. In addition, this double antipathy holds for both the critics who evaluate films dearly during their theatrical release and those who pass judgment after the film has entered the rental or purchase market for videos/DVDs. Even in the privacy of their home entertainment systems, critics prefer less excitement and more art. This preference is seen in their leaning toward cinema that deals with important life issues. Critics want a cinematic encounter both deep and stimulating, something that they will experience long after they leave the theater—besides a bad taste in the mouth. Sex and violence don't cut it.

In the end, it appears that violence is inserted for cash, but that sex has no obvious justification, judging by our three criteria of cinematic success. Chapter 7 may later help explain the presence of sex in cinema. That's where we'll discuss sexism in cinema.

Sequels and Remakes

They say that no two snowflakes are ever alike. Given how many fall at any one moment somewhere on the globe, this seems highly improbable. At the very minimum there might appear two that are indistinguishable to the untrained eye. By the same token, Netflix's inventory of DVDs cannot be said to consist of utterly unique films. Although technically the films will all have different scripts, in effect some scripts are closely related, even very similar. They will contain some of the same characters involved in similar plot situations. These related films fall into two major categories: sequels and remakes. The former continues the developments of an earlier film whereas the latter creates a revised version of an earlier film. In either case the problem of coming up with a creative script is minimized. The extreme case of that minimization is the nearly exact remake. The 1998 *Psycho* was a virtual shot-by-shot recreation of Hitchcock's classic 1960 *Psycho*. There were only two really substantial differences: (a) the remake was shot in color (to enhance the violence) and (b) it added a masturbation scene (to increase the sex). In any case, sequels and remakes have perceptible consequences with respect to cinematic success.

Financial Performance

The phenomenon of the sequel is proverbial. In the first place, sequels provide the bread and butter for many movie stars: Harrison Ford in *Raiders of the Lost Ark* (1981), *Indiana Jones and the Temple of Doom* (1984), *Indiana Jones and the Last Crusade* (1989), and, after a two-decade lull, *Indiana Jones and the Kingdom of the Crystal Skull* (2008), plus three appearances as Han Solo in the *Star Wars* franchise; Tom Cruise in *Mission: Impossible* (1995), *Mission: Impossible II* (2000), and *Mission: Impossible III* (2006); Sigourney Weaver in *Alien* (1979), *Aliens* (1986), *Alien³* (1992), and *Alien: Resurrection* (1997); and Sylvester Stone in *First Blood* (1982), *Rambo: First Blood Part II* (1985), *Rambo III* (1988), and *Rambo* (2008) and in *Rocky* (1976), *Rocky II* (1979), *Rocky III* (1982), *Rocky IV* (1985), *Rocky V* (1990), and *Rocky Balboa* (2006). Some specific series have become very long: *Halloween* (1978) had 7 sequels between 1982 and 2002, *Friday the 13th* (1980) 12 between 1981 and 2009. Even more amazingly, some series have merged to form combined sequels: *Predator* (1987) had one sequel before entering into mortal combat with *Aliens* to produce two more; and the *A Nightmare on Elm Street* (1984) went through six sequels before its protagonist Freddy Krueger took on Jason Voorhees of *Friday the 13th* in *Freddy vs. Jason* (2003).

Filmmakers like sequels for good reason: Such movies have a somewhat higher probability of making money than do original films. They open on a larger number of screens, sell more tickets on opening weekend, have longer theatrical runs, and earn a bigger domestic gross. Consumers seem to treat sequels as junk food: It's not the most nutritious fare, but you're pretty much guaranteed to get the same thing every time. This expectation is sufficient to ensure a lucrative theater attendance for each successive feature-length episode.

Sequels do have one financial liability, however: They cost more than the average film. Apparently, there's some pressure on the sequel to outdo the special effects of its predecessor. And besides, the lead actors can charge progressively more for their services. Arnold Schwarzenegger received $75,000 for *The Terminator* (1984), $15,000,000 for *Terminator 2: Judgment Day* (1991), and $30,000,000 for *Terminator 3: Rise of the Machines* (2003). The production budgets for the three films grew from $6,400,000 to $200,000,000, indicating that Arnold's contribution to the cost grew from 1% to 15%. This increase in budget meant that the series eventually became progressively less profitable, the box office not entirely recovering the enhanced expenses.

Remakes would seem to make more much business sense than sequels. After all, if consumers liked the original, why wouldn't they enjoy an updated version with contemporary stars, state-of-the-art techniques, and script enhancements? So let's redo *Psycho* with Vince Vaughn, Anne Heche, Julianne Moore, Viggo Mortensen, and William H. Macy! Let's use digital methods to increase the shock value of the blood in the shower scene! And let's show the murderer masturbating while he looks at the future victim through a peep hole—just so no one in the audience can doubt the killer's motives!

This may make sense, yet the economics of remakes are somewhat less conspicuous than sequels. Unlike sequels, they do not have substantially bigger budgets than other films. Although remakes are like sequels in that they open on more screens, earn a bigger first weekend, and attain a higher gross than average, they do not usually achieve the same magnitude of box office success as sequels do. It remains to be determined whether the lower costs compensate for the lower returns. The 1998 *Psycho* cost a mere $20 million—only about half the price of mainstream films of that time—but also grossed only $21 million. Yet the 1960 *Psycho* cost less than a million to make but made $32 million in the US and $50 million world-wide. As in the instance of sequels, remakes can't promise anything.

Movie Awards

I noted that sequels are prone to cost more than average, and suggested that a portion of that expense may be relegated to improved special effects. Compare *Terminator 2: Judgment Day* (1991) with *The Terminator* (1984) and you can appreciate the power of that added technical investment, especially in the superb visual effects. Consistent with this observation is the fact that sequels have a high probability of getting nominations and awards in the technical cluster—better visual effects, sound effects editing, and sound mixing. But that's the limit of the benefits. Sequels have lower odds of receiving honors for best picture and for the achievements that make up the dramatic cluster. I would speculate that of the components making up this cluster, it's probably the writing that's most severely affected. Having to write a sequel may tie the hands of the writer in ways that stifle the creative imagination. Unlike the original writer, who is free to invent characters and plots more or less at will, the sequel writer must confine his or her creativity to whatever was decided in the first version. This confinement even happens when the same writer creates both the original and the sequel. Screenwriters then become imprisoned in a cell of their own making.

Remakes also suffer when the movie awards and nominations are announced by the major professional organizations. They are not usually honored in any cluster, not even the technical. Yet like sequels, remakes are less likely to receive recognition in the dramatic cluster. It's clear that the writer can not earn much credit for updating a script for a remake. The directing and acting may experience a handicap as well. Unless it's a remake of an obscure predecessor—such as a foreign film not widely distributed in the United States—direct comparisons with the performances in the original version are almost inevitable. But often a film good enough to inspire a remake will also feature performances that are "a hard act to follow." If the performance strikes off on a totally different path, the result may not just be different but worse. But if the performance attempts merely to improve upon the original renditions, the outcome may look imitative or unnatural.

The remake of *Psycho* provides plenty of examples. It was apparent to critics and consumers alike that Vince Vaughn's portrayal of Norman Bates was not in the same league as Anthony Perkins's. Nor was Gus Van Sant's derivative direction comparable to Alfred Hitchcock's. Not only did the 1998 *Psycho* win a Golden Raspberry "Razzie" Award for Worst Remake or Sequel—tied for last place with *Godzilla* and *The Avengers*—but also Van Sant won the Razzie for Worst Director. Perhaps only William H. Macy's take on the private eye Arbogast came close to matching Martin Balsam's performance in the original movie.

Critical Evaluations

You can probably guess how the critics are going to weigh in on this script parameter. Whether at the beginning of the theatrical run or after the release of the video/DVD, critics like neither. This antipathy is stronger for sequels than for remakes. Thus, the critics appear to side with those who bestow the nominations and awards for best picture and in the dramatic cluster. In terms of the criteria that really count, sequels are less likely to be worth seeing than the original films that inspired them. Here are some concrete examples for a diversity of film types (averaged movie guide ratings on 5-star scale in parentheses): *The French Connection* (4.8) and *The French Connection II* (2.8); *The Sting* (4.5) and *The Sting II* (1.8); *Conan the Barbarian* (3.1) and *Conan the Destroyer* (2.3); *The Blair Witch Project* (2.9) and *Book of Shadows: Blair Witch 2* (1.9); *2001: A Space Odyssey* (5.0) and *2010: The Year We Make Contact* (3.0); *Men in Black* (3.9) and *Men in Black II* (2.6); *The Matrix* (3.9), *The Matrix Reloaded* (3.5), and *The Matrix Revolutions* (2.5); etc., etc. The decline from one film rating to the next can amount to a star or more. The series almost inevitably runs out of ideas.

I said "almost inevitably" because exceptions do appear from time to time. Sometimes the first sequel will surpass the original; the decline only setting in with the second sequel. A classic example is the following trilogy: *The Godfather* (4.9), *The Godfather, Part II* (5.0), and *The Godfather, Part III* (3.8). Even more rarely the last film will be the best of the set. A recent example is *The Lord of the Rings* trilogy: *The Fellowship of the Ring* (4.5), *The Two Towers* (4.7), and *The Return of the King* (4.9). However, these departures from statistical expectation are not just rare but also distinct in that there's often a clear reason for the exception. For instance, *The Lord of the Rings* films were all cut from the same cloth— J. R. R. Tolkien's classic—and all filmed together rather than separately. The last film was put in the ideal position of narrating the book's climax. Even the second part of *The Godfather*, though filmed two years after the first part, was based on the same source (Mario Puzo's novel) and was conceived as an ingeniously interwoven prequel and sequel. All in all, it takes some special conditions for a sequel to match or surpass its predecessor.

True Stories and Biopics

Every one of the films mentioned in the previous section concerned imagined persons and events. Conan the Barbarian and Don Vito Corleone are both pure fiction. The celebrated car chase in *The French Connection* and the mysterious monolith in *2001* are figments of a writer's imagination. Sometimes we are even warned that any resemblance to real people or events is purely accidental. Yet it's also clear that a large number of films make the opposite claim, namely that the script narrates a true story, or at least was "based on" or "inspired by" real events. An example is a movie like the 1981 *Chariots of Fire* that tells the actual story of two British track athletes who competed in the 1924 Summer Olympics (it's better than it sounds). One especially prominent subset of these "fact-based" films is the biopic, an attempt to narrate the life and works of some famous personality. Instances include the 2004 *Ray* (Charles), the 1994 *Ed Wood*, the 1982 *Gandhi*, the 1970 *Patton*, the 1962 *Lawrence of Arabia*, the 1952 *Viva Zapata!*, the 1942 *Ivan Groznyy I* (*Ivan the Terrible, Part One*), the 1933 *Queen Christina*, and the 1927 *Napoléon*. In these cases the titles reveal the subjects of biographical treatment, but other times the subject is not so obvious. The 2001 *Beautiful Mind* treats the life of John Nash, a Nobel laureate in economics. Given how frequently true stories and biopics appear on the silver screen, we must ask whether they have any special assets as business or as art.

Financial Performance

Let's start with the bad news: The popularity of true stories and biopics is not necessarily predicated on their box office draw. On the contrary, they are less likely to do well on opening weekend, and biopics are less prone to open in wide release. Their overall gross is somewhat slightly below average, albeit not to a statistically significant degree. The only saving grace is that they cost somewhat less to produce, but that difference is very small. To illustrate, compare *Gandhi* with *E.T.: The Extra-Terrestrial*, one of its rivals for the 1983 best picture Oscar. The former opened on 4 screens and earned a mere $131 thousand on its first weekend; the latter opened on 1,103 screens and had first-weekend earnings of over $12 million. Curiously, cinema consumers seem slightly more attracted to true stories in general than they are to biopics in particular. Perhaps that's because for most moviegoers biopics tend to evoke the déjà vu experience of a high school history lesson.

Movie Awards

Whenever a common screenplay characteristic does not predict financial performance it most often redeems itself from an aesthetic standpoint. In the Golden Age of Hollywood film, true stories and biopics were often the foundation of prestige products aimed more at status than cash. That emphasis hasn't really changed. First of all, such films enjoy a higher likelihood of receiving nominations and awards in the dramatic and visual clusters. Specifically, true stories and biopics are more likely to receive recognition for writing, directing, acting, editing, cinematography, art production, costume design, and makeup. The last plays an especially crucial role when the protagonist must undergo appreciable aging.

Additionally, true stories have an edge in the best picture category. *Gandhi* illustrates some of these assets. Besides winning the best picture Oscar, it won Oscars for best writing, directing, lead actor, editing, cinematography, art direction and set decoration, and costume design, plus got an Oscar nod for makeup. But scripts based on real persons or events do not have an advantage in the technical and music clusters—perhaps because the film is supposed to be carried by the "truth" or the "facts." This does not mean that such films cannot have great special effects and scores. *Lawrence of Arabia* still grabbed an Oscar for best score. It's just that the correlations are either zero or slightly negative.

Critical Evaluations

Although film critics are somewhat more ambivalent than the award voters, it remains the case that true stories seem to be preferred over creations of the unadulterated imagination. Nonfiction trumps fiction. This preference is witnessed in the evaluations that appear early in the film's theatrical run, but become even more evident in the movie guide ratings published after the videos/DVDs appear on the market. Although this holds for true stories in general, the positive relation is not nearly so large for biopics even if the latter constitute a subset of the former. But because biopics represent only about half of all true stories, it's possible that this cinematic type is not frequent enough to have the same consequences for critical evaluations—or movie awards besides. Furthermore, biopics most often describe the lives of famous people while true stories can extend to less historic events, such as notorious homicides—like *In Cold Blood* (1967), *The Black Dahlia* (2006), or *Zodiac* (2007). These homicides all involved killers and their victims, neither of whom have any claim to fame beyond the viciousness of the act that connected their fates. In the last two instances the murderers themselves remain unidentified—perhaps locked forever in an anonymous infamy.

Adaptations

Since the very first Oscar banquet of 1929, the Academy of Motion Picture Arts and Sciences has maintained a vital distinction between two types of writing: original and adapted. The former is a story conceived specifically for the big screen, whereas the latter is derived from some previous work already published in some other medium besides cinema. Of the two categories of scripts, the latter can be said to be the most heterogeneous in origins. After all, the prior work can entail (a) plays, such as the innumerable films based on William Shakespeare (e.g., the 1948 *Hamlet*); (b) novels or short stories, such as the many films adapted from Charles Dickens or Jane Austen (e.g., the 2005 *Pride & Prejudice*); (c) nonfiction, such as the 1987 *The Last Emperor* (from Henry Pu-yi's autobiography); (d) opera, operettas, and musical theater, such as the 1965 *The Sound of Music*; (e) epic poems and religious scriptures, such as the 2007 *Beowulf*; and even (e) television shows, comic books, and video games, such as *Star Trek: The Motion Picture* (1979), *Superman* (1978), and *Lara Croft: Tomb Raider* (2001), respectively. Moreover, many of these sources may have acquired a distinctive stamp of approval. The work may be recognized as a literary classic, or might have been a Broadway hit or a best-selling book or a prestigious award winner, such as a Nobel Prize for literature or a Pulitzer for fiction or nonfiction.

Whatever the specifics, adaptations are very common. In one investigation, fully 46% of the sampled films were adaptations (8% plays, 28% novels, 2% other fiction, 5% nonfiction, and 3% other material). Admittedly, sometimes it's difficult to draw a precise line that distinguishes adaptations from original screenplays. Often the writer's adaptation will take so many liberties with the source that it for all practical purposes constitutes an original screenplay. A prime example is the 2002 film called, significantly, just *Adaptation*. Here the real-life screenwriter Charlie Kaufman wrote about a character named Charlie Kaufman, a screenwriter struggling to adapt a nonfiction book, namely, Susan Orlean's *The Orchid Thief*. Meryl Streep plays the role of author Susan Orlean and Chris Cooper portrays the orchid thief (the real John Laroche), while Nicolas Cage performs as both Charlie Kaufman and as the latter's fictitious twin Donald. The cleverly convoluted script actually earned the real Charlie Kaufman as well as the script-created Donald Kaufman an Oscar nod for best adaptation! But why not best original screenplay given that the main story was a fictitious narrative about adapting the book?

These borderline cases be what they may, most adaptations can be sharply separated from original scripts. We can thus ask the question of whether adaptations are more or less likely to be successful. But that's not the only issue worth addressing. What type of adaptation is best? Plays, novels, TV shows, what? Does the quality of the source matter? Classics, hits, best sellers, prizewinners? And, finally, does it make any difference whether the author of the original material has any input into the adaptation? Should the playwright or novelist participate? Or is that best left to expert screenwriters?

Financial Performance

At first glance, the box office projections of an adaptation do not seem to differ from an original script. They do not differ with respect to production budget, the number of screens on opening weekend, the first-weekend gross, or the final domestic gross. On closer examination, however, adapted scripts do suffer a disadvantage relative to their original counterparts. The deficits are twofold:

1. Adaptations based on plays tend to open on fewer screens, earn less on their first weekend of release, and garner a smaller gross than do original scripts. Former plays are probably too strongly associated with art rather than entertainment. Besides, all too often when a play makes its way to the big screen it seems too small—too stagy, too claustrophobic—to take advantage of a medium which encourages the expansive use of space and time. A play's projection in live theater is often more vital than its cinematic embalmment.

2. The active participation of the original author only makes matters worse. No matter what the specific nature of the source—play, novel, or whatever—its creator tends to interfere with the process of producing a marketable script. The greater the involvement, the greater is the degree of interference. A script with the author as sole writer is worse off than a script with the author as co-writer. By worse off I mean that films based on such author adaptations tend to open on fewer screens and to bring in a smaller first weekend gross. Evidently the original author is too preoccupied with preserving his or her "artistic integrity" to heed the call for economic profitability. Integrity and profitability may be antitheses.

Hence, a producer would be especially wise to avoid play adaptations, particularly those in which the playwright wrote or co-wrote the script. The Tony award winning playwright Tom Stoppard adapted perhaps his most phenomenal play for the 1990 *Rosencrantz & Guildenstern Are Dead*. The cast included such notables as Gary Oldman, Tim Roth, Richard Dreyfuss, and Ian Richardson. The artistic upshot even garnered the Golden Lion at the Venice Film Festival. Yet its US domestic gross was more than a quarter million short of a measly million dollars. Just chicken scratch!

Movie Awards

Thus far it would seem that a producer would be a fool to get financial backing for an adapted screenplay. There's nothing to gain and much to lose. Still, we have already seen that the box office doesn't often jive with movie awards. The same opposition may apply here as well. And it does, albeit with a twist. First, adaptations are more likely to receive best picture nominations and awards, particularly if the original source was either a novel or a nonfiction book. Second, adaptations have higher odds of getting nominations and awards in the dramatic cluster of honors, an association especially pronounced for nonfiction works. Third, adaptations boast a higher probability of obtaining nominations and awards in the visual cluster of cinematic honors—an effect most strong for novels and nonfiction. Besides all this, adaptations of literary classics have a positive effect on recognition in the visual cluster. Nothing lends itself more to great cinematography, art production, costume design, and makeup than a script based on a great period work, such as a novel by Austen or Dickens. The 2005 *Pride & Prejudice* received nominations in all four categories defining the visual cluster, and the 1963 *Oliver!* was honored with nominations in all visual categories except makeup (which didn't exist back then), and actually won an Oscar for art direction-set decoration.

The foregoing inventory of positive adaptation-recognition relationships has to be qualified by just a small number of negative relationships. First, adaptations from plays are less disposed to receive honors in the technical and music clusters, and adaptations from novels are less disposed to receive honors in the technical cluster. Apparently, such literary adaptations shift the balance toward film as art and away from movies as entertainment. Second, author-adaptations are also less inclined to receive nominations and awards in the technical cluster. Perhaps when authors of the original sources have some control over the final scripts they are more likely to prevent the addition of unnecessary but attention-grabbing special effects and technological expertise. Whatever the reasons for these lone exceptions, it's clear that adaptations are more apt to obtain recognition in the award categories that matter most.

Critical Evaluations

We have already seen multiple times that the film critics are more likely to side with the award voters than with the ticket buyers. That agreement applies here too, albeit the concurrence is not exact. The main consensus is that award-winning and critically acclaimed films are much more disposed to be adaptations from material from some other medium. In addition, literary classics have a special status in this regard. Finally, of the various kinds of adaptations, nonfiction works seems to have the strongest positive effect. The last two results are somewhat curious because filmable nonfiction works are seldom literary classics. Edward Gibbon's *The History of the Decline and Fall of the Roman Empire* can be counted as a classic work of nonfiction literature, but nobody is going to make a movie adapted from its massive volumes. No, not even the 1964 *The Fall of the Roman Empire* was based on Gibbon's classic! As a consequence, it's probably best to view nonfiction works and literary classics—whether novels, short stories, or poems—as two independent sources of critically acclaimed adaptations.

Unanswered Questions

So far I have examined how three criteria of cinematic success are influenced by the following script characteristics: genre, running time, MPAA ratings, sex and violence, sequels and remakes, true stories and biopics, and adaptations versus original screenplays. The chief results are summarized in Table 5.1. Although the empirical findings are rather complex and

TABLE 5.1   Relationships between Screenplay Attributes and Three Sets of Success Criteria

Attribute	Financial performance[a]	Movie awards[b]	Critical evaluations[c]
Genre			
Drama	Negative: S;W;G	Positive: B;D	Positive: E;L
		Negative: T	
Comedy		Negative: V;T;M	
Romance		Positive: B;D;V;M	
Musical		Positive: V;M	Negative: L
Runtime	Positive: W;G	Positive: B;D;V;T;M	Positive: L
MPAA			
G	Positive: S	Negative: D	Negative: E;L
		Positive: M	
PG	Positive: S;W	Positive: V;M	Negative: L
PG-13	Positive: S;W;G	Negative: D	
		Positive: T	
R	Negative: S;W;G	Positive: D	Positive: E;L
		Negative: V;T;M	
Sex	Negative: G	Negative: D	Negative: L
Violence	Positive: G	Negative: D	Negative: E;L
Sequels	Positive: S;W;G	Negative: B;D	Negative: E;L
		Positive: T	
Remakes	Positive: S;W;G	Negative: D	Negative: E;L
True stories	Negative: W	Positive: B;D;V	Positive: E;L
Biopics	Negative: S;W	Positive: D;V	
Adaptations			
All types		Positive: B;D;V	Positive: E;L
Plays	Negative: S;W;G	Negative: T;M	
Novel		Positive: B;V	
Nonfiction		Positive: B;D;V	Positive: E;L
Classics		Positive: V	Positive: E;L
By author	Negative: S;W	Negative: T	

[a]Financial performance: S = screens first weekend; W = first weekend gross; G = domestic gross

[b]Movie awards: P = picture; D = dramatic; V = visual; T = technical; M = musical

[c] Critical evaluations: E = early (Metacritic); L = late (movie guides)

some results are more tentative than others, taken together they essentially support the following broad conclusion: There are two kinds of scripts.

On the one hand, there are the scripts that support film as art—as an aesthetic product. These are more likely to receive nominations and awards for best picture as well as in the dramatic cluster of honors. They also have a higher likelihood of receiving critical acclaim. The scripts that achieve these forms of recognition have some tendency to be R-rated dramas, to be true stories or biopics, and to be adaptations from literary classics or nonfiction works.

On the other hand, there are the scripts that support movies as business— as big, money-making entertainment. Any awards and nominations they receive are prone to be in the non-dramatic clusters, especially the technical. And they often receive the opprobrium of the critics. They are less likely to be adaptations—particularly not from plays or prizewinning works and certainly not adapted by the original author—and the scripts are less likely to be R-rated dramas, or true stories/biopics, but instead are prone to be sequels to or remakes of previously successful films. These scripts also cost considerably more to convert into a finished film.

The only characteristic these two cinematic types have in common is that the films tend to boast longer than average running times. Whether the film wins awards and critical acclaim or becomes a box office smash, it will most likely run for more than two hours.

Given these results, one might think that I would stop typing on my keyboard right this instant, move to Hollywood, and set up a business as a script consultant. Clients will knock on my door, hand me a new script, and have me forecast the odds that it would yield a blockbuster, inspire critical praise, and earn some awards for this or that cinematic achievement. But instead I'm going to keep on writing this chapter, and even finish writing this book. And for good reason: The screenplay characteristics studied so far do not completely explain a film's cinematic success.

This last point is convincingly established if we look at the squared multiple correlation, or R^2, that tells us the proportion of variance that can be explained by a set of predictor variables. In Table 4.2 we saw how much box office earnings, best picture awards, and critics ratings could be predicted using awards and nominations in the dramatic, visual, technical, and musical clusters. The R^2s ranged between .40 and .76, which looks impressive. But how do the script's attributes stack up against these statistics? Here's the answer: (a) production budget .38, number of screens .33, first weekend gross .43, and gross .35; (b) nominations and awards for best picture .09, the dramatic cluster .10, the visual cluster .16, the technical cluster .16, and the music cluster .11; and (c) the critical evaluations during the theatrical run .19 and after the video/DVD release .09. So the screenplay characteristics never explain as much as half of the total variance in a given variable—we can account for 43% of the variance in first weekend earnings—and can sometimes dip below 10%, as happens for the best picture honors and the movie guide ratings. Oddly, it's easier to predict the success of movies as business than it is to predict the success of films as art. Consumers are more predictable in their tastes than are the award voters and film critics.

It must be acknowledged, nonetheless, that the screenplay characteristics so far discussed by no means exhaust the inventory of relevant attributes. Any avid moviegoer could make up a list of omitted factors that go well beyond the findings reviewed in the previous section. Even though research has been conducted on some of these other features, the work has not been fully integrated into comprehensive prediction equations. Instead, the inquiries have often been piecemeal and mainly qualitative rather than integrative and quantitative. Nevertheless, I will discuss some of this work to give some idea of possibilities that may eventually inspire more precise predictions.

The relevant studies share one thing in common: All entail some form of content analysis. In other words, they involve the systematic application of some coding scheme for assessing the occurrence and frequency of specified themes, ideas, concepts, events, persons, conflicts, and so on. These content analytical studies can be grouped into two categories: indirect and direct.

Indirect Content Analyses

The feature-length narrative film is an artistic medium for telling an extended story about one or more characters. In this respect, it can be compared with other narrative forms—especially drama, the novel, and the short story—that have been around for ages. As a result, the factors that are known to contribute a successful narrative in these literary genres might also contribute to the success of a film script. Thus, content analytical studies of high-impact plays, novels, and short stories might yield some understanding of the content of high-impact films. This argument receives some endorsement from the fact that films adapted from these forms make up a large proportion of all films made each year. So can we learn anything by this indirect method? To answer, let's briefly look at each of the three genres separately.

1. *Plays*. A few empirical investigations have examined what it takes to make a great drama, concentrating on the masterpieces of the four classic Greek playwrights—Aeschylus, Sophocles, Euripides, and

Aristophanes—and William Shakespeare. The plays that are most frequently performed tend to have a larger number of quotable lines and to deal with many core issues of human existence, such as dysfunctional family relationships, emotional excess, and even outright insanity. Shakespeare's *Hamlet, Lear, Macbeth*, and *Othello* epitomize many if not all of these thematic attributes. It's also easy to imagine films whose scripts feature one or more of these traits, including such Shakespeare takeoffs as *Ran* (1985; from *Lear*), *Scotland, PA* (2001; from *Macbeth*), *O* (2001; from *Othello*), and *Hamlet_X* (2003) and *Hamlet A.D.D.* (2008).

2. *Novels*. Many films are adapted from best-selling novels. The prototypical example is Margaret Mitchell's *Gone with the Wind* that provided the basis for one of the all-time great films just three years after it swept through the book stores. Hence, it's evident that the content characteristics of such best sellers might provide some clues regarding great movie scripts. According to one systematic inquiry, "emotion is a major ingredient of the best seller," especially if that emotion is concentrated in the central male character. The emotion can be either positive (e.g., affection) or negative (e.g., anger) so long as it's at least moderately intense. Unlike in great plays, the intensity should not be excessively strong and certainly not so strong as to result in madness.

3. *Short-stories*. This literary genre might seem particularly apt because it lacks all the descriptive details, subplots, and minor characters that a screenwriter has to strip away. It was probably easier to adapt the E. Annie Proulx short story "Brokeback Mountain" for the 2005 film than to adapt her novel *The Shipping News* for the 2001 film. Although empirical research on this artistic form is even less frequent than that on the previous two, some potentially useful findings have emerged about the narrative properties of great short stories. For instance, sex (eroticism) and aggression (violence) appear to offer positive themes, as does romance, and it also seems helpful if the characters experience insight or empathy. To the extent that these narrative themes evoke strong emotional reactions, successful short stories seem akin to best-selling novels and oft-performed plays.

So what should we make of these reported findings? It's hard to say. Two separate considerations might lead us to downplay their implications for identifying great scripts.

First, none of the effect sizes is really huge. Each theme appears to account for only a tiny percentage of the variance in the success of the works in a given genre. For example, the correlation between the popularity of a Shakespeare play and whether it features "madness or frenzy due to emotional excess" is .46. This figure is too small to give us sufficient precision to enjoy a high hit-rate in our predictions. And the predictive precision would no doubt be smaller were we to extrapolate from the restricted world of Shakespeare's plays to the broader world of film scripts. However much scholars might like to point to the cinematic character of the Bard's plays, it's still the case that Elizabethan and Jacobean theater conventions cannot be easily generalized to those expected in today's multiplexes.

Second, it's far from established fact that the variables that govern the success of literary genre will prove equivalent to those that affect cinematic success. Cinema represents such a dramatically different medium relative to plays, novels, and short stories. And what works well in one medium may not work well in another. This disparity has been empirically demonstrated in the case of opera. Although opera can be considered merely a play set to music, the composer's music is so much more critical than the librettist's book that the latter has the most minimal consequence. In fact, some of the world's greatest operas have some of the most ill-conceived libretti. *Die Zauberflöte* depends far more on Mozart's music than on Emanuel Schikaneder's libretto, just as Verdi's music for *Il trovatore* easily eclipses the words that Leone Emanuele Bardare and Salvatore Cammarano wrote. Although the musical, technical, and visual clusters of contributions do not override the dramatic cluster as much as opera music dominates the operatic text, their cinematic contributions can severely alter the optimal mix of factors defining a winning script.

The opera world illustrates another critical point: Operas using libretti that are based on literary classics do not necessarily make superior products in that medium. As an example, William Shakespeare most likely outstrips Friedrich Schiller as a pure dramatist, but libretti based on Schiller's plays have generally proven more successful than those based on Shakespeare's. Even when we concentrate on just Shakespeare's works, some of his best plays have not always done well on the opera stage. The most effective operatic treatment of *Hamlet*, namely that composed by Ambroise Thomas, pales in comparison to the handling that *The Merry Wives of Windsor* received from Verdi (*Falstaff*) or even from Carl Otto Nicolai (*Die lustigen Weiber von Windsor*). Yet *Hamlet* is certainly the far superior play. Perhaps there's something intrinsically non-operatic about Shakespeare's most monumental tragedy. Is it even possible to conceive of Hamlet's famous soliloquy "To be, or not be" as being better sung than spoken? The theme seems fundamentally intellectual rather than emotional. Pure cerebral reflection!

The same lesson applies to film adaptations of plays, novels, and short stories. Whatever makes the latter attain classic status may not enhance the quality of any script adapted from those classics. Some of the great masterpieces of world literature may not lend themselves well to a change of artistic medium. Thus, not every novelist writes a work as filmable as Jane Austen's *Sense and Sensibility* (1995), Henry Fielding's *Tom Jones* (1963), E. M. Forster's *A Passage to India* (1984), Boris Pasternak's *Doctor Zhivago* (1965), or Lew Wallace's *Ben-Hur* (1959).

A recent instance is the 2005 *A Cock and Bull Story*. Nominally, this film is adapted from Laurence Sterne's *The Life and Opinions of Tristram Shandy*. Despite that attribution, the script has even less connection with the classic novel than *Adaptation* has with its nonfiction source. Despairing of doing the novel justice, the writer, Frank Cottrell Boyce, ended up creating a screenplay in which actors try to shoot an adaptation but never manage to do so. Scenes are shot, thrown out, and re-shot; major characters appear only to vanish forever from view (such as Gillian Anderson's Widow Wadman). No, it's not that the writer was incompetent. He had already written accomplished scripts for *Hilary and Jackie* (1998), *The Claim* (2000), *Code 46* (2003), and *Millions* (2004). It's just that *Tristram Shandy* is inherently unfilmable. The only solution was to tell *A Cock and Bull Story*.

The fundamental inference from all this is that we need to rely much more on direct content analyses if we wish to isolate the attributes of a great script.

Direct Content Analyses

The ideal content analytical investigation would begin with a large sample of films that exhibit extreme variation in cinematic success: blockbusters, award winners, and critically acclaimed films as well as box office flops that were panned by the critics and ignored by all award ceremonies (except the Razzies). Then researchers would either view the films or read the corresponding shooting scripts to identify the key predictors of success and failure by the several criteria. These predictors would then be entered into the same kind of multiple regression equations used earlier in this chapter in order to test the predictors in the context of the other screenplay characteristics that have already been discussed: genres, MPAA ratings, adaptations, and the like. Presumably, the result would be a set of prediction equations that can account for more variance in success than what has been accomplished to date. Ideally, because a certain amount of subjectivity would be involved in finding the relevant factors, the study should use multiple raters working independently of each other so as to maximize objectivity. Reliability coefficients could even be calculated to gauge the degree of agreement.

Sounds ambitious, doesn't it? In concrete terms, you would need to start with about a thousand films. Assuming that the average film is two hours long, a minimum of two thousand hours of watching time would be required.

This number would be multiplied by the number of independent raters, say at least two, to yield four thousand hours of scoring time. And if we allow the raters to use pause button whenever necessary to do the scoring, or review a film to double check the assigned scores, the number of person-hours gets larger still. Accordingly, we would not expect such scientific inquiries to be all that common. That expectation is amply confirmed: I can't think of a single published example in the research literature. However, it behooves me to mention what has been accomplished, even if the studies fall well short of my idealistic specifications. The following two investigations stand out:

1. *Protagonists*—Douglas Beckwith wanted to isolate the personal values displayed by the protagonists in two major types of successful films, best pictures and blockbusters. The films, which were distributed between 1996 and 2005, fell into three groups: (a) 43 films that were nominated for or actually won the Oscar for best picture; (b) 43 films that generated the highest worldwide revenues (taking the top five each year); and (c) 7 films that were both best pictures and blockbusters by the preceding definitions. Among 2003 films, *Lost in Translation*, *Master and Commander: The Far Side of the World*, *Mystic River*, and *Seabiscuit* occupy the first group; *Finding Nemo*, *The Matrix Reloaded*, *Pirates of the Caribbean: The Curse of the Black Pearl*, and *Bruce Almighty* define the second; and *Lord of the Rings: The Return of the King* is the lone representative of the third. In fact, no year between 1996 and 2005 had more than one film in the third group, and the three years 1996, 2004, and 2005 had no film in that group. So blockbuster best pictures are rather rare. Movies as business seldom converge with film as art.

   In any case, two independent raters then evaluated all 93 films on the values held by the protagonist, including how those values changed during the course of the film. The values concerned both goals (true friendship, mature love, family security, national security, sense of accomplishment, self-respect, inner harmony, and wisdom) and desirable behaviors (being responsible, honest, capable, courageous, ambitious, helpful, and loving). Although the protagonists often shifted their values from more selfish to more altruistic ends, Beckwith was surprised that the three groups of films were not distinguishable with respect to protagonist value hierarchies or their changes as the narrative unfolded in the film. The investigator argued that these films are perhaps too similar—as mainstream productions—to display any differences as these content analytical attributes. The mainstream may blend art and entertainment into a single homogeneous solution.

2. *Storylines*—Eliashberg, Hui, and Zhang adopted a totally different approach. Rather than content analyze the actual films on DVD, they subjected spoilers to content analysis. Spoilers are rather detailed summaries of the entire film storyline. The spoilers for 281 films released between 2001 and 2004 were downloaded from the website www.themoviespoiler.com. Because these thumbnail scripts are already in electronic form, it was fairly easy to subject them to computerized content analyses. For example, some words refer to "dialogue" whereas others to a "violent scene." The relevant words can be easily counted via content analytical computer software. These computer analyzes were supplemented by some expert evaluations concerning certain key features of the storyline. These evaluations included both basic genre categories, like action, thriller, drama, and comedy, as well as more subtle script characteristics, such as familiar setting, clear premise, sympathetic hero, character growth, logical story, and surprise ending. Then using sophisticated statistical methods—techniques that allowed for complex interactions among the content factors—these variables were used to predict the film's return on investment. The resulting prediction model could account for almost half of the variance in the film's profitability.

The investigators plausibly argue that the predictions could be improved all the more if the same content analytical methods were applied to actual scripts rather than spoiler sketches. Unfortunately, they did not apply the same method to forecasting critical acclaim or movie awards. But judging from what we've already learned, the predictors would not be the same. For instance, the action genre proved quite decisive in the prediction of returns on investment, a factor that would probably prove less valuable in predicting the success of film as art.

I believe that it's just a matter of time before the potential of a script can be adequately predicted for all of the diverse cinematic criteria of success. Yet it also must be admitted that these direct content analyses can only take us so far toward predictive precision. The predictions will only be adequate, never perfect, with many exceptions in either direction. Some films will be better warranted by the script's inherent characteristics, and others will be far worse. The script, however critical, remains just one part of the whole picture. The term "screenplay" notwithstanding, scripts are not made to be read as standalone works of literature. Their contents must be fleshed out by the cast in front of the camera and the crew behind the camera. Certainly even the best script cannot survive terrible acting. And the inferior acting may not even be the actor's fault. We'll probably never know how many potentially great scripts were sunk by horrid miscasting or by interpretational conflicts with the director.

It may be especially difficult to predict cinematic success as judged by the more aesthetic criteria—according to film critic evaluations and film awards and nominations. That's because the scripts behind commercial cinema are probably more formulaic than those behind artistic cinema. Indeed, this possibility has been documented in previous results. Why else would financially lucrative sequels and remakes be largely panned by the critics and ignored in the award ceremonies? Art cannot be just "more of the same." An essential component of creativity is originality. A script that merely echoes another script is as insubstantial as an echo. So scripts for great flicks as art are more likely unique.

Want a direct demonstration? Ponder the following films: *All Quiet on the Western Front* (1930), *Gone with the Wind* (1939), *Rebecca* (1940), *Casablanca* (1943), *The Lost Weekend* (1945), *The Best Years of Our Lives* (1946), *On the Waterfront* (1954), *The Bridge on the River Kwai* (1957), *Lawrence of Arabia* (1962), *Tom Jones* (1963), *A Man for All Seasons* (1966), *The Godfather: Part II* (1974), *Annie Hall* (1974), and *One Flew Over the Cuckoo's Nest* (1975).

What do the scripts have in common—besides all representing English-language, feature-length narrative films? Do the protagonists all share the same core values? Are the storylines all similar in some central manner? If so, what is the crucial common denominator? I myself can detect no feature that they share that set them well apart from thousands of other films that could not possibly have made this list—even from films that eventually won Razzies! I can only tell you where this list came from. It's a list of films that satisfied two conditions.

First, all received the highest possible evaluation from five distinct movie guides. If all ratings are converted to a five-star scale, then everyone is a five-star film. That's five full stars, not four and a half or even four and three quarters. Five stars from five critics.

Second, all earned the Oscar for best picture. All were considered by the voting members of the Academy of Motion Picture Arts and Sciences to be the single best film released that year. They were deemed good enough to beat out such rivals as *The Big House* (1930), *The Wizard of Oz* (1939), *The Grapes of Wrath* (1940), *Mildred Pierce* (1945), *It's a Wonderful Life* (1946), *The Caine Mutiny* (1954), *12 Angry Men* (1957), *To Kill a Mockingbird* (1962), *Lilies of the Field* (1963), *Who's Afraid of Virginia Woolf?* (1966), *Chinatown* (1974), *Nashville* (1975), and *Star Wars* (1977). That is to say, in most years the best picture Oscar was quite competitive.

In short, all satisfied the highest possible standards in cinematic creativity and aesthetics. Perhaps the only thing they have in common is that they have nothing in common. And maybe that's the key!

Postscript: What about the Writers?

The prior section seemed to end on a pessimistic note. It suggested that it may not be that easy to pick out great scripts from their run-of-the-mill rivals. At the very minimum this task will prove difficult if the aim is to achieve artistic acclaim rather than just monetary profits. Yet perhaps the solution to this problem requires only that we step back a bit, and view the issue from a more encompassing perspective. Why not move the unit of analysis up one notch? Rather than focus on scripts why not concentrate on writers? If we can determine the attributes of great writers then those findings will get us closer to the desired goal.

Surprisingly, although there has been lots of research on the characteristics of poets, novelists, and playwrights, very little has been done on the attributes of successful screenwriters. Not until 2007 was the first systematic inquiry conducted: The researcher was Steven Pritzker, a psychologist who once had a brief stint as a writer for a television series. Pritzker scrutinized the 100 writers who between 1935 and 2005 had won the Academy Award for best original screenplay. Here are some highlights of what he found:

1. Only 5 of these Oscar-winning writers were women, and 3 of these had received the award since 1991: Callie Khouri for *Thelma & Louise* (1991), Jane Campion for *The Piano* (1992), and Sofia Coppola for *Lost in Translation* (2003). Yet currently women make up almost a quarter of the WGA West membership. So women are apparently underrepresented among star writers.
2. The writers were between 25 and 67 years old at the time of receiving the award, with a median age of 42; 60% of the awards were received by writers between 34 and 48 years of age. These figures are comparable to what is seen in other forms of artistic creativity, including literary creativity. Most literary masterpieces appear when the author is somewhere between age 30 and 50, with the late 30s or early 40s representing the most likely age for producing a masterwork. As an instance, Jane Austen's *Pride and Prejudice* was published when she was 38.
3. The occupational backgrounds of award-winning writers are quite varied. The largest proportion consisted of journalists. According to Pritzker, "this could explain the image of the heroic wisecracking newspaperman" who figures so prominently in so many great scripts. This favorite vocation is followed by actors and playwrights—plus a smattering of writers with studio jobs or with careers in law. A very small number wrote for television. A similarly small number devoted

their entire career to writing for the silver screen. In a nutshell, the overwhelming majority of writers had to "keep their day jobs" before they could become fulltime professionals.

4. It is extremely rare for any writer to receive multiple writing Oscars. Just 4 writers received 3 Academy Awards in any writing category (including adaptations): Charlie Brackett for *The Lost Weekend* (1945; shared with Billy Wilder), *Sunset Blvd.* (1950; shared with Billy Wilder and D.M. Marshman Jr.), and *Titanic* (1953; shared with Walter Reisch and Richard L. Breen); Billy Wilder for *The Lost Weekend* (1945; shared with Charles Brackett), *Sunset Blvd.* (1950; shared with Charles Brackett and D.M. Marshman Jr.), and *The Apartment* (1960; shared with I.A.L. Diamond); Paddy Chayefsky for *Marty* (1955), *The Hospital* (1971), and *Network* (1976); and Francis Ford Coppola for *Patton* (1970; shared with Edmund H. North), *The Godfather* (1972; shared with Mario Puzo), and *The Godfather: Part II* (1974; shared with Mario Puzo). Another 10 won just 2 Oscars apiece. Meanwhile, 60% of all Oscar winners for original screenplay never again received a nomination in any of the writing categories. Even multiple nominees form an elite club. This club includes Ingmar Bergman and Federico Fellini, nominated 5 and 8 times, respectively. Yet, sadly, neither took an actual Oscar home.

When you think about it, the above empirical findings do not really help us much. Producers would be ill-advised to only green light scripts written by former male journalists between 34 and 48 years old who have already received one Oscar nomination. Furthermore, Pritzker's exploratory study was confined to a single criterion of cinematic success, namely, movie awards, and then only awards in just one category: original screenplay. Things might come out differently if we were to judge a writer's achievement by critical acclaim or box office returns. So we remain far from having a complete understanding of the creativity and aesthetics behind great scripts.

This ignorance notwithstanding, I have not yet reported what perhaps is the most provocative empirical result of Pritzker's investigation: A large percentage of the Oscar winners are combined writers and directors. Besides Jane Campion and Sofia Coppola, who both directed from their own scripts, these writer-directors include Preston Sturges for *The Great McGinty* (1940), Orson Welles for *Citizen Kane* (1941), Billy Wilder for *The Lost Weekend* (1945; also won best director), *Sunset Blvd.* (1950), and *The Apartment* (1960; also won best director), John Huston for *The Treasure of the Sierra Madre* (1948; also won best director), Woody Allen for *Annie Hall* (1977; also won best director) and *Hannah and Her Sisters* (1986), Mel Brooks for *The Producers* (1968), Quentin Tarantino for *Pulp Fiction* (1994), and Pedro Almodóvar for *Hable con ella* (2002). In concrete terms, over one-fifth of the Oscar-winning writers also did the directing, and in the last 13 years this percentage has increased to over three-fifths.

Notice that this synergism reinforces the positive impact of individual creative freedom on the receipt of nominations and awards—an association discussed back in Chapter 3. Those who occupy more than one position in the core crew are more likely to attain award-winning achievements. Writers who direct their own scripts enjoy the freedom to work out their unique creative vision. Better yet, films made by writer-directors are more highly appreciated by the critics both during the theatrical exhibition and the later DVD/video distribution. Film critics evidently recognize the artistic integrity that is often the trademark of such products. And as an additional asset, writer-directed films tend to have smaller budgets. Such films place more emphasis on storytelling than on expensive stars, production values, and special effects. Given these extensive virtues of writer-directed cinema, one must wonder why all films are not directed by the same person who wrote the script!

And here's the Catch-22: Such films tend to do more poorly in terms of financial performance. They open on fewer screens, earn less money on the first weekend, and gross less upon completion of their theatrical runs. Thus, we possess yet another criterion by which we can distinguish films as art from movies as business. Writer-directed films earn critical acclaim and award recognition, but they're seldom blockbusters. They get respect, not bucks.

Chapter 6

The Auteur: Are Directors Experts or Artists?

Film criticism is rich in concepts by which to analyze the cinematic product. As a psychologist, I can't help but take a special fascination in what has been styled *auteur theory*. This hybrid term merges the French word for author with the English word for … well … theory. This linguistic hybridism reflects the idea's history. Beginning as a distinctly French idea in the 1950s, it was later picked up by American film critics in the 1960s. In essence, the theory holds that truly great films have an author, a single creator who assumes responsibility for the cinematic product. Like creators producing in other domains of artistic expression, auteurs in cinema generate a body of work that is recognizably theirs—a certain style, a recurrent theme, a final touch … something. As the film's identifiable maître d'œuvre, they are the cinematic parallel to a Michelangelo, Vincent van Gogh, Ludwig van Beethoven, Fyodor Dostoevsky, Arthur Rimbaud, Martha Graham, or Antoni Gaudí.

To illustrate, the following filmmakers have all earned this appellation (albeit to varying degrees): Woody Allen, Pedro Almodóvar, Ingmar Bergman, Peter Bogdanovich, Robert Bresson, Luis Buñuel, John Cassavetes, Charlie Chaplin, Vittorio De Sica, Sergei Eisenstein, Rainer Werner Fassbinder, Federico Fellini, John Ford, Jean-Luc Godard, Alejandro González Iñárritu, D. W. Griffith, Howard Hawks, Werner Herzog, Alfred Hitchcock, Buster Keaton, Akira Kurosawa, Fritz Lang, Spike Lee, Sergio Leone, F. W. Murnau, Max Ophuls, Roman Polanski, Jean Renoir, John Sayles, Martin Scorsese, Josef von Sternberg, Andrei Tarkovsky, François Truffaut, John Waters, Orson Welles, Wim Wenders, Billy Wilder, John Woo, and Yimou Zhang.

What do they have in common except that they have nothing in common? Or almost nothing! For certainly all were directors. And, in fact, most versions of auteur theory view the director as the auteur. No other member of the core crew is better positioned to impose his or her will on the final print. The director as auteur alone has the power to make even the most spoiled movie star conform to a film's aesthetic ends.

Now you should be in the position to appreciate why a psychologist should be so fond of auteur theory. We psychologists like to focus on the individual. We prefer to study the person's thoughts, acts, values, interests, and emotions. Psychologists who study artistic creativity likewise concentrate on the individual artist as the unit of analysis. The sample may consist of dozens, even hundreds of cases, but the variables will be assessed on individuals, not groups. Yet because cinema appears to be a collective creative product, the medium seems resistant to the psychologist's individualistic modus operandi. But if great films are the creations of single artists, the cinematic auteur, then all is well in psychology land. By turning the microscope on the film's director, we can again view the joint product as emerging from a singular human intellect.

There's still another reason why auteur theory must be especially attractive to me as a psychologist. I'm a psychologist, not an economist. I've spent more than three decades studying creativity and esthetics, not film industry profits and product marketing. As has been amply demonstrated in the previous chapter, film as creative art is quite distinguishable from, even antithetical to, movies as money-making entertainment. This was certainly apparent in the divergent responses to the writer-director, a filmmaking entity that would seem to have prima facie status as an auteur. Films made by writer-directors are more likely to receive critical acclaim but are less likely to attain box office success.

Even if we turn our attention to directors in general, independent of whether they participated in the script's creation, directorial impact appears more artistic than economic. On the one hand, the presence of a top-notch director is positively associated with a film earning both critical acclaim and best picture honors. The direct involvement of a first-class director also increases the odds that a given film will eventually be canonized by the American Film Institute as one of the 100 greatest all-time films. So the impact of the first-rate director on a film's aesthetic prominence is both long- and short-term.

On the other hand, although a director's prior box-office success has a positive association with the financial performance of a current film, prior experience directing films has a negative association. The more films directed, the worse are the economic consequences! This ambivalent twofold repercussion helps explain why the net effect of star directors on financial performance is often zero. Complicating the picture even more, the economic performance of directors may be dependent on their establishing strong vertical ties with producers and distributors, whereas such connections are irrelevant to the aesthetic merit of their final products. Of these linkages, the producers probably prove more crucial to financial performance than the directors do. In fact, during the age of the big Hollywood studios, between 1936 and 1935, the career course of the production head was a primary determinant of the average profit per film. Fox studios did well when Darryl F. Zanuck was making good decisions, but Fox did not do well when Zanuck lost the knack for making profitable films—all the while directors under Fox contracts would come and go with an economic irrelevancy.

Given these facts, I now have permission to concentrate on directors as artistic auteurs. In this chapter I will adopt a novel strategy in doing so. Rather than scrutinize their characteristics—their family background, personality, training, and the like—I focus the entire chapter on their careers. How do high-impact directorial careers unfold over the life span? And what does this life-span development tell us about cinematic creativity and aesthetics? We will find this approach useful not just here but also in our analysis of acting in Chapter 7 and film music in Chapter 8.

Age and Artistic Achievement

It just so happens that the oldest topic in psychological science concerns how creative output changes across the life span. When does productivity begin, when does productivity reach a maximum, when does it start to decline, and how steep is that descent? The first scientific study on those questions was published in 1835 (yes, in the early 19th century)! Although that particular investigation looked at the age curve for producing great dramas—such as Molière's *Le Misanthrope* ("The Misanthrope"), *Tartuffe ou l'Imposteur* ("Tartuffe or the Hypocrite"), and *L'Avare ou l'École du mensonge* ("The Miser")—subsequent researchers have examined other forms of artistic creativity, such as fiction, poetry, painting, and sculpture.

Taken altogether, this scientific research yields an overall age curve that describes the typical career trajectory applicable to most artistic creators. In particular, creative output increases fairly rapidly until reaching a peak relatively early in the career—most often 10–20 years after the very first product appeared. After this optimum is reached, productivity starts to decline somewhat gradually, the descent often leveling off slightly so that the output rate at the end of the career is about half the level attained at the highest point. Figure 6.1 provides a graph of this age curve. This curve

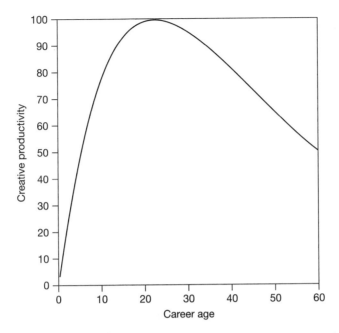

Figure 6.1 The general relation between creative productivity and a creator's career age. The vertical axis expresses productivity as a percentage of the maximum output rate occurring at the career peak (=100). Hence, after 60 years of productive output the rate is about half that shown at the career peak. To convert to chronological age, add about 20 years to the horizontal scale.

presents output as a function of career age—how many years the creator has been active producing works in an artistic genre—but the same basic curve holds when expressed as a function of chronological age (i.e., years since the creator's birth). Although investigators vary in whether they study career or chronological age, the two variables are highly correlated. That's because most artistic creators launch their careers sometime in their mid-20s.

It needs to be pointed out that the curve shown in the figure represents only a statistical aggregation. If you average creative output over a bunch of careers, that's what you get. It's not an iron-clad law like $E = mc^2$. Most creators will display fluctuations around this baseline. Even so, the curve still accounts for a significant proportion of output fluctuations even in individual cases, and even in creative domains beyond the arts. For instance, although Thomas Edison's output of his 1000+ inventions varied greatly over the course of his long career, the correlation is .74 between his actual output and that predicted using the generalized curve. Moreover, the peak of the curve for most inventors is located when they are between 30 and

40 years old, and the same holds for Edison as well. Despite being productive for over six decades, 39% of his inventions appeared when he was in his 30s—427 in all! So Edison's career closely parallels that of inventors in general.

Edison also illustrates another feature of this curve: A creator's best work normally appears during those periods in which he or she is most productive. The peak for output is roughly the same as the peak for impact. Edison invented the phonograph when he was 30, devised a practical incandescent light bulb when he was between 31 and 32, and discovered the "Edison effect" when he was 33. Probably the only highly influential invention left out of this age interval was his kinetoscope—the device that made him a pioneer in the emergence of the film industry. Yet even this invention came out when he was 41, just shortly into his 40s. So his most monumental contributions were conceived with a dozen years of each other.

Speaking in more general terms, the curve shown in Figure 6.1 also tends to express how creativity, influence, or impact of individual contributions fluctuates over the life span. A creator's single best work is most likely to appear in that period in which productivity peaks. In contrast, as productivity trails off toward the end of the career, masterpieces become ever more unlikely. There's also a lower likelihood of coming up with a masterpiece at the beginning of the career. In other words, the overall curve can be interpreted as the probability that creators will produce their best work as a function of career age. Because it is only a probability, exceptions will appear. But the prediction will work on the average. For example, the relation between a composer's age and the frequency that his or her music is performed in the classical repertoire follows a very similar age function, with a peak somewhere in the late 30s or early 40s, the intervals in which their most popular compositions are likely to appear. The same age curve is found to govern the popularity of the plays attributed to William Shakespeare, *Hamlet* appearing when the Bard was in his late 30s.

What makes the curve shown in Figure 6.1 so remarkable is not the rising portion before the peak but rather the downward slope after the peak. Why should output and impact decline with age? Particularly problematic is the decline in impact. After all, we can always argue that output can diminish because of declining physical health, increased family and professional responsibilities, and a host of other extraneous factors. Yet even if creators slowed down with the onset of aging, why shouldn't each creative product still get just better and better? Contributions might come out at slower rate, yet wouldn't the magnitude of the achievements more than compensate for the increased delays? Wouldn't creators have even more incentive to put all they've got into later works when those works are becoming few and far between?

This post-peak detriment in impact becomes all the more remarkable when we consider that some psychologists view creativity as a form of expertise. Creative achievement presumes that the creator acquires the knowledge and skills necessary to produce world-class work in the chosen domain of achievement. Typically, it takes about a full decade of deliberate practice and learning before reaching the point that you can start producing masterworks. This is the so-called "10-year rule." Hence, the ascending portion of the age curve can be simply taken as a sign of progressive expertise acquisition. It's like the typical "learning curve." Nevertheless, according to this explanation we should not expect a downturn after the creator attains domain-specific mastery. At worst the creator would just reach the "law of diminishing returns," creative capacity leveling off to approach some asymptote indicating maximal competence. And at best the creator would continue getting ever more competent with increased experience. Under the latter scenario, a creator's best work would be the last—their swan song perhaps. The artist must become most creative when they've become most expert.

By this point you may be asking what all this has to do with directors as auteurs. For the answer you need to go to the next section.

Creative Career Trajectories

The proponents of auteur theory view directors as artists, not experts. Auteurs are creators, not technicians. Accordingly, directors should exhibit the career trajectories associated with other great creative artists—the curve shown in Figure 6.1. Even more, this trajectory for individual artistic performance should correspond with the cinematic merit of the film that the artist directs. If directorial performance is described by a single-peaked function, then so should the quality of a director's films be described by that same age curve. Directors make their best films when they are doing their best directing. Let's examine the evidence for this connection. The evidence comes from film polls, movie awards, and critical evaluations.

Film Polls

The first relevant study was published in 1941 by Harvey C. Lehman, one of the top-notch early investigators on the relationship between age and achievement. Lehman took advantage of the results of an annual poll conducted by *The Film Daily*, a trade publication that had been published since 1915 (and which ceased publication in 1970). This poll asked critics from major print media to identify those who they believed to the single best director for that year. Lehman then looked up the nominated directors in *The Motion Picture Almanac* (another now-defunct publication). Using these data he could plot the curve showing the relation between chronological age and being chosen by critics as a best director. The resulting curve was single-peaked just like that shown in Figure 6.1, but with a far more precipitous decline. Specifically, the odds of being so honored increased rapidly from the late 20s and reached the peak in the late 30s but then dropped so that directors in their late 50s had a lower likelihood of being selected than those in their late 20s.

Lehman also provided a second graph based on just those directors who were listed among the top 10 in a given year, an obviously more elite group. Although the peak was still between 35 and 39 years of age, the variation around that interval was much smaller, and the post-peak decline much steeper. The cream of the cream of these directors were seldom younger than 30 and seldom older than 50 when entering the list of the year's top 10.

Unfortunately, Lehman did not give specific examples. But I can offer some cases using the Oscars for best director bestowed in the same years on which he based his investigation. Here are the winners along with their respective ages at the time that their film was released: Norman Taurog 32; Lewis Milestone 32 and 35; Frank Borzage 34 and 38; Frank Capra 37, 39, and 41; Leo McCarey 39; John Ford 41 and 46; Frank Lloyd 43 and 47; and Victor Fleming 50. The plurality of the awards were bestowed on directors between 35 and 39; no one was under 30, and only one person was as old as 50.

The latter, Fleming, was a special case. Although getting the final credit for directing *Gone with the Wind*, the original director was George Cukor, who was 10 years Fleming's junior. Besides doing all of the pre-production work on the film, Cukor shot a number of scenes before Clark Gable was able to convince producer David O. Selznick to dismiss Cukor from the crew. Two of these scenes were actually retained in the final cut, namely, Melanie's childbirth sequence and the shooting of the Yankee deserter at Tara. In addition, even after Cukor was kicked off the set he continued to offer private coaching to both Vivien Leigh and Olivia de Havilland, the two female stars in the movie. So perhaps we should average Cukor and Fleming's ages to get 45 as the more proper estimate!

The results of Lehman's study are consistent with what has been found for creative artists. The fact that the descent was more rapid may even be consistent as well. There's some indirect evidence that the age curves for artistic creativity can often be less favorable to older creators in comparison to the age curves for scientists and scholars. The latter forms of achievement tend to be driven more by knowledge than by imagination. Although Pablo Picasso lived into his 80s, the last 20 years of his life were not nearly so creative as during his career peak. Even aside from this matter, it should be manifest that this is not an outcome that would be expected were directors mere technicians. Experts should get ever better, or at least not worse. Furthermore, we have no reason to believe that someone past 50 is going to lack the physical and mental capacity for directing on the set. John Huston was 79 when he directed the 1985 *Prizzi's Honor*, an achievement for which he even received an Oscar nomination. So this decrement cannot be attributed to external factors having undermined the director's expertise. Once again, directors seem to be artists, not experts. Their careers follow the longitudinal course of creative imagination rather than professional experience.

Even though directors' career trajectories closely parallel those of creative artists, it's illogical to infer from that datum alone that they are also cinematic auteurs. Because film is a collective artistic product, the merit of that product can be decoupled from the value of the director's contribution. It's analogous to what can happen in team sports. The basketball player Kobe Bryant can have a hot hand while the Los Angeles Lakers lose the game, or the Lakers can win even while Kobe has a bad day on the court. Likewise, the director's creative tour de force might be wasted on an inferior film while a sub par directorial performance might not prevent a film from reaching the heights. This kind of dissociation truly happens in the case of other filmmaking participants, as we'll see in later chapters, so this conjecture is by no means purely hypothetical. Thus, what remains to be demonstrated is that a film's artistic success agrees with the director's creative trajectory. Directors at their career peak will make superlative films.

Movie Awards

The Oscars bestowed each year make it very clear: Awards and nominations for best picture and best director go together. Since the onset of the Academy Awards, only three films managed to win best picture without having their directors receive so much as a nomination. These were the 1927 *Wings*, the 1932 *Grand Hotel*, and the 1989 *Driving Miss Daisy*. Better yet, almost three quarters of the films receiving the best picture Oscar also had their directors take home the directing Oscar (i.e., 60 of the 81 as of 2009). The last exception was in 2005 when Ang Lee won best director over his fellow nominee Paul Haggis even though Lee's *Brokeback Mountain* lost out to Haggis's *Crash* for the best picture award. In fact, recognition in the directing category is the single best predictor of recognition in the picture category. And this predictive power is not confined to the Academy Awards either. Best picture awards and nominations received from seven major organizations correlates .70 with best director awards and nominations received from the same organizations. This correlation holds for 4,238 films released between 1927 and 2004. Consequently, great flicks and great directors are quite frequent concomitants, as expected.

Critical Evaluations

Final evidence for this relationship comes from a study that Zickar and Slaughter published in 1999. The investigators scrutinized the longitudinal performance of 73 directors who met two requirements: (a) their films had to be produced primarily in the United States and (b) they had to have directed no less than 20 major feature-length films. The first requirement ensured that all directors operated under the same occupational conditions, while the second requirement ensured that their careers were of sufficient duration to provide a meaningful indicator of their trajectories. All 73 directors were male, a fact reflecting the male-dominated nature of the Hollywood film industry (see Chapter 7). The average number of films per director was about 32, with a range from 20 to 72. Each of their films was assessed for critical acclaim using two popular movie guide ratings. As we have already seen in earlier chapters, the evaluations published in such guides are highly consistent among themselves and at the same time correlate with critics' judgments during the theatrical run as well as with best picture awards and nominations. Hence, this outcome measure provides a reliable and valid assessment of the aesthetic quality of each film.

Zickar and Slaughter then analyzed how this critical evaluation changed as a function of the order of the film in each director's body of work. Even though ordinal position is not equivalent to career age, it should closely approximate career age. A director's later films will necessarily appear when the director is older and perchance even wiser. More critically, if we're right that Figure 6.1 is valid for career age, it will be reasonably valid for film order. The single peak will emerge in both. In any case, the investigators analyzed how the movie guide ratings changed as a function of film order using a complex statistical analysis (hierarchical linear modeling) and introducing appropriate controls (for acting quality as gauged by Oscar awards and nominations).

The results of the analysis were telling: The overall curve across all 73 directors was quite similar to that shown in Figure 6.1. The quality of the films first rapidly improved until a peak was reached and then a decline set in, albeit cinematic quality tended to remain higher than during the outset of the director's career. The decrement usually appears after about 10 films, or, on the average, about one-third into the director's career. In rough terms, if the typical director made about 32 films, the first 10 showed progressive improvement, the next 2 stood at the director's career apex, while the last 20 suffered ever increasing decrements as judged by critical acclaim. Divide the numbers along the horizontal axis in Figure 6.1 by 2 and you obtain an approximate graph of the empirical results.

Michael Curtiz provides an approximate illustration of the general pattern. In 1912, while in his late 20s, he began as an actor and director in his native Hungary, and after World War I he continued filmmaking in Austria and Germany. This prior experience notwithstanding, his career may be said to have begun almost from scratch when he arrived in the United States in 1926, at age 40. Not only did he have to direct in English rather than in Hungarian or German, but he also had to learn to work within the Hollywood studio system (beginning at Warner Bros.). Besides that, he was compelled to make the crucial technical transition from directing silent films to directing "talkies." So his 1928 *Tenderloin* might be considered to mark the first year of his new career. It was only the second feature with talking sequences (using the same Vitaphone technique as the 1927 *The Jazz Singer*), and it was the first feature film in which actors could be said to actually speak their roles—albeit the spoken dialog lasted just 15 minutes and the acting was so horrid that the film no longer survives!

Nevertheless, his European experience directing silents was not totally for naught because his artistic growth was faster than the norm. Just 7 years after *Tenderloin*, his 1935 *Captain Blood* was nominated for best picture and he was nominated for best director. Three years later this double picture/director nomination was repeated for the 1938 *Four Daughters*, and *Angels with Dirty Faces* of the same year earned him a third best director nomination. Then a sequence of increasingly notable films came forth that culminated in 1942. In that year appeared two films that represent his career acme: *Yankee Doodle Dandy*, which received nominations for best director and best picture, and *Casablanca*, which won the actual awards in those same two categories, plus an additional Oscar for best writing along with nominations for lead actor, supporting actor, film editing, cinematography, and music score.

Curtiz was never again to be nominated for a best director Oscar. His last nomination in that category came from the Directors Guild of America for the 1951 *I'll See You in My Dreams*. Also, only one later film, the 1945 *Mildred Pierce*, received an Academy nomination for best picture. So his career optimum may be said to have lasted about a decade, from 1935 to 1945, after which the slow decline began. Even if these post-peak products are seldom as mediocre as those with which he launched his Hollywood career, the films still mark a noticeable decrement. His last film, the 1961 *The Comancheros*, staring John Wayne, garnered no awards or nominations from any major organization, and Curtiz died the very next year, having outlived his career peak by two decades. But that's acceptable: He was presumably an artistic creator, not just an expert technician. Other artists who lived into their late 70s also showed decrements—even the great

Michelangelo! If you need proof, just compare the Rondanini Pietà of the Master's final weeks with the Pietà of his mid-20s, the one that graces St. Peter's in Rome.

Creative Life Cycles

It has already been said but it bears repeating: The curve shown in Figure 6.1 is a statistical average. It delineates no more than probabilistic expectation. Any given director will depart from that likelihood in a number of ways. First of all, even when the curve has got the peak right, the merits of each consecutive film made by a director will oscillate randomly around the predicted baseline. Sometimes the films will be better than expected, and sometimes worse. The aesthetic value of a film is a product of many distinct factors, not all of which are under the director's control. Perhaps the lead actors can't get along off the set or can't show an ounce of chemistry on the set. Maybe the script is like Humpty Dumpy who fell off the wall and can't be put together again by all the king's horses and all the king's men. Or the extraneous inputs might even be positive—a memorable acting performance in an otherwise hopeless production. Remember what we learned in Chapter 3, namely, that both best picture honors and critical acclaim are affected by cinematic contributions to all four creative clusters— the dramatic, visual, technical, and even musical clusters. Because some contributions will subtract and others add, the upshot is a far more unpredictable product. And any synergisms implied by the interaction effects will undercut the predictability even more.

As an example, Michael Curtiz might not have ever matched his achievement in *Casablanca*, yet the subsequent decline was never steady and inexorable. The later *Mildred Pierce* and *I'll See You in My Dreams* showed that he still could be associated with some fine filmmaking, and the final *The Comancheros* surpasses the *A Breath of Scandal* that was released in the immediately prior year. Even during his career peak in the early 1940s he could direct some less than stellar films. According to movie guide ratings, *Casablanca* may have been a 5-star movie, and *Yankee Doodle Dandy* worth 4.7 stars, but *Captains of the Clouds*—which appeared in the same year and also starred James Cagney—weighs in at only 2.8 stars. Curtiz had good times, mediocre times, and bad times scattered sporadically across his career.

These seemingly random departures from the smooth curve are less irksome than more pronounced discrepancies. Some directors may crest much earlier than expected, and others may crest far later.

At one extreme is Orson Welles, whose 1941 *Citizen Kane* is often considered the greatest American film ever made. Yet it was the first feature-length film that he ever directed, and he pulled off that accomplishment when he was only 27 years old. In contrast to the 10-year rule, his prior film directing experience consisted of just two shorts, the first of which, the 1934 *The Hearts of Age*, he co-directed with William Vance. *Citizen Kane* was clearly a hard act to follow. Welles could only come close when he directed the 1942 *The Magnificent Ambersons* and the 1958 *Touch of Evil*. His first feature film brought him his only best director nomination as well. The sole Oscar he ever received was for co-writing *Citizen Kane*'s screenplay.

At the other extreme is John Ford. The acme of his directorial career is the 1956 *The Searchers*, which he made when he was 62 years old. This is not to say that the films prior to this one were undistinguished. On the contrary, he had already won best director Oscars for the 1936 *The Informer*, the 1940 *The Grapes of Wrath*, the 1941 *How Green Was My Valley*, and the 1952 *The Quiet Man*, and had received an Oscar nomination for directing the 1939 *Stagecoach*. Plus, these honors from the Academy were augmented by many other nominations and awards from the Directors Guild of America, the National Board of Review, the New York Film Critics Circle, and the Hollywood Foreign Press Association. Yet much of this recognition was for films that Ford directed in the latter part of his career. Besides *The Searchers* and *The Quiet Man* these included *The Long Gray Line* (1955), *Mister Roberts* (1955), *The Last Hurrah* (1958), and *The Horse Soldiers* (1959)—films all made when he was in his 60s.

The economist David W. Galenson argued that this contrast between Welles and Ford is no accident. Instead, these two directors represent diametrically opposed forms of artistic creativity, each with identifiable creative life cycles.

On the one hand are the *conceptual directors*. They use film as a vehicle for expressing their ideas or emotions through visual imagery. And they tend to mature early and decline quickly, often leaving behind a single great film that epitomizes their artistic vision. Besides Welles, conceptual directors include Ingmar Bergman, Sergei Eisenstein, Federico Fellini, D. W. Griffith, and Buster Keaton. When I say a "single great film" I don't mean that these directors are mere "one-shot wonders" but rather that they each have created a single film that "says it all"—that pretty much summarizes who they are as a cinematic auteur. If Eisenstein had stopped making films after his 1925 *Battleship Potemkin* his mark on world cinema would still have been fixed forever.

On the other hand are the *experimental directors*. Their films aim at depicting plausible characters in real-life conditions, and thus emphasize reality. Such creators slowly improve their cinematic methods with increased maturity so that their best films do not usually appear until much later in their careers. And rather than define their legacy in terms of a single great film, the experimental directors often leave behind a whole corpus of masterworks. Besides Ford, Charlie Chaplin, Howard Hawks, Alfred Hitchcock, Akira Kurosawa, Jean Renoir, and Billy Wilder are counted among the great experimental directors.

For a graphic demonstration, take Hitchcock: Figure 6.2 shows the relationship between the cinematic success of 53 films and his career age, where success is gauged by the user ratings published by the Internet Movie Database (as of March 19, 2008). This age curve accounts for about 42% of the year-to-year fluctuations in Hitchcock's success. Two points should be immediately evident. First, the peak of the curve occurs around career age 30, about a decade later than implied by the theoretical curve shown in Figure 6.1. Second, Hitchcock left behind not a single masterpiece but rather several divergent masterworks. A dozen films score 8.0 or higher, such as the 1940 *Rebecca* (8.4), and four weigh in at above 8.5, namely the 1954 *Rear Window* (8.8), 1958 *Vertigo* (8.6), 1959 *North by Northwest* (8.6), and 1960 *Psycho* (8.7). To put these scores in perspective, at the time this figure was constructed only three films in the entire Internet Movie

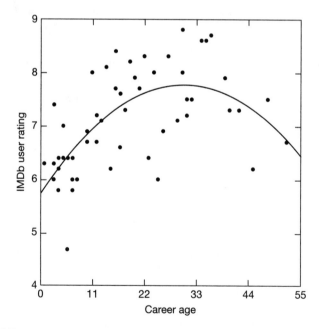

Figure 6.2 The curvilinear relation between cinematic success and career age for 53 extent feature films directed by Alfred Hitchcock. Success is assessed by the "user ratings" published by the Internet Movie Database on a 10-point scale (as of March 19, 2008). The curve is represented by a simple quadratic function that approximates the function shown in Figure 6.1.

Database received user ratings of 9.0 or higher (viz. the 1972 *The Godfather* and the 1994 *The Shawshank Redemption*, both at 9.1, and 1974 *The Godfather: Part II* at 9.0).

This distinction between conceptual and experimental creators is not confined to directors. Indeed, Galenson first introduced the distinction with respect to modern painters. Where Pablo Picasso was seen as the archetypal conceptual artist, Paul Cezanne was viewed as the emblematic experimental artist. Later, Galenson extended the dichotomy to all the arts. Sculptors, poets, novelists, and the like could also be categorized as either conceptual or experimental artists. Where T. S. Eliot was a conceptual poet, Robert Frost was an experimental poet; and where F. Scott Fitzgerald was a conceptual novelist, Thomas Hardy was an experimental novelist. The conceptual creators were also styled "finders" or "young geniuses" while the experimental creators were also called "seekers" or "old masters." The two types of creative artists have distinguishable aesthetic motives and practical styles of working. Galenson even went so far as to distinguish between conceptual and experimental economists!

The contrast between conceptual and experimental directors puts a new spin on auteur theory. In effect, there are two kinds of auteurs: the finders, young geniuses, or conceptual directors versus the seekers, old masters, or experimental directors. Each type leaves an impression on the body of cinematic work in a totally different fashion. On the one side of the divide are the directors who give us films like *The Birth of a Nation* (1915), *The Battleship Potemkin* (1925), *The General* (1927), *Modern Times* (1936), *The Seventh Seal* (1957), *La Dolce Vita* (1960), and *Citizen Kane* (1941); on the other side of the divide are those who directed *Grand Illusion* (1937), *His Girl Friday* (1940), *Seven Samurai* (1954), *The Searchers* (1956), *Some Like It Hot* (1959), and *Psycho* (1960). Neither type is superior to the other. They're just different.

Tying Loose Ends

This chapter seems to have started in one place and ended in quite another. I began with a brief discussion of auteur theory. That led me to demarcate two kinds of career trajectories, one characteristic of artistic creators and the other descriptive of experts. Where creative artists tend to exhibit single-peaked age curves, experts or technicians display positive monotonic functions. Hence, if directors are true auteurs, their careers should conform to the curve in Figure 6.1. Both their performance as directors and the quality of the corresponding films they directed should follow the rise-and-decline longitudinal pattern. Evidence from film polls, movie awards, and critical acclaim then lent support to the hypothesized curvilinear function. The peak of that function was usually in the late 30s (in chronological age), or somewhere around the 10th film (as proxy for career age).

Then all of a sudden I brought in the distinction between conceptual and experimental directors, and muddied up the waters. The former reaches their zenith slightly earlier than that interval, while the latter attains their zenith much later. Both of these creative climaxes present interpretive problems.

On the one hand, the first peak may sometimes appear so early as to violate the 10-year rule. If a director's first film is his best, then can we even say that direction requires the acquisition of domain-specific expertise? Was Orson Welles an unadulterated genius whose *Citizen Kane* could spring from his brain like Mineva from the head of Zeus? I don't think so. To begin with, he had acquired relevant experience in the theater and in radio that he could carry over to his first feature. In addition, he had the fortune of working with some very talented and more experienced collaborators—most notably the writer Herman J. Mankiewicz and the cinematographer Gregg Toland, both of whom had been active for over a dozen years. Moreover, it's relatively rare for even conceptual directors to peak so early as Welles. Only Eisenstein matched this level of precocity (also age 27). By comparison, Keaton peaked at age 32, Bergman at 39, Griffith at 41, and Fellini at 42. The latter four all fall well within the more inclusive 30–50 interval found in the top-director polls discussed earlier.

On the other hand, if the experimental directors peak really late in life, it would seem more appropriate to call them experts rather than artists. They just have a gradual learning curve in which they arduously acquire the directorial bag of tricks necessary to say what they want to say on the big screen. We might even stigmatize them as "slow learners." This potentially damning interpretation overlooks the fact that the experimental directors still display a single-peaked career trajectory. The summit may be shifted toward more maturity, but the summit and ensuing downward slope appears nonetheless. This conclusion is apparent when we look at the following estimated career acmes: Wilder at age 39, Chaplin 42, Hawks and Kurosawa 44, Renoir 45, Hitchcock 55, and Ford 62. This age range overlaps that for the conceptual directors. Wilder was actually younger than Fellini and Griffith and the same age as Bergman at their respective highpoints. Note, too, that every one of these experimental directors lived long enough to make lesser films after they had passed their prime. Even Ford, with the latest career optimum, continued to direct features for another decade after *The Searchers*. Yet his swan song, the 1966 film *7 Women*, is unequivocally inferior, his amplified cinematic expertise be what it may.

The end result is the inference that single-peaked trajectories apply to both conceptual and experimental directors. The former just crests about a dozen years before the latter. This difference can be easily explained by a theory of career trajectories that I have developed over the years. Although the theory is expressed in mathematical terms—one of its equations directly generated the curve seen in Figure 6.1—it's easy to provide a conceptual understanding of how the theory works. Assume that every creator begins with a certain amount of *creative potential*. This is roughly defined as the total number of original ideas he or she is capable of generating in an unlimited lifetime. Over the course of the career this potential is translated into actual creative products by a two-fold process of *ideation* and *elaboration*. Ideation converts potential ideas into "works-in-progress" while elaboration concerts those incipient ideas into finished works. The key is that these rates depend on the nature of the material making up the creative potential. If the ideas are highly abstract, relatively finite, and logically coherent, the rates will go faster than if the ideas are much more concrete, unlimited, and only loosely interconnected. The faster ideation and elaboration rates are responsible for early peaking trajectories, whereas the slower rates are responsible for later peaking trajectories. This theory has been successfully applied to creativity in a diversity of domains. As a case in point, poets tend to have faster rates than novelists, a difference reflected in the fact that the former have the earlier career pinnacle.

This same theory can explain the divergent trajectories of conceptual and experimental directors. The two types are obviously working with distinct inventories of cinematic material. The ideation and elaboration rates for filming images can be more rapid than the rates for filming reality, a far more elusive and intricate set of concepts. Conceptual directors are like poets, experimental directors like novelists. However, it must be stressed that these two directorial types definitely mark the extreme endpoints of the distribution in trajectories. The vast majority of directors will occupy some balance between conceptual and experimental filmmaking. Because they are dealing with both the abstract and the concrete, the finite and the indefinite, the coherent and the intuitive, and so forth, the pace of ideation and elaboration will be more middling.

And therein resides a final issue: How do these hybrid directors compare with the others at the extremes? It's conceivable that such inclusive directors are too nondescript to stand out as bona fide auteurs. Neither conceptual nor experimental, they may lack the necessary artistic unity or integrity to stamp their films with a recognizable logo. So this middle group may represent artists who mostly manifest their creativity in a more subtle fashion.

For the last time, I'll use Michael Curtiz as an example. Unlike the conceptual and experimental directors named earlier, Curtiz is not on anyone's list of auteurs. Not a chance! There's nothing particularly striking about his style or vision. He left no signature on his work. Yet, paradoxically, that very transparency itself may be his distinctive imprint. He may have focused on his actors' execution rather than on his own artistic expression. As a result, 10 different actors were inspired by his direction to deliver performances that received Oscar nods: Paul Muni (lead) in *Black Fury* (1935), John Garfield (supporting) in *Four Daughters* (1938), James Cagney (lead) and Walter Huston (supporting) in *Yankee Doodle Dandy* (1942), Humphrey Bogart (lead) and Claude Rains (supporting) in *Casablanca* (1942), Joan Crawford (lead), Ann Blyth (supporting), and Eve Arden (supporting) in *Mildred Pierce* (1945), and William Powell (lead) in *Life with Father* (1947). Two of these nominees, Cagney and Crawford, took the statuette home. Hence, over a 12-year period Curtiz's artistry may have consisted in bringing out the best performances possible. Unlike the genuine auteur, he was a collaborative rather than individual creator. But does that make *Casablanca* any less of a directorial triumph than *Citizen Kane*? Or any less a great flick?

Chapter 7

The Stars: Sexism in Cinema?

I'm a university professor by trade, so allow me to begin this chapter with a pop quiz: Name who you consider the top-10 movie stars in the Golden Age of Hollywood. What proportion of them are women? Half? A quarter? Even less? Now identify the top-10 Hollywood movie stars active this very day. What proportion of those are women? How do these two proportions compare? Has the proportion increased, decreased, or stayed the same? Does the change—or lack of change—correspond to changes in the status of women in American society? If not, why not?

Now another set of questions.

Recall the male and female actors who earned Oscars in the past few award ceremonies. Do the male and female winners differ in age, attractiveness, or any other physical feature other than gender? And what kinds of films did they appear in? Did those films also win Oscars? Were there any differences in the roles than male and female actors played?

Think of all the times that you went to see a blockbuster. Do you remember which blockbusters had male protagonists and which female? Does the relative proportion of male and female protagonists match the proportion seen in films that receive best picture awards? Or is there a striking discrepancy? Are there more heroes than heroines?

I began with these questions because I want you to think a bit about this issue before we get to the facts. That's necessary because the facts are sometimes unpleasant. These facts concern whether male and female stars compete on an even playing field. The facts regard whether there's sexism in the cinema—and whether that sexism has any association with the making of great films. Is sexism intrinsic to cinematic greatness?

Below I examine this question from four viewpoints: incomes, careers, characters, and kudos. Those words are all put in the plural because men and women differ from all four perspectives. There are two discrepant incomes, two contrasting careers, two opposed sets of characters, and two contrary kinds of kudos. And these discrepancies have consequences.

Incomes

In Chapter 5 we saw that "sex is cheap." That's because films with more graphic sexuality and nudity tend to cost less to make. One reason seems to be that such films contain a larger percentage of females: Female actors typically make a lot less money than male actors. In fact, the larger the representation of female actors, the lower the film's production costs. Although smaller budgets are also associated with a higher proportion of female producers, directors, and screenwriters, the women-cost-less-to-hire effect is especially strong for female actors. Apparently, this may partly reflect the fact that female actors seem to be hired more for their bodies than for their acting skills. At least we know that in film women are more likely to reveal more of their bodies than men. The 1972 *Last Tango in Paris* often shows a clothed Marlon Brando with a naked Maria Schneider—whether conversing or intercoursing—and only the latter is revealed in full frontal nudity. Other evidence reported in this chapter provides more support for this inference.

Significantly, the above gender gap cannot be dismissed as applying solely to actors who perform very minor roles. The contrast is even more striking among those actors who earn the top gross salaries. For instance, the dozen highest paid actors in 2003—those earning about $20 million per film and averaging about 12% of the gross—included only one woman, Julia Roberts. And she earned only half as much as the two top men in that year, namely, Tom Cruise and Bruce Willis. As the last two names hint, most of this gender differential can be attributed to the simple fact that men are much more likely than women to be the protagonists in blockbusters. In part, men make more money because they bring in more money. That's what stars are hired for, and that's what male headliners deliver.

For example, between 1996 and 2005 men occupied the protagonist role in 93% of the movies that ranked among the top five money-makers each year. Ruminate over the following movies: *Independence Day*, *Titanic*, *Armageddon*, *Star Wars: Episode I – The Phantom Menace*, *Mission: Impossible II*, *Harry Potter and the Sorcerer's Stone*, *The Lord of the Rings: The Two Towers*, *The Lord of the Ring: The Return of the King*, *Shrek 2*, and *Harry Potter and the Goblet of Fire*. These 10 movies claimed the highest worldwide gross during the respective years of their release. How many feature a woman as the primary protagonist? Can Kate Winslet's performance in *Titanic* really be allowed? Did her role even rise above being a mere sex object at the mercy of masculine testosterone?

The preceding list indicates another key fact: Many blockbusters are sequels, and male stars are more likely to carry such franchises than female stars. One of the rare exceptions is Sigourney Weaver's *Aliens* series. Renée Zellweger's two *Bridget Jones* flicks can hardly count: She may have earned over twice as much for her performance in the sequel but the film itself flopped. Although a third film may be in the offing, one would not expect it to do any better than the first sequel.

Nor are these gender disparities confined to recent times. A study of 1,687 movies released between 1956 and 1988 found that 78% of the star actors were men. In rough terms, for every female star there are three or four male stars. Or going back even more into the cinematic past, another study examined the box-office favorites from 1915 to 1939, using annual surveys of about 12,000 exhibitors. Men were over twice as likely to be named as the biggest money-making actor in a given year. Of course, different periods in film history would vary in whether audiences were willing to buy a ticket to see a woman perform in a central role on the silver screen. At one extreme, there were two years (1957 and 1983) that had no outstanding female stars in the sense of their being top box-office draws.

At the other extreme, women came closest to equality in the 1930s—the crowning decade of Hollywood's Golden Age. Indeed, the very last year of that decade can be considered the high-water mark for women in screen acting: Merle Oberon in *Wuthering Heights*, Greer Garson in *Goodbye, Mr. Chips*, Bette Davis in *Dark Victory*, Greta Garbo in *Ninotchka*, Irene Dunne in *Love Affair*, Judy Garland in *The Wizard of Oz*, and, naturally, Vivien Leigh in *Gone with the Wind* (or *GWTW*). The Academy nominated all of these films for best picture honors and the last one actually captured the Oscar. Better yet, the remaining stars or impending stars of the feminine gender were rounded up for *The Women*, namely, Norma Shearer, Joan Crawford, Rosalind Russell, Paulette Goddard, and Joan Fontaine, all superbly directed by George Cukor (recently fired from *GWTW* for allegedly being a "woman's director"). All in all, the year 1939 was as good as it got for female actors. Even so, who do you think earned more for their performance in *GWTW*, Vivien Leigh or Clark Gable? Well, the "man of the house" raked in almost 5 times as much! A $120,000 to her measly $25,000! Clark scored a "handsome sum" while Vivien got the lady's "pin money."

So it doesn't matter whether we're looking at 1915–1939, 1956–1988, or 1996–2005, female actress were at an economic disadvantage vis-à-vis male actors. Fewer strike it rich and even the best can expect to earn less cash. And they have an abbreviated life on the top of the charts.

Why these contrasts? The next two gender differences may provide a clue.

Careers

Every film star has a biography and a résumé. These provide details about the star's career origins and development. Nowadays this info is even made available free on the Internet, whether via the Internet Movie Database or an official or fan site devoted exclusively to the star. In any case, even though male and female actors are engaged in the same profession, they do not have the same developmental history. Some of these discrepancies can provide insights into their contrary status in making of great films. So let's discuss how actor career origins and career progressions vary by gender.

Origins

In 1989, Emanuel Levy (then sociologist now *Variety* film critic) published an empirical article entitled "The Democratic Elite: America's Movie Stars" that reports an extensive analysis of the origins of 129 top movie stars in the United States. The stars were identified according the annual "Motion Picture Herald Poll" in which film distributors and exhibitors were asked to name the 10 players who brought the biggest audience. Because the sample spans from 1931 to 1984, the study fills in some of the gaps in the results reported in the previous section.

Levy referred to these stars as the "democratic elite" because they often represent genuine instances of upward mobility. Unlike many institutional elites—such as politicians or academics—star actors often emerged from ethnic minorities and from lower socioeconomic backgrounds. In the case of gender, while it's true that more men than women make it to the very top, it's also undeniable that the proportion of women is far greater than in most other domains of high achievement. At a time when female politicians, entrepreneurs, and even academics were extremely rare, female film stars were more than countable. In fact, the women constitute 37% of Levy's sample! That amply exceeds the percentage of women who have become eminent literary creators, a field in which their gender has been unusually exceptional.

Nevertheless, the two genders differ on some factors that may help us comprehend the issue that drives this chapter. Although almost a third of the stars came from either New York or Los Angeles—two major centers of the US film industry—the women were likely to have been born in LA rather than NY. Given that Hollywood dominated film production, this difference may count as a geographical advantage favoring the women. Even more telling, the women were more prone to have come from families where one or both parents were involved in show business or entertainment. As an example, fully 42% of the women but only 17% of the men had "stage mothers." Finally, where men were more likely to attain higher levels of formal education, and even to have studied acting, the women were far more likely to have begun in modeling. An entire quarter of future female stars began as models whereas none of the future male stars did so. Marilyn Monroe (arguably the most celebrated female star of all time) modeled swimsuits before signing her first studio contract. Just to show that this route is not yet obsolete, Uma Thurman, Charlize Theron, and Lindsay Lohan all started out in modeling. Think about what we learned earlier about female actors revealing more of their bodies than male actors. Such is the professional modus operandi of the Hollywood starlet?

Given that the women have a higher likelihood of being born in LA, to come from parents involved in entertainment, and to have been models, they may be uniquely positioned to begin their careers early. Because they would have more opportunities to establish connections with others in the film industry, and because their modeling may make them noticeable at a relatively young age—even in their teens—they would probably get their first "big break" much sooner than men (especially in a world dominated by male producers and casting directors). In line with this inference, 31% of the women but only 10% of the men became professionals before reaching the age of 15. That is, female stars are three times more likely to start as young teenagers or even pre-teen. Lindsay Lohan started acting at age 10, Jodie Foster at 6, and Shirley Temple at 3.

Progressions

So you may ask: Where's the problem? Aren't female actors getting a head start? Yes, but getting a jump on the gun may not help in the long run. The women are not only less inclined to have studied acting, but they are also more inclined to have been selected for their "looks," often as advertised by their modeling portfolios. So the young starlets are more frequently cast for sex appeal than thespian prowess. While still in her 20s Marilyn Monroe was playing the "blonde bombshell" in movies like *Gentlemen Prefer Blondes* (1953) and *The Seven Year Itch* (1955). Because female physical attractiveness seems to have a short shelf life in comparison to the male, they may end up with more truncated screen careers besides. That's actually the case. Where the median length of careers is 25 years for the males, it's only 17 years for the female stars. Furthermore, women are about a third less likely to be top film attractions for more than 10 years. In Levy's sample, only Betty Grable, Doris Day, and Barbara Streisand were able to sustain stardom for over a decade. Accordingly, women sprint off sooner but pull out of the race sooner still. They may push out of the blocks faster than the men, but they don't make it all the way around the track.

Other researchers have replicated this astonishing result. One study found that although female actors attained maximal box-office popularity between 23 and 27 and male actors did so between 30 and 34, the male box-office draw was about twice as long as the female. The men stood on top of the charts 100% longer than the women. What's even more amazing is that the same disparity crops up in monthly assessments of "best performances" (according to the editors of *Photoplay Magazine*). Women were younger than the men when they began leaving their mark on the acting scene, and were disposed to reach their career climax about a decade younger as well. But their post-peak decline was considerably more precipitous. By this more demanding criterion, women were has-beens by the time they were 40 years old, whereas the men could still be going strong well into their 60s. A 10-year contrast in peaks expands into a 20-year contrast in the tails of the distribution. By these stats, it takes two female actors to equal one male actor.

Because the study just described was published in 1941, the results might be easily dismissed as woefully out of date. Surely women have made some progress toward equality since the Second World War, and a portion of this advancement should mitigate the sex contrast in career course for male and female actors. This pleasant if perhaps overly hopeful possibility was scrutinized in an investigation published in 2004. The investigators specifically focused on what they called the "double jeopardy" inherent in the dual effects of gender and aging. The adverse impact of being female is compounded by the ever growing handicap of getting older. The sample consisted of 318 stars who appeared in a total of 14,922 movies between 1926 and 1999. Hence, the typical star appeared in around 47 movies. Two distinct measures were then devised for assessing the course of the career. The first was simply the number of movies in which an actor appeared in a given year. The second was the average star presence in a given year. In this case the actor received more credit for top billing than for second or third billing. For example, the actor paying the lead role would get more credit than the one playing in a supporting role. Even if there are two leads, one will be billed before the other—often the actor whose name stands highest or first on the marquee.

Although the statistical analyses and empirical results are fairly complex, the central findings can be summarized as follows. In terms of number of movies made in a particular year, women not only had fewer roles than men, but also the age decrement was steeper for women than for men. With respect to average star presence, the career trajectories differed greatly for movies made up to 1942 and those made after 1942, when Hollywood film production dropped appreciably. In the earlier period, star presence was roughly equal for men and women, and slightly increased with age. But in the later period, from 1942 to 1999, aging brought on a slight increase in star presence for men whereas for women age was associated with a rather steep drop in star presence. These findings establish a patent case for female actresses facing double jeopardy in the movie business. The only period in which men and women stood on more or less equal ground was during Hollywood's Golden Age—a point that was indicated in Levy's 1989 study as well.

Putting this altogether, the careers of male and female actors have very different progressions. Women start younger and have shorter careers. Men get a later start but have longer careers. The gender divergence in career onset helps us comprehend an empirical curiosity: Women tend to earn the acting Oscars at much younger ages than men. Want some particularly dramatic examples? At age 20 Timothy Hutton became the youngest male to win an Oscar for supporting actor, and at age 29 Adrien Brody became the youngest male in the lead actor category. But these male exemplars of impressive precocity were completely outdone by Tatum O'Neal, who won the Oscar for female supporting at age 10 and by Marlee Matlin who did the same for female lead at age 20. This all averages to about a decade difference between the male and female awardees.

These cases are not atypical. One pair of investigators examined more than a thousand actors of both genders who were nominated for honors in both lead and supporting roles between 1927 and 1990. Whereas two-thirds of the male Oscar winners were 40 years old or older, only about one quarter of the female winners are so advanced in age. This age gap is also apparent in the Oscar nominees, and even holds for Emmy winners, the corresponding television awards for outstanding acting. No matter what the specific success criterion, female actors tend to max out at younger ages than do male actors.

Yet it must be remembered that women get out of the gates younger, too. It has been shown that once you control for the actor's age at the time of the first film, the gender gap becomes negligible. Women are nominated and awarded before men of the same age because the women began their acting careers first. This explanation was illustrated in the 2003 Oscar ceremonies. Four women and three men earned their first Oscar nod for best lead or supporting actor in that year. The women were Salma Hayek (lead in *Frida*), Diane Lane (lead in *Unfaithful*), Queen Latifah (supporting in *Chicago*), and Catherine Zeta-Jones (supporting in *Chicago*), and the men were Adrien Brody (lead in *The Pianist*), Chris Cooper (supporting in *Adaptation*), and John C. Reilly (supporting in *Chicago*). The average age of the four first-time female nominees was 34.5 whereas that for the three first-time male nominees was 39.0, yielding an age difference of 4.5 years. Male actors are older than female actors when they stand at the threshold of fame and fortune. But if you calculate career age instead of chronological age, the inference changes. The time from first film to first Oscar nod is 13.5 years for the four women and 13.7 for the three men. These lags in career ages should be reminiscent of the 10-year rule discussed in the previous chapter. Only, we can call it the "bakers-dozen rule." On the average, a future film star should be working in the trenches for over 13 years before he or she can expect to enter stardom.

Characters

The previous section seemed to end on a positive note. Men and women apparently have similar careers once due allowance is made for their contrasting career onsets. Yet the fact remains that male actors have much longer careers than female actors. So women have accelerated yet truncated careers while men have belated yet extended careers. These two career paths combined help explain a curiosity of movieland: The often tremendous age disparities between male and female leads supposedly involved in romantic relationships—like Sean Connery teaming up with the 40-years younger Catherine Zeta-Jones in the 1999 *Entrapment*. To be sure, such age gaps do occur in real life. A year after *Entrapment*, Zeta-Jones married actor Michael Douglas, a man born on exactly the same birthday as she but 25 years earlier. It still seems that such multiple-decade gaps are far more common in the movies than in the everyday world. A male actor can still play a romantic lead when he's past 60, whereas a female actor finds herself to be a more ephemeral motive for love or lust. As a male who turned 60 while writing the first draft of this chapter, I can only express envy at the masculinity purportedly displayed by those born the same year as I but who chose a different profession. Guys like Mikhail Baryshnikov who could play the "Sex and the City" lover opposite Sarah Jessica Parker despite being 17 years older.

Which leads us to ask: What are former female stars doing when they're past *their* supposed sexual prime? If they're no longer playing the objects of male affection or desire, then what are these women doing with themselves? Certainly they're doing something!

This query gets us to the larger question of what kinds of characters female actors are playing in films. How do those feminine characters differ from those played by men, and how do these differences change over the career course?

Below I address this issue from two angles: films that win acting awards versus movies that make big money in the box office.

Award-Winning Films

One year after Levy published the study of 129 movie stars he published a second with a quite different focus. Instead of studying the origins and development of film stars he was interested in how men and women are differentially portrayed by stars in the movies. In particular, he inspected the 218 screen roles that earned their actors an Academy award between 1927 and 1986. Of these 218, 116 were for lead roles (established since 1927) and 102 were for supporting roles (not bestowed until 1935). One asset of this sample is that male and female characters will be about equally represented. Oscars are given to both men and women in both leading and supporting categories.

Levy then systematically classified the types of roles that won this high honor. Doing so, he arrived at the following five sets of results:

1. Although fiction characters outnumber real-life characters by about fourfold, the contrast is much greater for female Oscar winners than for male Oscar winners, especially for the lead categories. Over one-third of the Oscars won for best male lead have gone to actors playing a real-life protagonist, whereas only about 16% of the corresponding women performed characters of this type. However, this disparity may be less decisive than it seems on first blush. After all, men outnumber women among famous personalities—whether creators, leaders, or other celebrities—and many real-life characters appear as the protagonists in biopics. If there are more eminent men than women, and if many Oscar-winning leads appear as protagonists in biopics, then male actors would naturally hold the advantage over female actors.

2. Oscar-honored men and women also differ in the genre of the film in which they performed their winning role. Although the differences for some film genres are rather small—like drama, comedy, and musicals—in two genres the differentials are rather pronounced. First, male Oscar winners vastly outnumber female Oscar winners in adventure films. The difference is between more than 19% for men and less than 6% for women. That's a threefold divergence. Even more intriguing

is the fact that if a female actor does win an Oscar for playing a character in an adventure film, that rare event is invariably associated with a supporting role. A woman can be the love interest or side kick, but not the hero who saves the day in a cliffhanger. The outcome for the genre of romance is even more dramatic: Then Oscar-winning roles, whether lead or supporting, are played by women, not men. Between 1927 and 1986 there was not a single male actor who won an Academy Award for his performance in a romance. No, not even Humphrey Bogart in *Casablanca*. They're probably too busy playing protagonists in adventure films!

3. The ages of the characters played by Oscar-honored actors are even more provocative. In some respects the gender contrasts reflect the actual ages of the performers, only with some exaggeration. On the one hand, almost a third of the male leads are most likely to play middle-aged characters, and over a fifth played old men. Putting lead and supporting roles together, over 80% of the male characters are either middle-aged or old. On the other hand, female actors are far more likely to play young characters—over three-fourths do so. In contrast, female actors are half as likely as the men to interpret old characters. Finally, although nobody in the sample won a lead Oscar for playing an adolescent, almost 4% of the performances that earned female supporting Oscars were in this age group. To sum up, whereas male characters are grownups, female characters are still growing up.

4. The characters enacted by Oscar-winning actors are dominated by certain key concerns. Male characters have a higher likelihood of being preoccupied with public or occupational aspirations, whereas female characters have a higher probability of being concerned with personal and domestic aims. From the perspective of traditional American sex-role stereotypes, men are men and women are women. This differentiation is so powerful that it overrides the distinction between lead and supporting roles. Male lead and supporting characters are cut from blue cloth, and female lead and supporting characters are cut from pink cloth, period.

5. Consistent with the preceding divergence are the occupations the characters ostensibly pursue. Male lead and supporting Oscar winners are most likely to play soldiers, followed by sheriffs, criminals, politicians, actors, writers, and laborers, with an additional smattering of businessmen, lawyers, journalists, prizefighters, priests, teachers, scientists, and monarchs. Fewer than 4% of the male characters have no gainful work. The female lead and supporting Oscar winners? By far the most popular occupations for them to pursue are "actress" and

prostitute—those two alone account for over a quarter of the characters played. After that comes a miscellany of heiresses, teachers, artists, hotel proprietresses, farmers' wives, secretaries, businesswomen, queens, politicians, nurses, seamstresses, and maids. Although a few items in these two lists overlap, the frequencies always seem to favor the men. Thus, male politicians outnumber female politicians, and the same superior representation holds for businessmen versus businesswomen. In general, women suffer from lower status employment. Even worse, more than a third of the characters that earn women acting Oscars seem to have no gainful employment whatsoever! They don't come home from work, nor do they bring any work home.

If the last "null" group is combined with the two most common female occupations, we arrive at this startling statistic: Over 60% of all Oscars for lead or supporting performances are presented to women who played characters who either were unemployed, acted for a living, or made ends meet by servicing the sexual needs of men. If you've repressed from your memory the many instances of the third option, here are some reminders: Elizabeth Taylor in *BUtterfield 8* (1960), Jane Fonda in *Klute* (1971), Jodie Foster in *Taxi Driver* (1976), Mira Sorvino in *Mighty Aphrodite* (1995), and Charlize Theron in *Monster* (2003)—Oscar performances all! Prostitution may or may not be the oldest profession, but who'd ever guess that would become such a ready path to an Academy statuette? As the 2003 example shows, a prostitute doesn't even need a "heart of gold" to get the gold.

Levy concluded that rigid screen stereotypes have consistently differentiated male and female film characters and that this consistent differentiation probably explains their prevalence. But rather than debate whether this is the best conclusion, I would like to add my own remark on these findings. A perceptive reader may have noticed that I have assiduously avoided as much as possible any use of the word "actress" in this book. That's because I find the word outdated at best and perniciously sexist at worst. The usage implies that women are doing something different, even inferior. Because men are acting but women are merely "actressing," the former are actors and the latter mere "actresses."

Yet the results of the above data analysis might be interpreted as actually endorsing this gender-specific lexical division. Actors and "actresses" are indeed playing different characters. Male characters are competent, active, courageous, mature, and realistic if not actually real. Female characters are naive, passive, young, vulnerable, and overly romantic, even fictionally so. Who most deserves an Oscar? Male actors playing the typical male character or female actors playing the typical female character?

Money-Making Movies

Before we blame all the sexist male producers and screenwriters, we must remember that film is a business as well as an art. If the characters played by male and female actors betray sexist attitudes, that may tell us as much about the movie audience as the industry. Perhaps sexism, unlike sex, really sells. To test this possibility we need to use box office success as the criterion. If blockbusters depict female characters in a more negative manner than male characters, then can the movie industry be fairly blamed for pandering to their consumers? If moviegoers decided that they preferred to see animated over live-action films, wouldn't we expect the producers to satisfy their tastes? No money, no movie.

Therefore, in this section on movie characters I will discuss another investigation that confined its analysis to 100 movies that were the box office smash hits from the 1940s to the 1980s (20 movies from each 10-year period). From these top-grossing movies the investigators isolated 829 characters: 252 of these were central to the storyline, another 281 were secondary, and a final 295 were considered peripheral. These characters were then rated by 12 independent judges, both male and female, and ranging between ages 28 and 60. More specifically, the characters were scored on age, goodness (sinner to saint), socioeconomic status, intelligence, friendliness, romantic activity, physical attractiveness, and life outcome (i.e., negative or positive end). With the exception of age, these attributes were assessed on a 10-point scale. The reliabilities of these ratings were excellent (between .76 and .98).

In line with earlier findings, female characters were underrepresented relative to male characters. For example, among the characters central to the plot, men outnumbered women by almost 2 to 1. Men were even more numerous among the secondary characters. Also supporting previous results, male characters tended to be older, sometimes by more than a decade. But the most fascinating findings concern how the other assessed characteristics varied according to the age of the characters. Consider the following seven results:

1. Although both male and female characters are depicted as becoming less friendly with age, the age drop is more conspicuous for the females. Women evidently turn into much nastier people as they get older. Do wrinkles and gray hair make women more bitter?

2. While older men are shown as being more intelligent than younger men, older women are shown as being less intelligent! So older women are not only more unfriendly but also increasingly stupid! It gets worse.

3. From the standpoint of goodness, male characters neither increase nor decrease with age. Young, middle-aged, and old men are all similarly good (or bad). Not so the female characters: Young women are moral, older women immoral—as if they develop from virgins to witches! Because goodness and beauty tend to be strongly associated, and because only women are said to lose beauty with age, they must suffer a double whammy.

4. Male characters increase in socioeconomic status as they get older, whereas according to this criterion woman gain nothing. Increase a man's wrinkles and gray hair, and you enhance his wealth and prestige.

5. Even though both male and female characters appear to decline in attractiveness with increased age, the decline is much more radical in the "gentler sex." What men lose in virility they may partially regain in looking "distinguished." Aging women on the silver screen do not enjoy any compensatory trends. On the big screen, it's either witch or bitch.

6. The final life course of the character also varies with age. Older men and women are more likely to have bad outcomes than younger men and women. Even so, the downward pull of tragedy is far stronger for female characters. In the movie world, fate hates hags.

7. The pattern for a romantic life is very similar to the preceding. Both male and female characters are less likely to experience cinematic romance as they get older, but the decline in love and/or lust confronts the women more than the men. This might be taken as another instance of a negative outcome for older female characters.

The final assessment? The article's title reads: "The Aging Woman in Popular Film: Underrepresented, Unattractive, Unfriendly, and Unintelligent." This only tells part of the story. Even when aging man suffers the same unfavorable trends, he doesn't have to suffer to the same degree.

I was trying to conjure up a specific film that illustrates all of the above findings at once. Failing to do so, I have come up with an illustration that may capture the essence. Contemplate the careers of two actresses from Hollywood's Golden Age: Joan Crawford and Bette Davis. Born only three years apart (in 1905 and 1908, respectively), both won Oscars for their lead performances, Davis in *Dangerous* (1935) and *Jezebel* (1938) and Crawford in *Mildred Pearce* (1945). They were also arch-rivals who came together to co-star in the 1962 *What Ever Happened to Baby Jane?* This was the film for which Davis received her last Oscar nod. Even if the characters the two stars embodied in the earlier movies are not all perfect, it's obvious that the squabbling and nasty characters in the later film score far lower on almost any human virtue. What we see is two former movie stars descending into poverty, disability, and insanity.

Kudos

So far I have investigated gender differences in acting with respect to incomes earned, careers achieved, and characters portrayed. Almost without exception the male actors come out on top: They earn higher incomes and are the favored protagonists in blockbusters; after a delayed start, the men have longer careers as stars; and men have roles in more films and portray more attractive characters in those films. It all seems pretty dismal for female actors.

Nonetheless, one last hope remains: Kudos for great performances. For here we must observe a most curious paradox. Whatever the disadvantages women may face relative to men, they are guaranteed the exact same chance to win major acting awards. Every organization that confers honors for acting ensures that male and female actors will receive the same level of recognition. During the usual Oscar gala, there will be a total of 20 acting nominees, 10 for men (5 lead and 5 supporting) and 10 for women (also 5 lead and 5 supporting), and exactly 2 men and 2 women will have their names inscribed in the secret envelope. Equality cannot get any more equal than that! The only time that this equality has been broken was in 1968 when a tie vote resulted in two Oscars for best female lead: Katherine Hepburn for *The Lion in Winter* and Barbara Streisand for *Funny Girl*. So that night the women walked away with the most awards!

Given everything else I've reviewed, this equality seems almost too good to be true. There must be a catch. If female actors are disadvantaged in almost every possible way, then how can they manage to earn exactly the same number of acting awards and nominations? A potential solution does present itself, and it's not pleasant: Perhaps the women's great performances do not appear in the best films. By "best" I do not mean top-grossing movies because we have already had to give up on that option. Instead "best" signifies films that earn high critical praise and haul in awards and nominations for best picture—artistic rather than economic standards. Is it possible that a woman's best acting performances are more frequently wasted on less important movies? Below I answer using both critical acclaim and best picture honors as criteria of cinematic achievement.

Critical Acclaim

I know of no empirical studies that investigate this question regarding critics' evaluations that appear early during a film's theatrical run. I am aware, however, of investigations based on movie guide ratings. Their implications are not all that favorable to women.

The first study was published in 2002 and concentrated on the Oscars. The specific criterion of cinematic success was the five-item composite of movie guide ratings discussed more than once in previous chapters. As before, this measure was highly reliable (i.e., the coefficient was .85). The sample consisted of 2,323 movies that had received nominations or awards between 1928 and 2000. Because the award categories for the supporting actors had not yet been established, the main results are confined to the male and female lead roles. In this case the gender contrast in best acting Oscar awards and nominations was strong. Although both male and female leads were positively associated with the movie guide ratings, the association for the men was almost twice as strong as that for the women. Indeed, the consequence of a female acting award was less potent than an award or nomination in cinematography and only slightly superior to Oscar recognition in art direction. In contrast, the only honors that exceeded a male acting Oscar statuette or nod were those for directing and writing. Hence, it seems that the Oscar performances of female actors are *less likely* to be found in critically acclaimed films.

A follow-up study published two years later replicated this result for 2,137 films that received major Oscar nominations or awards between 1936 and 2000. Because of the later start date for the sample, this inquiry could include the honors granted in the supporting categories. The results for the latter merely replicated the findings for the lead categories. Not only are Oscar-honored female supporting actors less likely to appear in critically acclaimed films, but there was no difference between lead and supporting female actors. Their apparent contribution to the critical evaluation was about the same. Worse yet, Oscar nominations and awards for male supporting performances had a stronger relation with the film's critical acclaim than female lead performances. Put differently, a female lead actor is less important to a film's cinematic success than a male supporting actor.

One might dismiss these findings as merely echoing the sexist attitudes of the nearly 6,000 voting members of the Academy. Perhaps they are handing the female acting awards to the wrong performances. However, the same follow-up investigation replicated these conclusions using a larger collection of acting awards and nominations, namely, those received from (a) the Academy of Motion Picture Arts and Sciences, (b) the British Academy of Film and Television Arts (BAFTA), (c) the Hollywood Foreign Press Association (Golden Globes), (d) the National Board of Review, (e) the National Society of Film Critics, (f) the Los Angeles Film Critics Association, and (g) New York Film Critics Circle. This time the sample consisted of 1,367 films released between 1968 and 2000. Once more, the female acting awards were far less likely to be associated with critics' assessments, and honors for female lead actors were less predictive of a film's acclaim than honors for male supporting actors. Given that these findings were based on the nominations and awards received from seven major organizations, it's manifest that the Academy voters cannot be condemned for this gender difference in performance impact. Female actors do seem less relevant than male actors to a film's artistic merit. On this point, professionals, journalists, and critics all agree.

But what happens when we change the criterion of cinematic success? What if we use best picture awards and nominations rather than the evaluations of film critics?

Best Picture Honors

Unfortunately, the change in scene does not make the story any better. The same old plot line just continues. To begin with, Oscar nominations and awards for best picture show the same pattern of relationships with Oscar nominations and awards in the categories of best male and female leads and best male and female supporting. Once more, noteworthy interpretations by men in supporting roles are more strongly linked with best pictures than similarly notable interpretations by women in lead roles. And regarding one comparison, the gender difference is even accentuated. For the Oscars in the two lead categories, females are only half as likely as men to have their outstanding performances appear in exceptional films!

Other researchers provide additional support for the conclusion that Oscar-honored films are less likely to feature Oscar-honored female acting performances. Specifically, we can add the following pair of findings:

1. One investigator scrutinized all films that were nominated for the best picture Oscar between 1996 and 2005. He determined that female characters made up only 28% of the protagonists in these top-flight motion pictures. Given that actors playing protagonists have more opportunity to win Oscar nominations or awards in the two lead acting categories, this low representation can only work against women. Even when women play the film's key protagonist, their attributes were distinguishable from men in such roles. Female protagonists tended to be much younger: More than two-thirds were between 21 and 30, whereas less than one-third of the male protagonists fell into this age range. The greater youth of the female protagonists suggests that they are realizing a more restricted range of characters, such as romantic leads. Remember the earlier observation that award-winning female actors are strongly disposed to appear in romances—a genre

that seems especially feminine. Even the best picture nominated *Brokeback Mountain* (2005)—which narrated a romantic relationship between two men—provided a supporting role for Michelle Williams sufficiently substantial to enable her to earn an Oscar nod.

2. In a second study the investigators examined a totally different question: What impact do Oscar nominations and awards have on a film's financial success? The authors began by confirming what is well known in the industry, namely, that a best picture nomination does enhance a film's box office returns. More relevant to the present problem are their results for nominations in the four acting categories. Not surprisingly, nominations in the lead acting categories have more of an impact than nominations in the supporting categories. But even more interesting was the finding that a nomination for best male lead has a bigger influence on success than does a nomination for best female lead. Indeed, the impact of a male acting nomination is about the same magnitude as a best picture nomination! Both increase income by over 200%. Even more fascinating is the fact that a female win in the lead acting category has a much larger influence on the film's earnings than does a male win. Why is this so? Apparently, a man's nomination is a stronger signal of cinematic quality. If a film earns the male lead an Oscar nod, then it must be really good, and moviegoers will head to the theater to see it. But moviegoers require that a female lead actually win the award before they'll draw the same inference about her film! In other words, an Oscar award for a female actor has about the same box office value as an Oscar nomination for a male actor!

These results might also be criticized for relying exclusively on the opinions of Academy voters. Yet that criticism won't withstand empirical scrutiny. The same conclusions emerge when both best picture honors and nominations/awards in the four acting categories are based on recognition received from seven major organizations, the same used in the previous section. Awards and nominations for male leads are almost three times as powerful as the same recognition for female leads, and even the male supporting category slightly surpasses the female lead category. Finally, female supporting actors have hardly any connection at all with best picture recognition. So one more time: Outstanding performances by male actors have a higher probability of being found in exceptional films than outstanding performances by female actors.

These statistical findings can be easily documented with concrete examples. A very large number of women have won best acting Oscars in films that were not even nominated for best picture Oscars. This list includes such big names as Mary Pickford, Helen Hayes, Katharine Hepburn, Bette Davis, Olivia De Havilland, Loretta Young, Ingrid Bergman, Joanne Woodward, Susan Hayward, Elisabeth Taylor, Sophia Loren, Anne Bancroft, Maggie Smith, Glenda Jackson, Jane Fonda, Ellen Burstyn, Meryl Streep, Geraldine Page, Jodie Foster, Kathy Bates, Jessica Lange, Susan Sarandon, Halle Berry, Charlize Theron, and Reese Witherspoon.

Of those listed, Streep's film career is perhaps most indicative of this odd phenomenon. If we count both lead and supporting categories, she can claim more Oscar acting nominations than any other woman in the history of the Academy Awards, including both Katherine Hepburn and Bette Davis. Yet only a small proportion of these nominations were for films that were also nominated for best picture honors. In fact, her only award for best lead acting came for *Sophie's Choice* (1982), a film that received no important best picture awards and only one best picture nomination of note (from the Hollywood Foreign Press Association). The films in which she received mere nominations did not do any better.

Congruent with what we learned earlier about women's acting careers Streep's biggest successes came early, when she was between 29 and 30 years of age. She then won Academy recognition for supporting roles in the award-winning films *The Deer Hunter* (1978) and *Kramer versus Kramer* (1979), the first as a nominee and the second as a winner. Yet later in her career this prominence in first-rate films gave way to acting nominations in films that were often far removed from the running for best picture awards. Examples include roles in *Ironweed* (1987), *Evil Angels* (1988), *Postcards from the Edge* (1990), *One True Thing* (1998), *Music of the Heart* (1999), *The Bridges of Madison County* (1995), *Adaptation* (2002), and *The Devil Wears Prada* (2006). Her stellar acting performances had become disconnected from the overall impact of the films in which she appeared. Hence, it would be reasonable to style this gender stigma the "Meryl Streep Effect."

This is not to say that some male actors never contribute award-winning performances to less than superlative films. We're talking about odds, not certainties: The separation of stellar acting from cinematic greatness has higher odds for women rather than for men.

Conclusions

We have toured through a massive amount of research on gender differences in the acting profession. We've pondered results regarding divergent incomes, careers, characters, and kudos. No matter where we look, female actors seem to be at a disadvantage with respect to male actors. Not only do women earn less money, but they have shorter and less illustrious careers, perform in unattractive roles as they get older, and often have their best performances ghettoized in less successful films. The chapter's title implies that these contrasts demonstrate the existence of sexism in cinema.

As suggested earlier, to some extent these sexist consequences may mirror the gender stereotypes and discriminating practices of the larger society. Filmmakers give the public what they're willing to pay for. It is for this reason that money-making movies display larger gender inequalities than do critically acclaimed or award-winning films. Yet I don't believe that the film industry is excused from all responsibility. The same sexism that affects what we see on the screen also affects what happens behind the camera. Women have been even more underrepresented among producers, directors, writers, cinematographers, composers, and so forth. Frequently women could only become prominent by making rather gender stereo-typical contributions to filmmaking. Edith Head garnered more Oscar recognition than any other woman in history, receiving 8 awards out of 34 nominations! But in what category did she receive these honors? Costume design! She's the exception that proves the rule.

If the observed gender contrasts are attributable to sexism, then we can hope that they'll slowly disappear. Women are achieving equality in ever more occupations and professions, including in the movie business. Even so, progress in Hollywood and elsewhere seems awfully slow. Among directors, for example, it was not until 1977 that a woman was first nominated for a best directing Oscar—Lina Wertmüller for *Pasqualino Settebellezze*—and a female director was not nominated again until 1994, when Jane Campion was honored for *The Piano*. The next instance had to wait until Sofia Coppola was nominated a decade later for *Lost in Translation*. If that's an upward trend it's more flat than up!

Regarding the acting profession, the data are even more ambiguous. This ambiguity can be traced in the historical trends for the Meryl Streep Effect with respect to the Academy awards and nominations. These trends are graphed in Figure 7.1. Plainly, the effect was the lowest in the 1930s. That is, in that decade male and female actors were equally likely to receive acting Oscar recognition for performances in films that received nomina-tions or awards for best picture. This fits what I said earlier about this par-ticular decade representing the high point for female actors in Hollywood. Feminine prominence may have also have inspired the Academy to offer separate acting awards for males and females, the only category of cine-matic achievement so divided. Given that other organizations followed this practice, it may have been very fortunate that the Oscars appeared during

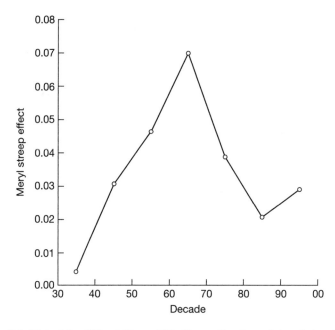

Figure 7.1 Plot of the "Meryl Streep Effect" as a function of decade in which the Oscars were awarded. This effect is a gauge of the gender difference concerning the likelihood of receiving an Academy nomination or award in an acting category for a performance in a film that received no best picture recognition, whether a nomination or an award. The value of zero indicates no gender difference.

the cinematic acme for female actors. If otherwise, men would have had complete liberty to dominate the acting honors just like they do in virtually all other categories.

But after that golden age of equality we see a steep increase in the disparity. In the 1960s the Meryl Streep Effect reaches its all-time peak. During this decade outstanding performances by women were least likely to be found in an Oscar-nominated or awarded film. After that low point in gender equality, the disparity gradually declined, albeit the effect shows a slight increase in the 1990s. During the latter decade the disproportion is about equal to that seen in the 1940s. Judging from this overall trend, we have a distance to go before great films feature great acting performances regardless of an actor's gender. The line has to go all the way down to the zero point.

Admittedly, Figure 7.1 stops at films released in 2000. Consequently, it's conceivable that the effect has utterly vanished in the current millennium. Interestingly, the Academy decided to double the number of films that can be nominated for best picture—a change that took effect for the 2010

Oscar ceremony. By increasing the nominations from 5 to 10, a larger number of stellar female performances may become featured in pictures having received nods for best picture. It will take perhaps another decade or so before we can know for sure. Perhaps sexism in cinema is indeed on the wane. Maybe one day Streep herself will receive a best-acting Oscar in a film that won the best-picture Oscar! When that happens, the eponymic term becomes obsolete.

Chapter 8

Music: Is Silence Golden?

Judging from most moviegoers' experiences, the answer to the question posed in this chapter's title should be a resounding "No!" It's exceptional for a great film to get by without some sound, and especially without any music. Alfred Hitchcock's 1963 *The Birds* had no score to speak of, and certainly no songs. Yet instances like this are rather uncommon. In truth, it may be easier to go without spoken dialogue than without music. The 1956 *Le ballon rouge* ("Red Balloon") had music without any significant speech—and it still won an Oscar for best original screenplay! And think about cinema's early years, the time before the talkies: So-called silent films were seldom silent. At the very minimum a pianist provided a live accompaniment, an essential component that dates from the very first film showings by the Lumière Brothers in 1895 Paris. Large city theaters would usually replace the pianist with an organist or perhaps a whole orchestra.

Sometimes music even participates in a film's production, not just its exhibition. Music on the set would be used to get the actors and crew in the proper mood. This technique was implemented in both the silent and sound eras. When Stanley Kubrick shot *2001: A Space Odyssey* (1968), the director had music played on the set to put everyone in the right frame of mind. Notwithstanding the fact that Alex North was busy composing the score, Kubrick was so pleased with the result that the final soundtrack consisted solely of compositions by Johann Strauss, Richard Strauss, Aram Khachaturyan, and György Ligeti! Poor North had to publish his film music as music sans film.

We also must acknowledge that some of the world's most loved music was first written directly for film. Sometimes the music takes the form of an unforgettable song, such as "Over the Rainbow" from the *Wizard of Oz*, "Moon River" from *Breakfast at Tiffany's*, "Mrs. Robinson" from *The Graduate*, "On the Road Again" from *Honeysuckle Rose*, and "My Heart Will Go On" from *Titanic*. Other times instrumental music is used to highlight a central character, scene, or moment, such as "The March of the Charioteers" from *Ben-Hur*, the "The Murder" in *Psycho*, "Zorba's Dance" from *Zorba, the Greek*, and the "Hymn to the Fallen" in *Saving Private Ryan*. Still other times the music constitutes an orchestral composition that practically encapsulates the entire film. Examples include the main themes from *Gone with the Wind*, *The Magnificent Seven*, *Exodus*, *Lawrence of Arabia*, *Doctor Zhivago*, *The Godfather*, *Jaws*, *Rocky*, *Star Wars*, *Chariots of Fire*, *Dancing with Wolves*, and *Schindler's List*. So effective are these compositions that many are often featured in concert performances and classical music radio stations alongside more traditional art music compositions by Bach, Mozart, and Beethoven. Moreover, since 1959, outstanding film music has received special recognition at the Grammy Award ceremonies, joining not just classical but also rock, country, jazz, blues, rap, and numerous other styles of musical expression.

As remarkable as this music may be, we should never forget that these renowned compositions were once an integral part of a complex cinematic product. The music was just one component of numerous other contributions, such as the screenplay, direction, acting, cinematography, art direction, costume design, special effects, and editing. With the exception of musicals and music videos, the original purpose of these sonic pieces was always to be no more than part of the whole. Like the other components, the music was inserted, incorporated, appended, or amended to boost the film's overall impact as either art or entertainment. Indeed, sometimes the director or the producer has summarily rejected a composer's music if it did not serve the film's cinematic goals, no matter how excellent the music might be as a standalone creation. A notorious example is Bernard Hermann's score for Alfred Hitchcock's *Torn Curtain*, its rejection ending a director-composer collaboration involving nine films, including the classics *Vertigo*, *North by Northwest*, and *Psycho*. But is there any evidence that music actually has a cinematic benefit?

Pros and Cons

Below I provide an overview of the arguments for and against the proposition that great music makes great films.

The Case for Music

One potential article of positive evidence is that many organizations that bestow annual honors for cinematic achievement include one or more awards for film music. These awards include the Oscars for Best Original Score and Best Original Song, the Golden Globes for Best Original Score and Best Original Song, and the Anthony Asquith Award for Achievement in Film Music bestowed by the British Academy of Film and Television Arts. It must be deemed significant that the Academy Awards for the two film music categories began in 1935 (for films released in 1934), just shortly after the advent of the sound era—the Oscar for Best Sound was first given in 1931. The first best score Oscar was bestowed to *One Night of Love* (1934), the first best song for "The Continental" from *The Gay Divorce* (1934). Significantly, the film music honors appeared before other awards strongly associated with filmmaking. Editing wasn't so honored until 1936, supporting male and female acting until 1937, film special effects until 1940, costume design until 1949, and makeup until 1968. Hence, industry professionals have long recognized music to constitute a critical feature of films.

Furthermore, award winning scores and songs include works created by an impressive diversity of eminent composers. Among the most distinguished are:

1. *Classical musicians*—Arnold Bax, Leonard Bernstein, Aaron Copland, John Corigliano, Tan Dun, Philip Glass, Erich Wolfgang Korngold, Sergei Prokoviev, Dmitri Shostakovich, and Toru Takemitsu;
2. *Jazz, rock, and pop musicians*—Phil Collins, Neil Diamond, Bob Dylan, Duke Ellington, Eminem, Elton John, Mick Jagger, Madonna, Barry Manilow, Paul McCartney, Prince, Ryuichi Sakamoto, Carly Simon, Sting, Bruce Springsteen, Vangelis, and Stevie Wonder;
3. *Musical theater composers*—Jerome Kern, Frederick Loewe, Alan Menken, Richard Rodgers, Stephen Sondheim, and Andrew Lloyd Webber;
4. *Songwriters*—Harold Arlen, Burt Bacharach, Irving Berlin, Isaac Hayes, Giorgio Moroder, Randy Newman, Cole Porter, Diane Warren; and, of course,
5. *Film music specialists*—both the legendary: Elmer Bernstein, Bernard Hermann, Maurice Jarre, Henri Mancini, Ennio Morricone, Alfred Newman, Alex North, Miklós Rózsa, Max Steiner, Franz Waxman, Dimitri Tiomkin, and Victor Young, and the contemporary: John Barry, Jerry Goldsmith, Marvin Hamlisch, James Horner, Michel Legrand, Rachel Portman, Zbigniew Preisner, Howard Shore, and Hans Zimmer.

As if these names were not sufficient proof, each year since 1987 the American Society of Composers, Authors and Publishers (ASCAP) has been recognizing the "Most Performed Songs from Motion Pictures," "The Most Performed Theme," and the film composers of the "Top Box Office Films." So not only do film industry professionals acknowledge the power of music, but also the music industry professionals do so. Everybody who should know seems to agree that great films presume great music.

Finally, because I'm a psychologist, and because psychologists love to conduct laboratory experiments, and because some of those experiments are devoted to aesthetics, I would be remiss not to cite the research showing how music can contribute directly to the cinematic experience. This music not only helps establish the appropriate mood, emotion, or arousal, but also facilitates the cognitive understanding of the film's narrative course. Moreover, both music and film have comparable temporal structures for the expression of dynamic transformations (e.g., a beginning, middle, and an end, and the time-wise placement of conflicts and their resolution). These parallels should enable music to reinforce the progression of the visual and verbal content. Score and song can thus underline key moments in the script and their realization on the big screen. Research in experimental aesthetics seemingly reinforces the apparent opinions of the professionals. Music matters.

The Case against Music

Pretty convincing evidence? Not really! If you think about it carefully, nothing said in the previous section directly addressed this core issue: Is the music's impact as an independent aesthetic experience positively related to the film's own cinematic effectiveness? For instance, although laboratory experiments show that music influences visual interpretation, it does not establish whether excellent music does a superior job than mediocre music. Admittedly, one could argue that a positive association would be implicit in the empirical findings. If music works then why not assume that great music works better? But that assumption is far from justified. In fact, one could easily defend the opposite position, namely that effective film music must retreat to the background, providing subliminal priming of cognitive and emotional associations. If so, then music that's so outstanding that it becomes foreground could divert attention from the narrative, obliging audiences to pay attention to the music itself rather than to its cinematic connotations. Great music could be a distraction rather than a contribution.

To document the last statement we need look no farther than the unused music that Alex North wrote for *2001: A Space Odyssey*. His score is no doubt competent. North had already received nearly a dozen Academy nods for his work on other films, so he was no newcomer to the profession. Yet it should be evident to any listener that his score was much more nondescript than the adapted music that Kubrick selected. Just compare North's "Fanfare" to that taken from the opening of Richard Strauss's *Also sprach Zarathustra* to hear the difference. North's score was not designed to upstage the film. He was writing film music, not opera. Not surprisingly, his unused score has failed to enter the repertoire as an autonomous composition.

What about all the movie awards bestowed by various organizations? It turns out that the evidence here is not as strong as first meets the eye. For instance, the ASCAP Awards on closer scrutiny are irrelevant to this issue. Honoring those composers whose films are box office successes or those songs that are most frequently performed does not indicate whether the composers or the songs themselves had positive cinematic consequences. In particular, the awards cannot rule out the possibility that the same composers wrote even more exceptional music for box office failures or that the popular songs appeared in films that critics considered "bombs" or "turkeys." In 2007, the ASCAP Award for Top Box Office Films was bestowed on *The Break-Up* (2006), with music composed by Jon Brion and John O'Brien, and *Eight Below* (2006), with music composed by Mark Isham. Yet neither film received so much as a single nomination in any music category from any organization. This is not to say that the composers are not outstanding. Brion received Grammy nominations for his music for *Eternal Sunshine of the Spotless Mind* (2004) and *Magnolia* (1999), and Isham got an Oscar nod for *A River Runs Through It* (1992). What's at issue is whether the music they wrote for the two 2006 films had anything to do with box office performance. The same argument applies to the music contributions of all composers and songwriters, no matter what their personal track records.

Likewise, the bestowal of Oscars, Golden Globes, and Asquith Awards cannot be taken as direct empirical support unless it is demonstrated that these honors are most likely to be granted to movies that also receive best picture awards or earn critical acclaim. We have already seen how the outstanding performances of female actors can often be relegated to films that are less than extraordinary. Score and song composers might see their top work similarly ghettoized. In point of pure fact, the awards for best score and best song are often given to films that have only one claim to fame, namely, that they have been nominated for having exceptional film music. This disconcerting result has emerged in three separate empirical investigations.

The first study focused on the Oscars, looking at how well the Academy Awards in the major categories predicted two separate criteria of cinematic success, the best picture award and the number of stars the film received in movie guides. Although both best score and best song awards exhibited positive correlations with best picture, these correlations were small and, in the case of songs, not always statistically significant. In the instance of movie guide ratings, the score awards did not make a significant contribution and, even worse, the song awards were slightly negative predictors. Critically acclaimed films were less likely to feature Oscar-honored songs. This outcome held for 1,523 films released from 1948 to 1999—that's more than a half century of Oscar films. This doesn't mean there aren't exceptions. "Over the Rainbow" won an Oscar and *The Wizard of Oz* rates 4.8 stars in the movie guides. Yet just the year before, the Oscar went to "Thanks for the Memory" from *The Big Broadcast of 1938* which scored a mediocre 3.0 stars—noticeably below average for Oscar-nominated films.

The second study used factor analysis to determine how the awards given by seven major organizations clustered together. The results of this analysis were already reported earlier in Chapter 3 (see Table 3.1). As we saw then, the score and song awards formed a separate "musical cluster" that was largely uncorrelated with the other factors, namely, the dramatic (directing, writing, acting, and editing), visual (cinematography, art direction, costume, and makeup), and technical (visual effects, sound effects editing, and sound mixing). As also reported in Chapter 3 (see Table 3.2), although the musical cluster had a very small positive association with the number of nominations and awards received for best picture, the cluster had a negative correlation with the ratings received in movie guides. Therefore, the Oscars are not unique in suggesting a weak and possibly negative relation between great films and great music. The same held for 1,327 films appraised by the Academy and six other organizations between 1968 and 1999.

The third and last study was discussed in Chapter 4. As was seen in Table 4.1, a film's budget was positively correlated with recognition received for score and song from seven major organizations. By inference, it costs money to purchase the services of acclaimed composers and songwriters. Even so, judging from Table 4.2, this cash was not necessarily well spent: Film music honors did not display significant associations with best picture awards, critical acclaim, movie guide ratings, or box office earnings, whether on the first weekend or the final gross. Strikingly, the musical cluster was the only one of the four creative clusters that did not correlate with any of the five success criteria. Neither score nor song seems relevant to film as art or film as business.

Taken together, these studies imply that award-winning film music may not be associated with successful films. And, with respect to songs, the association might even be negative. Music seems like a pricey spice that spoils the broth—like sprinkling saffron on clam chowder.

Two Follow-Ups

I must hasten to add that none of the three investigations just discussed was specifically designed to examine the main question of the present chapter. As a consequence, the studies may not constitute the best tests of the great-music-goes-with-great-film hypothesis. Indeed, when these findings are more closely scrutinized it's easy to conjure up methodological objections that undermine the force of the case against this thesis. Five criticisms are probably the most important:

1. Score and song awards and nominations were most often combined into a single composite indicator of the music cluster. Yet the reliability of the latter measure does not compare favorably with the reliabilities of the other creative clusters. In particular, whereas the dramatic, visual, and technical clusters had internal-consistency reliabilities of .88, .83, and .73, respectively, the music cluster's estimated reliability was only .55. That's partly because score and song honors do not strongly correlate with each other. Films with great scores do not necessarily have great songs, and vice versa. A major reason for this disconnection is that the composer of the film score is seldom identical to the composer of a film song. Thus, Howard Shore composed the score for *Lord of the Rings: Fellowship of the Ring* whereas the song "May It Be" was composed by Enya and Nicky Ryan (to lyrics by Roma Ryan). Scores and songs do not even have to be composed in a coherent musical style. Often the score might be representative of the classical-style music of Hollywood's Golden Age while the song is written in some contemporary genre.

2. Because prior studies were not particularly designed to assess the impact of film music, the awards and nomination counts frequently came from organizations that did not always include an award category for film music. For example, the New York Film Critics Circle, the National Board of Review, and the National Society of Film Critics do not honor these two categories of cinematic achievement. One immediate repercussion is that the components of the music cluster will be measured with less reliability than the components of most other clusters. Only the components of the technical cluster are more frequently overlooked than score and song.

3. The earlier investigations used samples that excluded animated films and films in non-English languages even though that exclusion unavoidably deleted many award-winning musical compositions. Some instances include the animated films *Lion King* and *Toy Story* and the foreign-language films *The Umbrellas of Cherbourg* and

Crouching Tiger, Hidden Dragon. How can we trust a negative result if some of the best music is deleted from the sample?

4. No relevant study introduced all of the control variables suggested by previous research, such as each film's production budget, year and season of release, genre, runtime, and the MPAA rating. As an example, it is certainly necessary to control for genre given that prize-winning songs are highly likely to appear in musicals, a genre that may not do well by many criteria of cinematic success, particularly now that the heyday of glitzy Hollywood musicals is mere history.

5. Most prior investigations failed to consider the fact that the success of a film can be assessed by more than one criterion and that these criteria do not necessarily correlate with each other—a point that I fully established in Chapter 4. Specifically, cinematic success can be evaluated four major ways: the evaluations of critics at the time of the film's release, the film's box-office earnings, the best picture awards and nominations the film receives, and the evaluations that the film receives in movie guides published a year or more after the completion of the film's theatrical run. It's conceivable that the impact of film music—or its separate score and song components—varies according to the criterion of cinematic impact.

The forthcoming study attempted to overcome all of these deficiencies. The aim was to provide a fairer scientific evaluation of film music's role in the making of great films.

Film Music

The sample began with all films that were nominated for awards in major film categories from the following organizations: the Academy of Motion Picture Arts and Sciences ("Oscars"), the Hollywood Foreign Press Association ("Golden Globes"), the British Academy of Film and Television Arts ("BAFTAs"), the Los Angeles Film Critics Association, the Chicago Film Critics Association, the Broadcast Film Critics Association, and the Online Film Critics Society. These seven organizations were chosen because they all had at least one award category for film music. Because the Online Film Critics Society did not start offering awards for film music until 1999, the sample began with films released in 1998. To ensure that the sampled films would possess evaluations in movie guides, the sampling was terminated at films released in 2003. Although animated and foreign-language films were included, documentaries were excluded, thus confining the sample to feature-length narrative films. Documentaries seldom feature outstanding music—Melissa Etheridge's Oscar-winning song

"I Need to Wake Up" from *An Inconvenient Truth* (2006) is an extremely rare exception—and in any case the function of music in documentaries may be distinct from that in a film that has a plot and characterization. The final sample consisted of 401 films. This amounts to about 67 films per year, or more than a film per week—and hence a high percentage of the approximately 200 major films that are widely shown in a given year. Occasionally this sample size had to be reduced somewhat because of missing information on the measures discussed next.

To the extent possible, the films were then assessed on a large number of variables already introduced and discussed in previous chapters. In the first place, as in Chapter 4 (see Table 4.2) each film was accessed on both Metacritic and movie guide ratings, best picture honors, and domestic gross. In addition, besides measuring all films on the dramatic, visual, technical, and musical clusters, the latter cluster was also split into separate score and song tabulations of awards and nominations. Finally, a respectable number of control variables were also defined in a manner consistent with earlier studies: production costs, release date, release season (Christmas, summer, and Easter), runtime, MPAA rating (G, PG, PG-13, and R), and genre (drama, comedy, romance, and musical, plus animation and foreign language).

Nonetheless, before turning to the results I must note that the measures based on awards and nominations were constructed in a slightly different fashion than all previous studies. Although the measures used the same 0-1-2 coding scheme introduced in Chapter 2, the organizations on which the counts were based were changed in two ways.

First, the same organizations used to determine the sample also were used to create the measures. This means that the New York Film Critics Circle, the National Board of Review, and the National Society of Film Critics replaced by the Chicago Film Critics Association, the Broadcast Film Critics Association, and the Online Film Critics Society—this because only the latter three organizations bestow awards for music.

Second, additional points were added using awards and nominations from the Producers Guild of America (picture), Directors Guild of America (direction), the Writers Guild of America (screenplay), the Screen Actors Guild (all four acting categories), the American Cinema Editors (film editing), the American Society of Cinematographers (cinematography), the Society of Motion Picture and Television Art Directors (art direction), the Costume Designers Guild (costume), the Motion Picture Sound Editors (sound effects editing), and the Grammy Awards (score and song). Consequently, the more important categories of cinematic achievement were assessed by the honors granted by eight organizations rather than just seven. For the less prominent award categories, such as sound, fewer than eight scores make up the composite.

The latter change means that the resulting measures tended to have higher reliabilities, especially for the most important award categories. The final reliability coefficients were as follows: picture .85, direction .90, screenplay .86, lead male acting .89, lead female acting .89, supporting male acting .81, supporting female acting .87, film editing .79, cinematography .88, art direction .79, costume design .58, makeup .78, visual effects .72, sound effects editing .40, sound .75, score .80, and song .81. Only costume design and sound effects editing seem to have mediocre reliabilities, and these two categories are least crucial for testing the impact of film music. Lastly, the reliabilities for the music cluster also came out much better than in previous studies, namely, .65 (up from .55). Clearly the opportunity for finding a connection between great music and great cinema has been enhanced.

I'll divide discussion of the results according to a sample that includes all films and another sample that excludes animated and foreign-language films.

Inclusive Sample (with Animated and Foreign-language Films)

Table 8.1 gives the basic correlation coefficients between the four cinematic success criteria and the four creative clusters, but also including the music cluster subdivided into score and song. It should be apparent that these correlations are quite encouraging. The musical cluster of awards and

TABLE 8.1   Correlation Coefficients between Cinematic Success Criteria and the Four Creative Clusters With and Without the Music Cluster Separated into Score and Song

Composite variable	Critic evaluations		Best picture	Gross
	Metacritic	Movie guides		
Creative cluster				
Dramatic	.38***	.50***	.67***	.24***
Visual	.15**	.27***	.51***	.29***
Technical	.04	.17***	.38***	.43***
Musical	.18**	.26***	.46***	.34***
Separate music categories				
Score	.22***	.31***	.56***	.28***
Song	.10	.15**	.25***	.30***
n	316	393	401	387

*$p < .05$. **$p < .01$. ***$p < .001$.

nominations correlates with critic evaluations, best picture honors, and gross domestic earnings. Although the correlations are not usually as high as the dramatic cluster—with the exception of gross!—the coefficients are about as high as those for the visual cluster. It would seem that outstanding scores and songs contribute as much to cinematic success as does cinematography, art direction, costume design, and make up. Even so, when the musical cluster is separated into its score and song components, it becomes more patent that the former kind of music has more impact than the latter kind of music. With the repeated exception of gross receipts, songs have about half the influence of scores.

Before we begin speculating about the reason why songs seem to have a unique effect on box office performance, we must recognize that these correlations do not control for a large number of contaminating variables. As we observed in Table 3.2 of Chapter 3, the regression coefficients can look quite different from the correlation coefficients. Not only must we control for the influence of each creative cluster controlling for the other creative clusters, but we must also introduce the many control variables defined earlier. When we make these statistical adjustments we obtain the results in Table 8.2.

The outcome has changed considerably. Now only the dramatic cluster correlates positively with all four criteria of cinematic success. The visual

TABLE 8.2   Regression Coefficients for Cinematic Success Criteria as a Function of the Four Creative Clusters With and Without the Music Cluster Separated into Score and Song

Composite variable	Critic evaluations		Best picture	Gross
	Metacritic	Movie guides		
Creative cluster				
Dramatic	.38***	.49***	.63***	.19***
Visual	.00	−.00	.15***	−.01
Technical	.13	.14*	.12**	.08
Musical	.15*	.09	.13***	.08
Separate music categories				
Score	.14	.07	.18***	.01
Song	.06	.04	.01	.07
R^2	.46***	.48***	.79***	.65***
n	232	291	291	289

Note. The estimated standardized partial regression coefficients include the following control variables: production costs, release date, release season (Christmas, summer, and Easter), runtime, MPAA rating (G, PG, PG-13, and R), genre (drama, comedy, romance, and musical, plus animation and foreign language).

*$p < .05$. **$p < .01$. ***$p < .001$.

cluster correlates with only best picture honors, the technical cluster with movie guide ratings and best picture honors, and the musical cluster with Metacritic and best picture honors. Curiously, although four creative clusters correlate with best picture honors, the dramatic cluster has more impact than all of the other three clusters put together. In any case, the effect of the musical cluster does not improve when it is sliced into its score and song components. Score awards and nominations are now correlated solely with best picture honors, and song awards and nominations are correlated with absolutely nothing! No negative effects, but no positive effects either.

Exclusive Sample (without Animated and Foreign-language Films)

The findings presented in Tables 8.1 and 8.2 included all types of feature films except for documentaries. This inclusiveness was introduced in recognition of the fact that much outstanding music appears in animated and foreign-language films. What happens when we confine the sample to just English-language, live-action narrative feature films? Do results strongly differ? Table 8.3 gives the answer, and the answer is that the findings differ only a little. Best picture honors are still associated with awards and nominations in all four creative clusters, including the musical cluster.

TABLE 8.3 Regression Coefficients for Cinematic Success Criteria as a Function of the Four Creative Clusters with and without the Music Cluster Separated: Animations and Foreign-Language Films Deleted

Composite variable	Critic evaluations		Best picture	Gross
	Metacritic	Movie guides		
Creative cluster				
Dramatic	.42***	.53***	.69***	.23***
Visual	.02	.07	.11**	.02
Technical	.13	.17**	.11**	.09
Musical	.10	.02	.18***	.01
Separate music categories				
Score	.13	.04	.20***	−.03
Song	.01	−.01	.04	.03
R^2	.46***	.53***	.82***	.63***
n	203	252	252	252

Note. The variables are production costs, release date, release season (Christmas, summer, and Easter), runtime, MPAA rating (G, PG, PG-13, and R), genre (drama, comedy, romance, and musical, plus not animation and foreign language). The regression coefficients are all standardized ("betas").

*$p < .05.$ **$p < .01.$ ***$p < .001.$

Also, the separate indicator of score still predicts best picture awards and nominations. The only notable difference is that the musical cluster is no longer strongly predictive of the Metacritic ratings. But that falls more in line with what holds for the movie guide ratings.

So what's the upshot of all these correlations and regressions, inclusive and exclusive samples? Just three major conclusions.

1. Awards and nominations for outstanding film music are dependably linked only with awards and nominations for best picture. Music makes no reliable contribution to success judged by either critical evaluations or financial performance.
2. The contributions of film music to best picture honors are as least as potent as any other creative cluster besides the dramatic cluster. This inference becomes all the more justified when we toss in the third and last conclusion.
3. The predictive power of film music must be credited to exceptional scores, not songs. Once we introduce appropriate controls, songs become absolutely irrelevant to a film's success by any criterion whatsoever. Although this might seem a discouraging result if you're a songwriter, it must be remembered that some earlier studies found a *negative* association between great songs and great films. Additionally, the findings compensate by being especially encouraging to the score composers. As evident in Tables 8.2 and 8.3, their input to a film's prospects for best picture honors exceeds that of the cinematographers, art directors, costume designers, and make-up artists in the visual cluster and those executing the special visual effects, sound effects, and sound mixing in the technical cluster.

Despite the seeming reinstatement of score composers, we must confront a reasonable protest: Awards and nominations for best score are only related to awards and nominations for best picture. This is a problem because often it's the same voters casting their ballots for both awards. A case in point is the Academy whose voting members decide the Oscars. They are given a ballot that asks them to vote on all categories, including both best picture and best score. This means that a "halo effect" may intrude that makes a member more prone to vote for a composer whose creativity is featured in a film up for best picture. It's feasible that the reason why recognition for best score is uncorrelated with the other criteria of cinematic success—critical judgments and box office proceeds—is simply because the latter standards are not contaminated by this problem. Film composers don't earn enough money to pay critics for positive reviews, nor do they buy enough theater tickets to grant a film blockbuster status just because they like the score. How can we know for sure that film scores make a genuine contribution to a film's success as art or as business?

Cinema Composers

Perhaps we should tackle this difficult issue from a different angle. Rather than concentrate on film music we should turn our attention to cinema composers. This type of shift was already implemented in the previous two chapters. After spending Chapters 2–5 scrutinizing films as the unit of analysis, Chapters 6 and 7 looked mostly at directors and actors, respectively. Moreover, a large portion of both chapters were devoted to discussing the development of their careers. Particularly in Chapter 6 directorial careers were used to shed light on the auteur theory. We asked whether the careers follow the same trajectory as creative artists or whether the career trajectory is more like that expected of expert technicians. A version of that same question can be applied to composers as well. That is, film composers can be seen from two rather contradictory perspectives.

On the one hand, many composers are formally-trained musicians who appear to be continuing the compositional tradition of European classical music. For instance, famous film composers like Max Steiner, Wolfgang Eric Korngold, Bernard Herrmann, Nino Rota, and John Williams have all composed so-called "serious" music, such as symphonies, ballets, and operas. Many also have been trained under recognized classical composers and have received formal training at prestigious conservatories. John Williams was privately tutored by composer Mario Castelnuovo-Tedesco and studied at Julliard under Rosina Lhevinne. And as noted earlier, eminent classical composers will themselves venture into film composition from time to time. It would seem that film composers are merely classical composers who happen to write "incidental music" for the screen rather than for the stage. As such, they are full-fledged creative artists whose patrons just so happen to be film producers rather than princes, the idle rich, or plump funding agencies.

On the other hand, cinema composers have often been looked down upon in comparison to authentic classical composers. In contrast to the serious music written by composers who are now largely employed in university music departments, film music is far more immediately accessible. Thus, it seldom involves atonal, serial, or avant-garde compositional techniques. On the contrary, in many ways film composers appear retrogressive, even reactionary, steadfastly adhering to the luxuriant symphonic style favored by the Romantic composers of the late 19th and early 20th century— watered-down imitations of Brahms, Wagner, and Mahler crassly transported to a movie theater's sound system.

In addition, film music is essentially an exemplar of applied rather than pure creativity. Rather than being entirely self-expressive in the manner of symphonic and vocal music in the classical repertoire, the composer's ideas must fit the specific needs of particular segments of a given film. As a result, effective cinema composers have to "write on command," every such composition counting as an indisputable *pièce d'occasion*. Normally this means that they must create in a variety of musical styles—including jazz, blues, rock, folk, country, and other popular forms—suggesting that such composers may lack an identifiable style of their own.

Want an illustration? The low woodwinds that introduce the Overture to the 1941 *Citizen Kane*, the eerie electronic sounds of the theremins in the 1951 *The Day the Earth Stood Still*, the high-pitched violins violently accentuating the shower murder in the 1960 *Psycho*, and the poignant lament of the jazz saxophone in the 1976 *Taxi Driver* have virtually nothing in common—except that they are all the musical creations of Bernard Herrmann.

So film composers might appear to lack the artistic integrity expected of a true creative individual. If so, they are mere technicians with a specialized expertise.

But why is all this germane to the question that drives this chapter? If the second option holds, then it's hard to understand why great film music fails to correspond with great films. After all, the composers are like hired guns with the needed bag of tricks to get the job done. Pay more, and you get more. At the very least, because a film's budget correlates with both award-winning music and financial performance (see Table 4.1 in Chapter 4) then blockbuster movies should have chartbusting music. Furthermore, insofar as the director has creative control, and can get the composer to comply with his or her artistic vision, we might expect a greater correspondence between outstanding music and critical acclaim.

But what if the first option applies? Then it could very well be that film composers are behaving more like creative artists than as bona fide collaborators in filmmaking. In other words, they may be serious composers first and cinema composers second, writing music to meet their own intrinsic standards rather satisfying the extrinsic needs of the films for which they are nominally writing music. Accordingly, the quality of their compositions can decouple from the quality of the films in which their music appears. Instead of their musical creativity responding directly to the extrinsic demands imposed by particular films—such as great films providing the inspiration for great music—their output will emerge as the intrinsic outcome of the creative process itself. In more technical terms, a film composer's creativity will be determined endogenously (internal causes) rather than exogenously (external causes)—dedicated more to "art for art's sake" than to raking in the cash as a "hired gun."

The latter interpretation implies that cinema composers will display the same career trajectory as serious composers whose artistic creativity is driven by an internal impetus rather than external commands. At least since Ludwig van Beethoven, composers enjoyed sufficient autonomy that they could largely create what they wanted to create rather than have their creativity always at the mercy of others who could dictate what they could and could not compose. Even when such composers received a commission, they would tailor their response to satisfy their personal artistic direction. A classic case is Hector Berlioz's 1834 *Harold en Italie*. Written at the invitation of the great virtuoso Niccolò Paganini, who wanted a composition to show off his newly-acquired Stradivarius viola, Berlioz refused to write the anticipated virtuosic concerto. Instead, Berlioz wrote a "Symphony with Viola obbligato" which dared to include rests for the soloist notwithstanding the fact that Paganini had explicitly wanted to play non-stop as in his customary mad-musician act. It was not until four years later that Paganini relented, having heard the work performed by another violist, and Berlioz finally received his proper commission. Paganini wanted Berlioz to manufacture a showpiece for his fireworks, but Berlioz instead created an inspired masterpiece. As Oscar Wilde once said, "Genius is born—not paid."

If film composers are most comparable to classical composers in disposition, then we can take advantage of the empirical research on the career trajectories of the latter. Of special relevance are the inquiries concerning the ages at which the creator produces three career landmarks. These three landmarks are the first major composition, the single best composition, and the last major composition, where the middle career landmark is approximately coincident with the age at peak output (see Figure 6.1 in Chapter 6). The first landmark is the composition that first became part of the standard repertoire, the last landmark is the last composition that made it into the repertoire, and the middle landmark is the composition that is most frequently performed and recorded. Most commonly, the first landmark occurs in the late 20s or early 30s, the second in the late 30s or the early 40s, and the last in the early 50s, with the output rate maximizing in the late 30s. Beethoven's career is fairly typical. His "Pathétique" Piano Sonata appeared when he was 28, his Fifth Symphony when he was 37, and his last string quartets—who would dare to pick the best of these five!—when the Master was in his mid-50s.

However, the specific ages at which these three landmarks appear are contingent on a number of other factors that influence the career trajectory.

Especially crucial is the lifetime output of the composer. Those who create the most total compositions will usually produce their first career landmark at an earlier age and their last career landmark at a later age. Yet the age of the middle career landmark, the single best work, is not associated with lifetime productivity. One final expectation is also worth noting: If we control for (or hold constant) the age of the middle landmark, then the correlation between the ages of the first and last middle landmarks becomes negative. In different terms, given a set of composers who produced their single best hit at the same age, those composers whose first hit came earlier will have their last hit come later. More succinctly, precocity is positively related to longevity.

Below I offer the results of two studies that subject these expectations to empirical test. Are cinema composers principally serious composers only incidentally earning a living writing film music? The first study examines popular soundtrack composers, the second Oscar-winning composers.

Popular Soundtrack Composers

Besides testing the predictions derived from previous research on classical composers, this first inquiry will make a direct comparison between two kinds of film music—original and adapted. Original music was composed immediately for the film in which it appears whereas adapted music was written years earlier for other purposes. Many compositions in the classical repertoire have become extremely well known in movie sound tracks. A striking example is Richard Wagner's "Ride of the Valkyries" used by Francis Coppola to accompany the helicopter attack scene in *Apocalypse Now* (1979). These music adaptations provide a unique baseline for comparing original music. Is the most popular classical music adapted for film composed at the same age as the most successful cinema music composed originally for film? The answer could be affirmative if the best film music is endogenously driven by the composer's career trajectory rather than exogenous influence of the filmmaking collaboration.

All 153 composers in this study had created at least one composition recorded in several CD anthologies devoted to great film music. The composers were born between 1685 (Johann Sebastian Bach) and 1975 (Lauryn Hill), with an average birth year of about 1910. One quarter were strictly defined as classical composers—like Beethoven, Chopin, and Tchaikovsky—whereas 75% were primarily popular composers of various kinds, including jazz, rock, blues, pop, hip/hop, and, last but not least, film scores and songs. Indeed, 70% of the composers created original music for the silver screen, whereas 30% had their music adapted for such use. Because 48% of the composers were still living at the time of the investigation, special control was introduced to adjust for that fact. Each composer was also assessed on their ages at first hit, best hit, and last hit. By "hit" I just mean that the composition made it into the anthology, the "best hit" indicating that composition that was included in the most anthologies. Lastly, for each composer was also tabulated the total number of hits—compositions honored with tracks on the CD anthologies.

To illustrate, Miklós Rózsa, who was born in 1907 and died in 1995, was credited with four hits. His first hit was the score for the 1940 *The Thief of Bagdad*, which he composed at age 33, and his last hit was the score for the 1961 *El Cid*, at age 54. Between these two films appeared the scores for 1951 *Quo Vadis?* and the 1959 *Ben-Hur*, composed at ages 44 and 52, respectively. Can you guess the single best hit? Open the envelope, please: Yes, it was *Ben-Hur*, most often represented on CD anthologies by the "Parade of the Charioteers." This score also earned its composer an Oscar. So the composer's age at best hit is 52.

Table 8.4 gives the averages for all 153 composers. The typical composer's first hit appeared at around age 39, the best at around 41, and the last at around 43, with the average number of hits just shy of 2. The years between the late 30s and the early 40s define the manifest career peak. Yet as the table also shows, the variation for each of these statistics is substantial. The number of hits may range from 1 to 15. The low score is received by the many composers who can be considered "one hit wonders." An example is Anton Karas whose fame rests entirely on his zither theme for the 1949 *The Third Man*; his first, best, and last hits were all one and the same! The high score was received by Wolfgang Amadeus Mozart, who's the absolute favorite source for adapted music. The second highest score, 14 hits, was earned by John Williams, the most prolific creator of original film music (and still counting). The ranges for the ages at the three career landmarks are also quite extreme. The first hit can appear as young as 17 years (Mozart's Symphony No. 25 in G Minor used in the 1984 *Amadeus*) and the last as late as 72 (Williams's score for the 2004 *Harry Potter and the Prisoner of Azkaban*). Even the age at best work can range from 21 (Paul Anka's music for the 1962 *The Longest Day*) to 65 (Arnold Bax's music for

TABLE 8.4   Popular Soundtrack Composers: Variable Means, Standard Deviations, and Minimum-Maximum Values

Career variables	*M*	*SD*	Min	Max
Age first hit	39.24	9.49	17	65
Age best hit	40.89	9.55	21	65
Age last hit	43.29	11.24	21	72
Total hits	1.92	2.13	1	15

Note. $N = 153$ for all variables except for age best hit, where $n = 136$.

the 1948 *Oliver Twist*). According to subsequent regression analyses, this variation in the placement of the career landmarks was found to have three main sources:

1. Part of this variation can be considered an artifact produced by the fact that some of the composers were still living at the time that the data were collected for the study. Although those who are still alive would not be expected to produce a different first landmark, it's a bit presumptuous to assume that we have identified the correct second and third landmark. How can we know for sure that their best hit is yet to come? And how can we be so confident that the last hit in this investigation will actually be their last hit? The data show that in comparison to those still-living, the deceased composers produce their best hit almost four years later and their last hit almost five years later. Presumably, if we waited until all composers died before compiling the statistics these two differences would vanish.

2. The career landmarks for the composers of music adapted for film have their career landmarks occur a handful of years earlier in contrast to the composers of original film music. To give the numbers, the composers of original film music have their first, best, and last hits appear about 5, 4, and 6 years later, respectively. Expressed differently, it takes specialists in film composition about a half decade longer to achieve the same performance levels as other composers, both classical and popular. Remember the discussion of expertise acquisition and the "10-year rule" in Chapter 6? It's logical to think that composition directly for film requires knowledge and skill beyond that needed for regular composition (e.g., creating exactly the specified minutes of music with precisely the right style, dynamics, and instrumentation). But because the expertise overlaps to a high degree—such as the basic rules of harmony, counterpoint, and orchestration—it would not take a full decade to attain an expert level of competence. So the period of apprenticeship is about halved.

3. The final source of variation was already predicted on the basis of past research on non-film composers. As a composer increases in total productivity, the first hit appears earlier and the last hit appears later, while the placement of the best hit remains unchanged. That's precisely what's found for these 153 composers. For each additional hit their first hit appears one year earlier and their last hit two years later, without any change in the age at best hit. To be sure, the count of total hits used in the current study is not the same as a count of total compositions. Nevertheless, because quality of output is a direct function of the quantity of output, a hit count should serve as a good proxy for

a total productivity. Hence, the highly prolific are both early bloomers and late finishers.

The last finding fits what would be expected if the careers of cinema composers were governed by the same endogenous pattern as found for classical composers. As additional support for this connection, the correlation between age at first hit and the age at last hit becomes negative once you control for the age at best hit. Given two composers with the same career peak, the one who's the most precocious in the production of hits will outlast the other in the production of hits. It doesn't seem fair, does it? The first shall be best and the last shall be least. But who said the life of the creator, composer or otherwise, had to be fair?

Speaking of the beginning and ending of the hit-producing career, an astute reader may have spotted one sizeable discrepancy between the careers of classical composers and the careers of cinema composers. I had said that the former tended to create their first successful works in the late 20s or early 30s, their most successful work in the late 30s or the early 40s, and their last successful work in the early 50s. The figures in Table 8.4 seem to contradict this statement. The first landmark shows up about a decade too late and the last landmark about a decade too early. In short, the cinema careers seem truncated. However, this difference may also be a methodological artifact of a different sort. The criterion for identifying hits in film music was much more stringent than the criterion for identifying hits in classical music. In the former case the composition had to claim a track in one of 10 CDs devoted to great film music, whereas in the latter case the composition only had to have become part of the standard repertoire. Given that the standard repertoire in classical music would probably require appreciably over a 1000 CDs to record fully, the film composers were probably judged by more rigorous standards, and thereby narrow the time interval between first and last hit. Taking this artifact into consideration, cinema composers remain akin to serious composers.

Oscar-Honored Composers

This second investigation started with the same 153 composers in the preceding study but then deleted all composers (a) who did not compose directly for the screen and (b) whose hits failed to receive a single Oscar nomination or award for best score or best song. The result is a reduced sample of 78 cinema composers who created at least one hit that earned an Oscar nod or statuette. The composers were born between 1885 (Jerome Kern) and 1961 (Enya), and the average birth year increased by more than a quarter century, with 58% of the sample still living. This is obviously a much more contemporaneous sample that can be used to address a set of questions complementary to those addressed previously. To be specific, if the longitudinal creativity of cinema composers parallels that seen in classical composers, will that same pattern be reflected in nominations and awards that the cinema composers receive for their work? If such recognition is based on the actual merit of the music rather than the success of the film for which the music was written, then the age at first major work should correspond with the age at first nomination and the age at last major work should correspond with the age at last nomination. Moreover, the age at best work should be proximate to the age at first award. The results are shown in Table 8.5.

The Oscar nominations range from 1 to 45, the latter honor actually belonging to two film composers—Alfred Newman (43 for score and 2 for song) and John Williams (40 for score and 5 for song). Turning to the average ages for the career landmarks, the first point to notice is that the ages of first, best, and last hit for this select subsample has been shifted upwards by a couple years from what was shown for the same variables in Table 8.4. This shift likely reflects the fact that these statistics are now confined to only original music rather than including music adapted for film. More interestingly, Table 8.5 shows that the age at first hit closely coincides with the age at first nomination, the age at best hit with the age at first award, and the age at last hit with the age at last award. The three appear roughly at ages 40, 43, and 46 or 47, respectively. This correspondence implies that the Oscar awards and nomination trace a career trajectory in a manner congruent with the three hit measures. The only oddity is the age at last nomination. This event occurs about 5 years after the last award and the last hit. So the last nomination may be acknowledging something beyond actual artistic creativity, a point that I'll return to in a moment.

Everything else in Study 2 appeared to replicate the key results in Study 1. If we view total nominations as an indicator of total productivity in a manner

TABLE 8.5   Oscar-Winning Composers: Variable Means, Standard Deviations, and Minimum-Maximum Values

Career variables	M	SD	Min	Max	n
Total nominations	6.42	8.29	1	45	78
Age first nomination	40.15	8.24	21	63	78
Age first award	42.69	9.38	29	63	51
Age last award	46.94	10.35	29	66	51
Age last nomination	52.28	11.24	32	80	78
Age first hit	40.46	8.11	26	64	78
Age best hit	42.45	8.46	26	64	69
Age last hit	45.87	10.79	26	72	78

similar to total hits—because quality is a positive function of quantity—then it makes sense that total nominations correlates negatively with age at first nomination, positively with age at last award and last nomination, and zero with age at first award. Here age at first nomination functions like age at first hit, age at first award like age at best hit, and ages at last award and nomination like age at last hit. Even more remarkably, the correlation between age at first nomination and age at last nomination becomes conspicuously negative once the ages at first and last award are controlled.

I could get a lot more technical in reviewing the statistical results, but rather than do so, may it suffice to say that the findings are consistent with theoretical expectations. The receipt of Academy awards and nominations for outstanding composition are closely linked with the actual output of high-impact music. This connection is especially true at the career's beginning. The Oscars are quick to recognize new musical talent. But the gap between musical creativity and professional recognition expands later in the composer's career so that the last nomination lags behind the last hit.

My suspicion is that this final Oscar nod might often be used to provide the Academy with one last chance to honor a film composer who has never yet received an Oscar. I pointed out in Chapter 2 how sympathy votes can influence the award process. Accumulate lots of unsuccessful nominations and your prospects of another nomination may be augmented. As a potential illustration, Ennio Morricone produced many remarkable film scores—including the 1964 *A Fist Full of Dollars*, 1984 *Once Upon a Time in America*, and the 1986 *The Mission*—but never won an Oscar. He had been repeatedly nominated for less outstanding work from the 1987 *The Untouchables* to the 2000 *Malèna*, but to no avail, until finally he received an honorary Oscar in 2007 for lifetime achievement in film music.

Coda

I began this chapter by dissecting the connections between honors for film music and the film's corresponding cinematic success. Despite introducing methodological improvements over previous investigations, we discovered that awards and nominations for best score are only associated with awards and nominations for best picture. Otherwise, recognition for best score has no strong relation with either critical acclaim or box office gross. That minimalist inference for the film's score became even more minimal for any songs that might accentuate the film. That is, nominations and awards in the best song category are largely irrelevant to a film's success by any major criterion—*Titanic*'s "My Heart Will Go On" be what it may!

These mostly null findings then obliged me to switch from film music to cinema composers. The basic thesis was that composers for film behave like classical composers of days long past. Film scorers and songwriters can even be called classicists incognito. Like their seemingly outdated pre-decessors, cinema composers create music according to a trajectory that's decided more by their intrinsic creative growth than by the extrinsic require-ments of their cinematic assignments—more endogenous than exogenous. This personal trajectory generates their first, best, and last hits that then receive outward confirmation at the Oscar ceremonies when the composers are honored with their first nomination, their first award, and their last award. Yet these honored compositions may or may not match the quality of the cinematic product. Sometimes the production of creative music may correspond with an outstanding film—whether judged by critical acclaim or box-office performance. But just as often exceptional music will appear in motion pictures that are otherwise undistinguished. So the composers just do what they do best without regard to whether the resulting film is truly worthy of their creativity.

In a sense, filmmakers have replaced the patrons of earlier periods. Instead of getting a commission from a cultured aristocrat or wealthy con-noisseur, the modern composer signs a contract with a producer to supply music for a film, making the movie theater the new venue for the debut of musical creativity—a debut soon consolidated by the separate release of the soundtrack on CD or mp3 download. Perhaps this has become the only feasible career for a composer who wishes to write approachable music in a grand symphonic style. The choice is between writing film music for broad audiences or writing academic music for cognoscenti who want to read long essays that specify why some highly esoteric and inaccessible chamber music has immense theoretical interest. And, besides, a good film composer earns a great deal more income than even the best academic composer. So maybe the classical composers of yesteryear have become the cinema composers of today.

These results make one ponder this intriguing counterfactual: What if John Williams were born in 1832 rather than 1932? He would then have been a contemporary of Johannes Brahms, but without any chance of becoming a composer for film. What would've happened to his quite obvi-ous musical talent? To what extent would his career have paralleled that of Brahms? As young teenagers both Williams and Brahms had aspired to become concert pianists, and both began their compositional careers at age 19 by premiering a new piano sonata. So would Williams have pursued a similar career trajectory? Would his first, best, and last masterworks have appeared at about the same ages, or perhaps a half decade earlier? Only the masterpieces would have been symphonies and operas rather than scores and songs? Or did Williams need film as a vehicle to realize fully his genius? And, just as importantly, did the films for which he composed require his best compositional efforts to maximize their cinematic impact? Or would Williams's music on an off day suffice to do the trick?

Chapter 9

Razzies: Is Bad the Opposite of Good?

I have now been collecting data on great films for over a decade. Each year I routinely update my database by gathering raw information on a new set of films. And each year that data collection is timed to the movie-award season. That season begins in early January when many major critic organizations—such as the New York Film Critics Circle and the National Society of Film Critics—bestow their awards in the principal categories of cinematic achievement. A week or two later the National Board of Review will announce its award recipients. About the same time or a little later will come the Golden Globes awarded by the Hollywood Foreign Press Association. Scattered throughout this period are various guild awards, like those of the Directors Guild of America and the Screen Actors Guild. Then I turn my eyes across the Atlantic to witness the outcome of the BAFTA ceremony in London. But Hollywood is not going to be upstaged by anyone. So in recent years the biggest and the best is most often saved for last: The Oscars announced by the American Academy of Motion Picture Arts and Sciences in late February or March. With the history, the industry, and the stars now all converging on Kodak Theatre, this event is the proper capstone of the award season. By the end of that evening, I can identify the films that constitute that year's addition to my database.

Yet the day before the Oscar gala a totally distinct and much less sensational event takes place: the Annual Golden Raspberry Awards—or the plain "Razzies." Begun in a home living room in 1981, the awards or "'dis'honors" (as in "to diss" someone) have been handed out in varied venues, including elementary schools, the Hollywood Roosevelt Hotel, and most recently the Abracadabra Theatre at the Magicopolis in Santa Monica, some miles away from Hollywood's glitter and splendor. Razzie awards and nods are handed out in such major categories as picture, director, screenplay, and the four acting prizes. Just as the Oscars purport to honor the brightest and the best cinematic contributions in a given year, the Razzies strive to do the reverse—to point the finger at the dumbest and the worst.

Want some concrete examples? Well, the Worst Picture Razzie has gone to such cinematic duds as *Catwoman* (2004), *Gigli* (2003), *Battlefield Earth: A Saga of the Year 3000* (2000), *Showgirls* (1995), *Ghosts Can't Do It* (1990), *Leonard Part 6* (1987), and *Inchon* (1981). As these examples indicate, Razzies are not inflicted on obscure indie films with tiny budgets. That would be most unfair. Instead, the dishonor is saved for mainstream productions that fail in spite of themselves. The filmmakers had at their disposal all the financial resources and even the best stars, but blew it royally. These are often the films that make a critic cry out in despair "What *were* they thinking?!"

Now, in a book devoted to great flicks, why do I waste a whole paragraph even mentioning these anti-awards? The answer is simple: These negative film appraisals raise the question of whether bad movies are the simple opposite of good movies. If the Razzie awards are just the mirror image of the real awards, then they can give us additional insights into the basis for cinematic success. Look back to Figure 2.1 in Chapter 2. If the Oscars and other honors help us comprehend the upper right-tail of the distribution, why can't the Razzies aid our understanding of the lower left-hand tail? The negative honors allow us to round out our knowledge of the full range, from turkeys to masterpieces.

Admittedly, it could be the case that the positive factors that cause films to win Oscars may operate in a very different manner than the negative factors that make films earn Razzies. This possibility is suggested by psychological experiments on attitudes and emotional evaluations: Negative appraisals might not be the simple inverse of positive appraisals. Instead, the positive end of a "bipolar" dimension can differ from the negative end of the same dimension. At the most basic level, negative information and events tend to have bigger effects than do positive information and events. In the specific case of films, for instance, the baseline expectation for performances may be sufficiently high that a movie may lose more from bad acting than it gains from good acting.

Even more strikingly, the contrasts between the two poles of an evaluative dimension could be qualitative as well as quantitative. For instance, the negative ends of evaluative dimensions may be more complex and varied in terms of cognitive representations and behavioral consequences. Moreover, it is possible that that these dimensional disparities partly reside in the phenomena themselves and not just in subjective perception of those phenomena. Tolstoy opened his novel *Anna Karenina* with the provocative observation "Happy families are all alike; every unhappy family is unhappy in its own way." In a similar fashion, it is conceivable that there are more ways to make a bad film than to make a good film. While a five-star and much-awarded film cannot contain any serious flaws, each bomb may contain its own distinctive collection of deficiencies.

It's the goal of this chapter to find out the relation between great and horrid flicks. I'll carry out this goal by pitting the Oscars against their supposed opposites, the Razzies.

Four Big Questions

The above abstract speculations can be converted into the following four concrete issues:

1. *Are bad films the inverse of good films?* In other words, are the cinematic criteria that determine whether a film is good the same as the criteria that determine whether a film is bad? And do those standards have the same weights? The research findings that I've reviewed in previous chapters show that Oscars in some award categories correlate more highly with the critics' evaluations than do Oscars received in other categories. Will Razzies bestowed in the same categories display a similar pattern of correlations? For instance, if an Oscar for best direction has an especially large positive association with critical acclaim, will a Razzie for worst direction have an usually large negative association?

2. *Are bad films as bad as good films are good?* In Chapter 2 I indicated that the Oscars do an excellent job predicting the evaluations of film critics. Will the Razzies do equally well? Or might they have even more predictive power? Does a Razzie more strongly assure that a film is a bomb than an Oscar promises that a film is a masterpiece?

3. *Are bad films as cohesively bad as good films are cohesively good?* In Chapter 3 we learned that film awards in certain categories tend to cluster together. Thus, the awards in the dramatic categories—directing, acting, and screenwriting—tend to be highly intercorrelated with each other. Would the same magnitude of cohesiveness be found for negative forms of recognition? Or is Tolstoy correct in suggesting that the "horn effect" is less unified than the "halo effect" discussed in Chapter 2?

4. *Are bad films' positives/negatives good films' negatives/positives?* More specifically, if the Oscars exhibit associations with a given set

of variables, will the Razzies display associations with the same set, the associations having the same magnitude but opposite sign? In light of what has been noted above, the pattern of correlations might differ substantially for positive and negative recognition. However, if the Oscars and the Razzies truly anchor the opposite ends of a simple bipolar evaluative dimension, the correlates of one should closely reflect those of the other. As seen in Chapter 5, positive film awards are associated with particular screenplay characteristics. Presumably, the Razzies will be associated with the same characteristics but in the reverse direction. Especially interesting is whether the Oscars and Razzies have contrary correlations with gauges of a film's performance at the box office.

If negative evaluations are simply the inverse of positive evaluations, with equal weights and cohesiveness, and with comparable correlations with other cinematic variables, then bad films can be considered as the straightforward opposite of good films.

Four Big Answers

My sample started with all films nominated for Golden Raspberries in the following eight categories: worst picture, worst director, worst male lead, worst female lead, worst male supporting, worst female supporting, worst screenplay, and worst song. These are the only categories that have exact counterparts in the Academy Awards and that have been granted since the beginning of the Razzies in 1981. For obvious reasons, I completely ignored films that were only dishonored in the following categories: Worst Remake or Rip-Off, Worst Excuse for a Horror Movie, Worst Prequel or Sequel, Worst Screen Couple, Worst New Star, Worst Reckless Disregard for Human Life and Public Property, and Worst Written Film Grossing Over $100 Million. Although it is unfortunate that the Razzies are not normally bestowed for the worst in cinematography, art production, score, and other aspects of filmmaking, we've already seen in earlier chapters that the picture and dramatic awards are by far the most crucial to cinematic success.

The next step was to incorporate all films that received Oscar nominations or awards in the same eight categories—picture, director, male lead, female lead, male supporting, female supporting, screenplay, and song—also beginning with the 1981 Academy Award ceremony. Because both Razzies and Oscars are allotted to the films that were released in the previous year, the first films in the sample were released in 1980. The most recent films were released in 2003 and recognized in 2004. The films of later ceremonies could not be included at the time of the investigation because of the time lag between release and the appearance of certain key measures, particularly the movie guide ratings. Omission of the 2005 awards was inadvertently fortunate because the Razzies departed from the modus operandi by granting worst acting awards (male lead, male supporting, and female supporting) to George W. Bush, Donald Rumsfeld, and Britney Spears for their appearances in *Fahrenheit 9/11*—a documentary with no bona fide acting! This announcement was manifestly a political statement rather than cinematic assessment.

Following prior practice, the sample was restricted to English-language, live-action, feature-length narrative films. The result was 877 films, 445 according to the Razzie selection criterion, 483 according to the Oscar criterion, with 51 films satisfying both criteria. The latter oddity is illustrated by *Godfather, Part III*. Although it garnered Oscar nominations for best picture, best director, best male supporting actor, and best song, it also managed to win a Razzie for worst female supporting actor—bestowed on Sophia Coppola, the daughter of the director, producer, and screenwriter Francis Coppola. The part was originally going to be played by the far more experienced and talented Winona Ryder, but she had to withdraw at the last minute. Poor Sophia is often blamed for helping make *Part III* inferior to the previous two.

To the extent possible, these 877 films were then subjected to the full battery of measures already seen in previous investigations. These measures fall into the following four categories:

1. *Film awards and anti-awards.* Eight variables were created for each award category for both the Oscars and Razzies. That is, variables were defined for the categories of best/worst picture, director, male lead actor, female lead actor, male supporting actor, female supporting actor, screenplay, and original song. Each variable was coded using the same scheme used in earlier chapters: 2 = received the honor or dishonor, 1 = just nominated for same honor or dishonor, and 0 = neither of the preceding applied. Later I will combine these 16 measures in various ways to address the questions that drive this chapter.

2. *Critic evaluations.* These included both Metacritic and movie guide ratings, the latter based on 5 separate guides, as in earlier chapters. The scores on the Metacritic measure ranged from 9 to 95, with a mean of about 55 on a 100-point scale. The scores on the movie guide measure could range from 1 to 5, with a mean of almost exactly 3 stars. Because the quality of these movies extends the full range from bomb to masterwork, the reliability of the movie guide ratings increased to .91, which is about .10 higher than what is found in research

discussed in previous chapters. Film critics can more reliably discriminate the best from the worst than discriminate great films from merely good films.

3. *Film attributes*. This set included: (a) g*enre* indictors for *drama* (58%), *comedy* (37%), *romance* (20%), or *musical* (4%); (b) *runtime* defined by the number of minutes that it usually takes to show the film (range from 74 minutes to 356 minutes with a mean of 114 minutes); (c) *MPAA ratings* for *PG* (26%), *PG-13* (25%), and *R* (48%); (d) *writer-director* indicating whether the director was directly involved in the writing process; (e) *real-life origins* indicators to record whether the screenplay was based on a *true story* (10%) and whether the screenplay was an outright *biopic* (4%); (f) *cinematic predecessor* indicators to register whether or not a film was a *remake* (6%) and whether or not it was a *sequel* (7%); (g) *adaptation* indicators to gauge whether the script was based on a *play* (5%), *novel* (23%), other *fiction* (2%, i.e., short story), *nonfiction* (5%), and *other* (5%; comics, video game, television program, etc.), whether the source of the adaptation was a recognized *classic* (4%; e.g., Shakespeare's *Hamlet*), a *bestseller* (3%; e.g., on the New York Times Bestseller Lists), or a *prizewinner* (1%; e.g., Pulitzer, Nobel, National Book Award), and, finally, whether the script was an *author-adaptation* involving the author of the original source.

4. *Financial and box office*. This category included: (a) *production budget* in units of a million U.S. dollars, rounded off to the nearest million (ranging from 0 to 200 but with a mean cost of about $37 million); (b) *season of release* recorded as Easter (March and April; 11%), summer (May through August; 32%), and Christmas (November and December; 29%); (c) *number of screens* on which the film was shown when first released (with a mean of about 1323 screens but with a range from 1 to 3703); (d) *first weekend earnings* in the United States with the figures expressed in millions of dollars rounded off to the nearest million (ranging from 0 to 93 with a mean a bit over 10); and (e) *gross earnings* at the termination of its US run expressed to the nearest million in US dollars (ranging from 0 to 601 with a mean just below 47 million).

Taken altogether, the above measures give us the means to address the questions raised earlier.

Are Bad Films the Inverse of Good Films?

The first question is answered by scanning the correlations in Table 9.1. Here I give the correlations between the Oscar and Razzie award in each

TABLE 9.1   Correlations of Oscar and Razzie Awards with Critic Evaluations

Category	Movie guide		Metacritic	
	Oscars	Razzies	Oscars	Razzies
Picture	.49***	−.44***	.38***	−.41***
Directing	.48***	−.42***	.40***	−.43***
Male lead	.38***	−.43***	.32***	−.50***
Female lead	.32***	−.40***	.30***	−.36***
Male supporting	.38***	−.31***	.32***	−.31***
Female supporting	.34***	−.29***	.32***	−.28***
Screenplay	.63***	−.42***	.56***	−.42***
Song	.12**	−.25***	.21***	−.09

Note. $N = 877$. The correlations involving the Metacritic ratings are based on $n = 183$.

*$p < .05$. **$p < .01$. ***$p < .001$.

category and the two alternative critic evaluations, the movie guide and Metacritic ratings. In general, the pattern appears to be fairly consistent across the four columns, with the Razzies being just the inverse of the Oscars. In both cases the picture, director, and screenplay categories tend to have the highest correlations, the song category the lowest correlations, with the acting categories falling in the middle. However, there are also some minor discrepancies. The screenplay Oscar is more strongly correlated with critic evaluations than is the screenplay Razzie. In more concrete terms, a terrific script is more apt to be associated with a terrific film than is a terrible script with a terrible film. Lastly, the song category displays an inconsistent pattern of correlations. For the movie guide ratings the song Razzie has a higher correlation than the song Oscar, but the reverse is true for the Metacritic scores.

These minor departures notwithstanding, it seems fair to conclude that the Razzies are very nearly the inverse of the Oscars. The former gauge the lower end of the distribution much like the latter gauge the upper end.

Are Bad Films as Bad as Good Films Are Good?

The results in Table 9.1 also indicate that the Oscars and Razzies have about equal influence in most award categories. Although the Oscar correlations are more often larger than their Razzie counterparts, the advantage is not consistent across all pairs. However, to get a better picture of any differential, the critic evaluations were regressed on the two sets of awards. This will let us see whether the judgments are better predicted by the positive or negative measures. In the case of the movie guide ratings, the eight Oscar measures accounted for 51% of the variance whereas the eight Razzie measures accounted for 43% of the variance. Yet the pattern was partially reversed for the Metacritic scores: The Oscars explained 48% of the variance while the Razzies explained 49% of the variance.

Hence, the negative assessments have approximately the same weight as the positive assessments. Certainly there is no reason to believe in this case that bad is stronger than good. If anything, good films are slightly better than bad films are worse. That's how it came out for the movie guide ratings.

Are Bad Films as Cohesively Bad as Good Films are Cohesively Good?

One way to assess their relative cohesion is to calculate the internal-consistency reliability coefficients (alphas) for composites obtained by summing up the scores on the awards in the eight categories within each set of awards. The two resulting composite scores yield reliabilities of .72 and .77 for the Oscars and Razzies, respectively. Thus, the two composites are about equally coherent, with the negative awards showing slightly superior coherence relative to the positive awards. The basis for this modest difference can be attributed to the differential standing of the song award.

This last conclusion was based on a factor analysis of the two sets of indicators. The results are shown in Table 9.2, which gives the loadings on the first factor for each set of awards. For the most part, the loadings are fairly similar across the two factors. Hence, picture, director, and screenplay display very high loadings, whereas the four acting categories exhibit more moderate loadings. Moreover, across both factors males tend to have higher loadings than females within the acting categories of lead and supporting. The Meryl Streep Effect discussed in Chapter 7 applies to bad

TABLE 9.2   Factor Analysis of Oscar and Razzie Award Measures: Loadings on Single Factor and Percent of Total Variance Explained

Category	Oscars	Razzies
Picture	.88	.93
Directing	.85	.84
Male lead	.59	.54
Female lead	.37	.39
Male supporting	.47	.55
Female supporting	.45	.35
Screenplay	.82	.88
Song	−.01	.46
Percent of total variance explained	38.42	42.71

films as much as good films! Not only will a male actor's best performance more likely appear in a wonderful film, but a male actor's worst performance will more likely appear in a lousy film. I doubt that any female actor would take this last finding as any consolation for the first finding.

Nevertheless, although the worst song Razzie has a moderate loading on its factor, the best song Oscar has essentially a zero loading on its factor. Bad songs are more prone to be found in bad movies than good songs are likely to be found in good movies. This difference is largely responsible for the result that the factor for the Oscar accounts for less variance in the eight items than does the Razzie factor. Therefore, if anything the eight Razzie award categories are more consistent with each other than are the eight Oscars.

Even so, if the song category is deleted, the difference between the positive and negative assessments noticeably declines. Coefficient alpha becomes .76 for the Oscars and .77 for the Razzies. Likewise, one factor accounts for 44% of the variance in the seven Oscar measures and another factor accounts for 47% of the variance in the corresponding Razzies. Consequently, the two sets of assessments seem equally cohesive so long as the categories are limited to a film's dramatic qualities. Because these are the very qualities most responsible for a film's aesthetic success, Razzie films are bad in the same way that Oscar films are good.

Are Bad Films' Pluses/Minuses Good Films' Minuses/Pluses?

Rather than respond to this question with separate correlations for each award category across both awards, it was deemed more efficient to consolidate the measures into three composites: (a) total Oscars is the sum of the scores on picture, director, male and female lead, male and female supporting, and screenplay; (b) total Razzies is the sum of the scores on the corresponding negative assessments; and (c) bipolar is the difference between total Oscars and total Razzies (i.e., the Oscar total minus the Razzie total). The song category was omitted because of its null correspondence with the other award categories in the case of the Oscars. As noted in the previous section, the internal-consistency reliabilities are .76 and .77 for the Oscar and Razzie composites. The reliability for the bipolar composite is .81. These three composite measures are strongly correlated with the two critic evaluations, as seen in Table 9.3. Although the Oscar composite has a higher correlation than the Razzie composite, the difference is trivial in the case of the Metacritic scores. It is noteworthy, too, that the bipolar Oscar-versus-Razzie composite displays even higher correlations. This bipolar measure does a good job of distinguishing the must-see works of genius from the must-not-see turkeys or bombs.

TABLE 9.3   Correlations between Oscar and Razzie Awards and Critic
Evaluations

Critical evaluation	Oscars	Razzies	Bipolar
Movie guide	.68***	−.59***	.77***
Metacritic	.60***	−.58***	.71***

Note. $N = 877$. The correlations involving the Metacritic ratings are based on $n = 183$. The bipolar measure is the Oscar measure minus the Razzie measure (i.e., goodness minus badness).

*$p < .05$. **$p < .01$. ***$p < .001$.

These three measures were then correlated with the film attribute variables. Table 9.4 includes the results for only those attributes that produced at least one statistically significant correlation. One general finding should be evident at once: The Oscars and the Razzies invariably have correlations with opposite signs. This is true even when one or the other correlation is not statistically significant. Accordingly, the two correlations will necessarily be significantly different from each other (because statistical significance is gauged against the baseline of a zero correlation). Moreover, both correlations are significant for more than a majority of the items. Therefore, the answer to the fourth question is affirmative. The positive and negative

TABLE 9.4   Correlations between Oscar and Razzie Awards and Film
Attributes

Film attribute		Oscars	Razzies	Bipolar
Adaptations (total)		.18***	−.09**	.17***
Type:	Play	.08*	−.11**	.11**
	Novel	.12***	−.03	.09**
	Nonfiction	.17***	−.09**	.16***
Status:	Prizewinner	.11**	−.06	.10**
Author adaptation		.11**	−.09**	.12***
Writer director		.09*	−.05	.09*
Origins:	True story	.19***	−.13***	.19***
	Biopic	.16***	−.09**	.15**
Predecessors:	Sequel	−.15***	.14***	−.18***
	Remake	−.10**	.07*	−.10**
Genre:	Drama	.32***	−.23***	.33***
	Comedy	−.16***	.04	−.12***
	Musical	−.07*	.06	−.08*
Runtime		.37***	−.17***	.33***
MPAA rating:	PG–13	−.08*	.01	−.06
	R	.11**	−.06	.10**

Note. The bipolar is the Oscar measure minus the Razzie measure.

*$p < .05$. **$p < .01$. ***$p < .001$.

assessments reflected in the Oscars and Razzies correlate with the same attributes but with opposite signs. The only qualification to impose on this conclusion is that the Oscar correlations are usually larger in absolute value than are Razzie correlations. The results reported in Table 9.5 merely reinforce this generalization. The Oscar and Razzie composites always correlate in the opposite direction with the financial and box office variables, and with only one exception both correlations are statistically significant.

TABLE 9.5   Correlations between Oscar and Razzie Awards and the Financial and Box Office Data

| Financial and box office data | Award composites | | | n |
	Oscars	Razzies	Bipolar	
Budget	−.17***	.22***	−.24***	484
Release season				
Easter	−.09*	.02	−.06	877
Summer	−.20***	.22***	−.25***	877
Christmas	.24***	−.20***	.26***	877
First weekend				
Screens	−.31***	.28***	−.36***	409
Gross	−.24***	.24***	−.29***	448
Domestic gross	.28***	−.10**	.23***	802

Note. The bipolar is the Oscar measure minus the Razzie measure.

*$p < .05$. **$p < .01$. ***$p < .001$.

The Good, the Bad and the Ugly

Using the overall findings just reported, we can proffer a typical profile of the great flick as opposed to the miserable movie. Besides receiving lots of stars in critic evaluations and earning Oscar nominations and awards in the dramatic categories, exceptional films are more liable to be adaptations of prize-winning literature (especially of plays, novels, or nonfiction works), to have had the original author or the film's director immediately involved in writing the screenplay, to be based on a true story (perhaps even a biopic), to be dramas more than any other genre, to have very long runtimes, to be R rated, to be released during the Christmas season, and to do well in total gross earnings. In comparison, excellent films are less prone to be sequels or remakes, to be comedies or musicals, to have gigantic budgets, to be released in the summer months, to be rated PG-13, to open on thousands of screens, or to do an impressive box office the first weekend. Reverse the direction of these positive and negative characteristics, and the result is the attributes of the truly bad, even ugly film. When it comes to cinematic assessments of Razzie and Oscar films, bad is largely the opposite of good.

In the context of relevant research in experimental psychology, this outcome may seem a bit surprising. In the first place, negative assessments have mostly the same structure as the positive assessments. The various cinematic criteria have about the same relevance whether one is identifying the five-star or the zero-star films. Furthermore, the positive and negative assessments have about the same force. Bad is not stronger than good. On the contrary, bad seems a little weaker than good. Why is this so?

One explanation would concentrate on the Golden Raspberries as the sole indicators of negative assessments. In certain ways the Razzies cannot be considered the exact obverse of the Oscars. At the most superficial level, the amateur critics and film aficionados who make up the Golden Raspberry Award Foundation do not take themselves nearly as seriously as do the professionals who form the voting membership of the Academy of Motion Picture Arts and Sciences. Indeed, the Razzies are driven by a sense of parody to serve as an anecdote to the excessive pomposity of the Oscars and other film awards. As a result, the Razzies are often bestowed with more humor, a levity sometimes taking the guise of tongue-in-cheek honors. An example is the 1987 *Jaws: The Revenge* which earned a worst actor nomination for "Bruce the shark." Other examples include female acting nods for male actors performing in drag, such as Kurt Russell in the 1989 *Tango & Cash*, or simultaneous lead and supporting nods for the same actor, such as Arnold Schwarzenegger playing the main character and the clone of the same character in the 2000 *The 6th Day*.

Nonetheless, these mocking departures from Oscar practice cannot account for the results. When all such flippant assignments were removed by recoding all of the presumably inappropriate scores to 0, the correlations reported in the tables did not change in any noticeable manner. In fact, any changes that did take place only surfaced beyond the second or third decimal place. Such aberrancies are too infrequent to make a substantial difference. They occur in fewer than half of the years in which Razzies were granted, and then usually in just a single nomination or award (before 2005, that is). The lone deviation represents the single biggest joke of the evening.

A more likely explanation concerns the type of films on which Razzies are bestowed. The focus is on high-profile, big-budget, widely-distributed Hollywood productions. This fact is evident from the correlations in Table 9.5. The total Razzie composite correlates positively with budget, the number of screens and gross earnings on first weekend, and release in the prime summer season. These are obviously films that the studios had hoped would become blockbusters, hopes that were dashed by the weak returns after opening weekend. In line with this judgment, the Razzies have a negative correlation with the gross earnings measure. Therefore, the Razzies are seldom bestowed on small-budget, art-house, film-festival works that lack the means to attract a wide audience. Instead, Razzie-recognized films most often feature A-list actors, top directors, excellent production values, state-of-the-art special effects, and so forth. That probably raises the minimum level of quality. In the case of acting, for instance, a bad performance by Lawrence Olivier (in the 1981 *Inchon*) or Marlon Brando (in the 1996 *The Island of Dr. Moreau*) cannot be ascribed to amateurish talents but rather to overacting, complacency, or miscasting. Hence, films that win Razzies could have been so much better, but failed miserably to exploit their substantial cinematic resources. Even so, their threshold level of quality is probably several degrees higher than the typical run-of-the-mill film.

But it could also be the case that similar findings would have been obtained had the negative assessments come from other sources besides the Razzies. In particular, in the case of cinematic assessments bad may actually be the opposite of good, only a bit weaker. The reason may reside in the fact that bad films have a very different standing amongst viewers than do good films. Unlike many other circumstances in everyday life, a potentially negative cinematic experience does not have to become an actual bad experience. Movie goers are not forced to view all movies released each year whether they want to or not. They can be selective instead. Even if viewers make the mistake of buying a ticket or renting a DVD for a bad film, they can always walk out of the theater or press the eject button. In contrast, if a film is really good then it can be enjoyed until the final credits run. Thus, whereas a good film will almost always be completely experienced, a bad film will be granted that opportunity much less often, thereby diminishing its adverse impact. In many instances, if it were not for the heavy pre-release marketing maneuvers—the star-studded posters and exciting trailers—no one would even have showed up for the first weekend.

Aside from this unresolved issue there resides a related matter that's all the more perplexing: The bipolar dimension linking masterpieces at one pole with utter trash at the other pole sometimes curves around to become a circle. Certain rare films can be so achingly dreadful that they attain cult status as untainted "camp." Indeed, on occasion critics will assign two different sets of stars to films, one designating how bad the film is and the other how good the film is because it's so awesomely wretched—so incredibly "campy." A classic instance is Ed Wood's 1959 *Plan 9 from Outer Space*, which earned Wood a posthumous Golden Turkey Award for all-time Worst Director. Yet an entry in a popular movie guide tells us: "Hailed as the worst movie ever made; certainly one of the funniest.... So mesmerizingly awful it actually improves (so to speak) with each viewing."

To be sure, the director did not intend to make a comedy, but rather a serious sci-fi thriller and horror actioner. Perhaps it's unjust (or overly generous) to give credit where discredit is due.

But I will say no more than this about this latter question. In all likelihood the subject deserves another lengthy monograph dedicated entirely to the scientific study of campy flicks.

Chapter 10

Epilogue: The Science of Cinema

We've traveled very far through the scientific intricacies of cinema creativity and aesthetics. Are we there yet? To find the answer, make one last quick pass through the entire text, pausing only to process the section headings. Scan all the figures and tables as well. And skim through the list of references. Shouldn't we be impressed? Dozens upon dozens of scientists have studied film from diverse disciplinary perspectives, using a multitude of methods to address an array of significant questions. The samples have often amounted to hundreds of motion pictures, and the statistical analyses have frequently been state of the art. The end result of these studies is well over a hundred technical articles and monographs on the subject—not even counting the book you're reading.

So do we now know what makes a great flick? Well, yes and no.

What Do We Know?

Lots! Perhaps the single most critical lesson is that there's more than one kind of great film. There are movies that make big money, motion pictures that rake in the awards, and films that garner critical acclaim. And even these three groups of criteria have subgroups. In the case of movie awards, for example, we must take care to distinguish the honors defining the four creative clusters—the dramatic, visual, technical, and musical. Not only are these four awards largely independent of each other, but they also feature contrasting correlations with other criteria of film greatness, including box office returns, best picture honors, and rave reviews.

Whatever the specific standard of greatness, it's also evident that researchers have constructed an impressive inventory of factors that predict cinematic success. These include various aspects of the screenplay, the direction, and the acting, as well as the budget necessary to implement these components of the final product. Also important are certain features of distribution and exhibition—particularly in the case of financial performance. At the same time, we have learned what factors may be less relevant to certain standards of greatness. For instance, filmmakers can skimp on expenditures on special effects if the goal is to produce a first-rate, critically acclaimed film. Even first-class music is often optional. Drama is self-sufficient. In such cases the movie theater becomes tantamount to the Globe Theatre in Elizabethan London showing a Shakespeare play or the Theater of Dionysus in Periclean Athens staging a play by Sophocles.

Finally, I think this research lets us appreciate why it's extremely rare to see a film that "has it all." There are just too many participating influences. Worse yet, these influences often are unrelated and uncoordinated, often operating at cross purposes. Hence, each film must achieve greatness in its own unique way. This fact is evident in the three movies that are tied for receiving the most Academy Awards—11—at the time of this writing:

1. The 1959 *Ben-Hur* won its Oscars for picture, directing, male lead, male supporting, editing, cinematography, art direction, costume design, special effects, sound, and score, plus a nomination for screenplay. It got no Oscar nods whatsoever in the categories of female lead, female supporting, or song. Women and song (but not wine) were seemingly left out of the picture without detriment to aesthetic impact.

2. The 1997 *Titanic* took home Oscars for picture, directing, editing, cinematography, art direction, costume design, visual effects, sound effects editing, sound, score, and song, but only received nominations for female lead, female supporting, and makeup. It claimed absolutely no Oscar nominations in the categories of lead male actor, lead male supporting, or screenplay. This time, in terms of greatness, male actors and an original script went AWOL.

3. The 2003 *The Lord of the Rings: The Return of the King* received its Oscars for picture, directing, screenplay, editing, art direction, costume design, makeup, visual effects, sound mixing, score, and song, but earned no nominations in any other categories, including male lead, female lead, male supporting, female supporting, cinematography, or sound editing. All four acting categories, and even one visual and one technical category, had to yield to five better films in each category. Imagine! A great picture without so much as a single nod for acting!

Nor are these three films equivalent by other gauges of cinematic success. According to five movie guide ratings, the films average 4.4, 4.3, and 4.9 stars, respectively, which indicates that only the last can count as a legitimate 5-star film. Furthermore, although all did well in the box office, their earnings were inversely related to the number of stars received. That is, their respective rankings, adjusted for inflation, are 13th, 6th, and 49th. All three were surpassed in domestic gross by *Gone with the Wind, Star Wars, The Sound of Music, E.T.: The Extra-Terrestrial,* and *The Ten Commandments*—films that did not win anywhere near the same number of Academy Awards. So to some undetermined extent great flicks are unique flicks. No one pattern covers them all.

What Don't We Know?

Also lots! None of the prediction equations explain all of the variation in the diverse yardsticks of cinematic success, and many account for less than half—sometimes considerably much less than half. That means that we still have a long ways to go before we can provide an exhaustive treatment of the phenomenon. Some films will be more successful than predicted, others less. There will still remain unexpected flops, surprising sleepers, and out-of-nowhere hits.

Nor should we be especially embarrassed by our residual ignorance. A survey of all the variables so far investigated would reveal to any avid moviegoer that many likely predictors have yet to be tested. It doesn't take much knowledge of cinema to notice a strange gap between Chapters 5–7 and Chapter 8. Where are the chapters on film editing, production design, cinematography, and special visual or auditory effects? What's more, no one has yet scrutinized the (negative) consequences of egotistic stars "chewing up the scenery," "cheesy special effects," or "plot holes you can drive a truck through." Nor has anyone yet isolated that fine line that divides the manipulative and maudlin tearjerker from a truly profound and enduring tragedy. Why does the former leave a bad taste in your mouth as soon as you walk out of the theater while the latter still puts a lump in your throat just recalling the film years later?

Moreover, although the list of the already examined factors is reasonably long, no investigation to date incorporates all variables in a single inquiry. Instead, the research effort seems piecemeal. One study may include variables *A, B,* and *C,* while another *C, D,* and *E,* and yet another *E, F,* and *G.* Until a study accommodates not just *A* to *G* but also *H* through *Z,* we cannot identify with any certainty the most crucial traits of cinematic greatness, however it may be assessed. Aggravating the problem all the more is the fact that the film samples, success criteria, and predictor variables are often defined differently from one investigation to the next. It too often seems that each investigator starts from scratch, reinventing the wheel from a block of crude rock instead of speeding off in a state-of-the-art sports car.

In fact, I've compiled Table 10.1 just to give an idea of what's necessary for research in this area to produce a full-fledged science of cinema. To date absolutely *no* published investigation has come close to satisfying these "minimum" requirements. No study by me or anyone else. So perhaps the table might be better styled a "wish list." As a consequence, it should be apparent that the scientific study of cinema has not yet reached the point

TABLE 10.1   Minimum Specifications for Scientific Studies of Cinematic Creativity and Aesthetics

Sample:
   All films released within a *specific* interval that are (a) *English-language* (to equalize acting comparisons), (b) *live-action* (no animations), (c) *feature-length* (no shorts), (d) *narrative* (no documentaries), and (e) *widely exhibited* (including art house circuit)
Criteria:
   Box office: first weekend gross, length of run, and total domestic gross;
   Popular appeal: consumer surveys (e.g., Netflix customer and IMDB.com user ratings);
   Movie honors: best picture, dramatic, visual, technical, and musical awards and nominations bestowed by major professional, critical, and guild organizations;
   Critical acclaim: both early during the theatrical release (e.g., Metacritic.com) and later movie guide ratings (e.g., Leonard Matlin).
Predictors:
   Budget: total costs to produce the film (including any pre-production marketing);
   Script: genres, runtimes, MPAA ratings, sequels and remakes, true stories and biopics, adaptations (source, status, author-adaptors), storyline and protagonist traits;
   Personnel: actors and crew (producer, director, production designer, cinematographer, composer, etc.) assessed on attributes both individual (gender, age, prior credits, honors, box office) and collective (creative freedom, repeated ties, coreness, team quality);
   Distribution: (a) distributor, (b) timing, (c) screens, and (d) competition;
   Promotion: (a) advertising (e.g., trailers) and (b) merchandizing (e.g., tie-ins);
   Exhibition: word-of-mouth causing positive and negative information cascades.
Analyses:
   Statistical methods that (a) provide controls for potential *spurious* relationships, (b) allow tests for hypothesized *interaction effects* and *curvilinear functions,* (c) incorporate adjustments for the highly *skewed distributions* for box office performance, and (d) permit complex models that accommodate *indirect causal effects* and possible *two-way causal relations* (such as illustrated in much econometric research in macroeconomics).

where I can quit my day job to become a Hollywood consultant. A producer shouldn't ask me the question: What do I need to do to make a blockbuster that that earns five stars from the critics and sweeps the Oscars in all the major categories? To be sure, I could provide hints, suggestions, and clues. But I couldn't offer precise formulas. I would feel terrible guilt collecting the most nominal consulting fee. Perhaps what we now know is worth a mere 500 bucks per project!

Yet, in time, the picture may change. As researchers increase the number of variables and the size of their samples, and as they enhance the sophistication of their statistical methods, we may eventually be able to sell our advice with a good conscience. At the minimum, the cinema scientist may be sufficiently proficient to specify a probability for this or that desired outcome. Considering the tremendous complexity of the cinematic product, we probably could not hope to do more. Even so, given the costs of making a feature-length film, that specification may be help enough. After all, if the industry can make fewer turkeys more cash will be available for producing masterpieces. Whether a blockbuster, a best picture, or a critical favorite, we can then anticipate the creation of more great flicks.

Notes

Here I will not provide documentation for every single factual statement presented in this book. If the information is readily available on the Internet—especially the Internet Movie Database (imdb.com)—then anyone with online access can check those facts. Instead, I'll focus on the original sources for direct quotations and scientific conclusions.

Chapter 1—Prologue: Scientist as Cinema Connoisseur?

Film's emergence as art form: Baumann 2001. General discussion of awards and their significance: Frey 2006. Seventh art: http://en.wikipedia.org/wiki/Ricciotto_Canudo. Top 100: American Film Institute 2000. Titanic: De Vany & Walls 2004. Scientific research on box office: De Vany 2004.
   Science. Films released 2000-2006: Simonton 2009a.
   Caveat. For explanations for the dominance of English-language (and especially US-made) motion pictures, see: Acheson & Maule 1994; Bakker 2005; Jayakar & Waterman 2000; Marvasti & Canterbery 2005; Waterman 2005; see also Ginsburgh & Weyers 1999.

Chapter 2—Oscars, Golden Globes, and Critics: Consensus or Dissension?

Unofficial Oscar histories: Holden 1993; Wiley & Bona 1993. Second guessing example: Peary 1993.

Oscar quality. Unless otherwise noted, the research reported in this whole section—including the next four subsections—is based on Simonton 2004c. The 7 organizations:

1. Academy of Motion Picture Arts and Sciences: http://www.oscars.org/
2. Hollywood Foreign Press Association: http://www.hfpa.org/
3. British Academy of Film and Television Arts: http://www.bafta.org/
4. New York Film Critics Circle: http://nyfcc.com/
5. National Board of Review: http://www.nbrmp.org/
6. National Society of Film Critics: http://en.wikipedia.org/wiki/National_Society_of_Film_Critics/
7. Los Angeles Film Critics Association: http://www.lafca.net/

Agreements and alternatives. From nomination to win about same as from no nomination to nomination: Deuchert, Adjamah, & Pauly 2005; Faulkner & Anderson 1987; Ginsburgh 2003; Simonton 2002; Sochay 1994. "it don't make no nevermind": Wainer 1976. Other research using the 0-1-2 coding scheme: Basuroy, Chatterjee, & Ravid 2003; Cattani & Ferriani 2008. Table 2.1 adapted from Table 1 in Simonton 2004c. Reliabilities for personality traits and emergent leadership: Ilies, Gerhardt, & Le 2004.

General and guild awards. Guild awards:

1. Directors Guild of America: http://www.dga.org/
2. Writers Guild of America: http://www.wga.org/
3. Screen Actors Guild: http://www.sagawards.org/
4. American Society of Cinematographers: http://www.theasc.com/
5. Art Directors Guild: http://www.artdirectors.org/
6. Costume Designers Guild: http://www.costumedesignersguild.com/
7. American Cinema Editors: http://www.ace-filmeditors.org/
8. Grammy Awards: http://www.grammy.com/

Table 2.2 modified from Table 3 in Simonton 2004c (with the addition of the two correlations for film editing).

Oscar wins and nods. Table 2.3 adapted from Table 2 in Simonton 2004c.

Movie awards and critic evaluations. Five-item movie-guide ratings used here and in later chapters based on: Bleiler 2004; Craddock 2008; Maltin 2007; Martin & Porter 2006; Walker 2004 (or earlier editions). "Bones": Craddock 2008. For additional evidence on the reliability and validity of movie-guide ratings: Boor 1990, 1992; Holbrook 1999, 2005;

Simonton 2002, 2009c; Zickar & Slaughter 1999. More on correlation between Metacritic.com scores and movie-guide ratings: Simonton 2009a; see also Hennig-Thurau, Houston, & Sridhar 2006. Table 2.4 adapted from Table 4 in Simonton 2004c. Figure 2.1 based on raw data previously collected for Simonton 2004c (see also Figure 2 in Plucker, Holden, & Neustadter 2008). Additional evidence that critical evaluations correlate with movie awards: Holbrook & Addis 2008.

Oscar qualified. New reliabilities: Simonton 2007c. New organizations:

1. Chicago Film Critics Association: http://www.chicagofilmcritics.org/
2. Broadcast Film Critics Association: http://www.bfca.org/
3. Online Film Critics Society: http://www.ofcs.org/
4. Producers Guild of America: http://www.producersguild.org/

"Academy does much better" Ginsburgh 2003, 104; cf. Allen & Lincoln 2004.

Voter clustering. Main study: Collins & Hand 2006.

Past history. Main study: Pardoe 2005. See also: Pardoe & Simonton 2008; cf. Bennett & Bennett 1998.

Conclusion. "Fame, we may understand" in Barrett 1876, 179 (originally from essay on Goethe). Oscar predictions: Pardoe 2005. See also: Pardoe & Simonton 2008.

Chapter 3—Story, Sights, Tricks, and Song: What Really Counts?

Oscars best picture, directing, screenplay, and film editing: Simonton 2002.

Creative clusters. Main study: Simonton 2004d. Table 3.1 adapted from Table 1 in Simonton 2004d. For more detailed analysis of collaborative relations: Ferriani, Corrado & Boschetti 2005.

Cinematic success. Main study: Simonton 2004d.

Correlation: What goes with what? Table 3.2 constructed from coefficients reported in text of Simonton 2004d.

Regression: What predicts what? Table 3.2 constructed from the standardized partial regression coefficients reported in text of Simonton 2004d. All "regression coefficients" discussed in this book will be the standardized partial regression coefficients or so-called "betas" (β's). See also Simonton 2009a. For an alternative approach: Ginsburgh & Weyers 2006.

Collaborative creativity. Consumer priorities: e.g., Linton & Petrovich 1988. The main results reported in this section were originally based on a 2006 manuscript that Cattani & Ferriani had submitted for publication to

Organization Science. The manuscript subsequently went through extensive revision and resubmission until it eventually ended up being split into two different articles, one accepted for publication in *Organization Science* (Cattani & Ferriani 2008) and the other a working paper (Cattani & Ferriani 2007). With the exception of the repeated ties measure (and the introduction of certain control variables in later versions), the overlap among the three manuscripts is substantial. The main substantive difference is that the final version of the *Organization Science* article no longer contains the repeated ties variable.

Linear effects: More is better. Individual creative freedom: Cattani & Ferriani 2007, 2008. For changes in creative freedom: Faulkner & Anderson 1987; Baker & Faulkner 1991. Team quality: Cattani & Ferriani 2007, 2008.

Curvilinear effects: Not too much nor too little. Coreness: Cattani & Ferriani 2007, 2008. Repeated ties: Cattani & Ferriani 2007. For more on collaborative ties: Ferriani, Corrado & Boschetti 2005. Figure 3.1 constructed from results reported in Cattani & Ferriani 2007.

Chapter 4—Rave Reviews, Movie Awards, and Box Office Bucks: Which Doesn't Belong?

Production costs mainstream film: Simonton 2005a. "We all make mistakes ..." Wiley & Bona 1993, 120.

Film as art versus movies as business. Main study: Simonton 2005a; see also follow-up Simonton 2009a. Sampling strategy: Simonton 2004c, 2004d. Correlation between Metacritic and RottonTomatoes: Plucker, Holden, & Neustadter 2008; see also Hennig-Thurau, Houston, & Sridhar 2006. Tables 4.1-4.3 modified from Tables 1.3 in Simonton 2005a.

Comparisons and contrasts. Recent reviews: Hadida 2008; Simonton 2009b. Contradictory findings by same investigator: e.g., Litman 1983; Litman & Kohl 1989; Litman & Ahn 1998. Single year: e.g., Holbrook & Addis 2008. Samples based on films nominated for a major award: Simonton 2002; Sommers 1983-1984. Receiving a certain number of critical reviews: Eliashberg & Shugan 1997. Movie stars: Wallace, Seigerman, & Holbrook 1993. Box office earnings: Chang & Ki 2005; Dodds & Holbrook 1988; Simonet 1980; Smith & Smith 1986. Using random sample: Basuroy, Chatterjee, & Ravid, 2003. Whether or not to include foreign-language films, documentaries, and animations: Chang & Ki 2005; Simonoff & Sparrow 2000; Simonton 2007c. Different empirical outcomes depending on genre: Simonton 2007c. Movie stars defined as award winners: Basuroy,

Chatterjee, & Ravid 2003; Delmestri, Montanari, & Usai 2005. According to moviegoer surveys: Canterbery & Marvasti 2001. Financial performance of recent films: Chang & Ki 2005; Chisholm 2004; Hennig-Thurau, Houston, & Sridhar 2006; Litman 1983. Total prior films: Chang & Ki 2005. "100 powerful," or "bankable" or "marquee value," or "A" and "A+" list performers: De Vany & Walls 1999; Kindem 1982. Different outcomes using distinct techniques: Walls 2005a; cf. Terry, Butler, & De'Armond 2005.

Budget. Positive association with box office: e.g., Basuroy, Chatterjee, & Ravid 2003; Chang & Ki 2005; De Vany & Walls 1999; Hadida 2009; Hennig-Thurau, Houston, & Sridhar 2006; Jansen 2005; Holbrook & Addis 2008; Lampel & Shamsie 2000; Litman 1982; Litman & Ahn 1998; Litman & Kohl 1989; Simonton 2005b, 2009a; Sochay 1994; Terry, Butler, & De'Armond 2005; Walls 2005a, 2005c; Wyatt 1994. Profits: e.g., De Vany & Walls 1999; Sedgwick & Pokorny 1999.

Making a profit? $R^2 = .118$: De Vany & Walls 1999. Buck spent less than half buck earned: Litman 1982; Litman & Ahn 1998; Litman & Kohl 1989; cf. Prag & Casavant 1994. Trump: Trump 1987. Backward-J function: Litman & Ahn 1998. Third of big budget films lose: Sedgwick & Pokorny 1999. "In fact, of any 10 major" in Vogel 1998, 31. 78th percentile: De Vany & Walls 1999, 2004. 6% earns 80%: De Vany & Walls 2004. Average gross exceeds average cost: Prag & Casavant 1994; Simonton 2005a.

Reducing the risk? "Heavy spending" De Vany & Walls 1999, 308. For producer/director effects: Hadida 2009. "If a star is paid": Walls 2005b, 185. "Curse of the superstar": De Vany & Walls 2004, 1035. Stars positive effect: Canterbery & Marvasti 2001; Faulkner & Anderson 1987; Hadida 2009; Kindem 1982; Litman & Kohl 1989; Sochay 1994; Wallace, Seigerman, & Holbrook 1993; Sawhney & Eliasberg 1996; Wyatt 1994. Stars no effect: Ainslie, Drèze & Zufryden 2005; Delmestri, Montanari, & Usai 2005; De Silva 1998; De Vany & Walls 1999, 2004; Litman 1983; Litman & Ahn 1998; McKenzie 2009; Prag & Casavant 1994; Smith & Smith 1986; cf. Reddy, Swaminathan, & Motley 1998 (for parallel findings involving Broadway shows). Stars negative effect: Chang & Ki, 2005; Simonet 1977. Star power uncertain: De Vany & Walls 1999. Star on medium-budget film: Pokorny & Sedgwick 2001; Sedgwick & Pokorny 1999. Not all stars have effect: De Vany & Walls 1999. Effect unstable over time: Wallace, Seigerman, & Holbrook 1993. Stardom vs. talent: Adler 1985; see also Chung & Cox 1994; Rosen 1981.

Critics. Additional findings not in Tables 4.1 and 4.2: Simonton 2005a; see also Simonton 2005b, 2009a. More critic-budget negative correlations: Holbrook & Addis 2008; Lampel & Shamsie 2000. Complexities associated with film critics: Hsu 2006.

Film reviews during theatrical run. Critics positive relation with box office: Collins, Hand & Snell 2002; Jansen 2005; Lampel & Shamsie 2000; Litman 1983; Litman & Kohl 1989; McKenzie 2009; Meyer et al. 2001; Plucker, Holden, & Neustadter 2008; Sawhney & Eliasberg 1996; Simonton 2009a; Sochay 1994; Terry, Butler, & De'Armond 2005; Wyatt 1994; cf. Reddy, Swaminathan, & Motley 1998 (for parallel findings for Broadway shows). Critics no relation: Delmestri, Montanari, & Usai 2005; Reinstein & Snyder 2005. Critics negative relation: Hirschman & Pieros 1985; Simonton 2005a. Critics mixed relation: Hennig-Thurau, Houston, & Sridhar 2006. Critics predict gross but not first weekend: Chang & Ki 2005. Influencers versus predictors: Basuroy, Chatterjee, & Ravid 2003; Chang & Ki 2005; Eliashberg & Shugan 1997. Negative versus positive reviews: Basuroy, Chatterjee, & Ravid 2003. Interaction effects: Basuroy, Chatterjee, & Ravid 2003; cf. d'Astous & Touil 1999; Levin, Levin & Heath 1997. Budget and stars: Basuroy, Chatterjee, & Ravid 2003; see also Desai & Basuroy 2005.

Film reviews after video/DVD release. Movie-guide ratings and financial performance positively related: Hennig-Thurau, Houston, & Sridhar 2006; Prag & Casavant 1994; Simonton 2005b; cf. Simonton 2009a. U-shaped relation: Wallace, Seigerman, & Holbrook 1993. "It appears that a bad movie" Wallace, Seigerman, & Holbrook 1993, 11.

Awards. Positive relation between nominations/awards and box office: Dodds & Holbrook 1988; Gemser, Leenders & Wijnberg 2008; Hadida 2009; Litman & Ahn 1998; Nelson, Donihue, Waldman, & Wheaton 2001; Simonton 2005b, 2009a; Sochay 1994; Sommers 1983-1984; Terry, Butler, & De'Armond 2005; see also Taylor 1974; but see Hirschman & Pieros 1985. Mixed together: Gemser, Leenders & Wijnberg 2008; Hadida 2009. Temporal instability: Smith & Smith 1986. Major versus minor distributors: Gemser, Leenders & Wijnberg 2008. Nominations versus awards: Deuchert, Adjamah, & Pauly 2005; see also Wyatt 1994; but see Gemser, Leenders & Wijnberg 2008; Ginsburgh, 2003; Nelson, Donihue, Waldman, & Wheaton 2001; cf. Tony awards and Broadway productions: Boyle & Chiou 2009.

The big problem with box office performance. Popular appeal versus expert judgments: Holbrook 1999; see also Wanderer 1970; cf. Austin 1983; Holbrook 2005. Critic-audience correlation: Chang & Ki 2005; see also Holbrook 2005; Plucker et al. 2009. Consumer differences: Austin 1983; De Silva 1998; Holbrook & Schindler 1994. High consumer-critic agreement but low agreement with popular appeal: Holbrook 2005; see also Hennig-Thurau, Houston, & Sridhar 2006; Holbrook & Addis 2008.

Distribution. Major distributor: Litman, 1983; Litman & Kohl, 1989; Wyatt 1994; cf. Chang & Ki 2005; Jansen 2005. Variation: Litman &

Ahn 1998. Seasonal market: Chang & Ki 2005; Litman & Ahn 1998; Litman & Kohl 1989; Sochay 1994; Wyatt 1994; but see Terry, Butler, & De'Armond 2005. Wide release: De Vany & Walls 1999; Gemser, Leenders & Wijnberg 2008; Lampel & Shamsie 2000; Litman & Ahn 1998; Litman & Kohl 1989; Neelamegham & Chintagunta 1999; Simonton 2005b, 2009a; Terry, Butler, & De'Armond 2005; see also Jedidi, Krider, & Weinberg 1998; cf. Radas & Shugan 1998. Competition: Ainslie, Drèze & Zufryden 2005; De Vany & Walls 1997; Krider & Weinberg 1998; Litman & Ahn 1998; Litman & Kohl 1989; Sochay 1994; see also Jedidi, Krider, & Weinberg 1998.

Promotion. Advertising: Prag & Casavant 1994; see also De Silva 1998; Gemser, Leenders & Wijnberg 2008; Hennig-Thurau, Houston, & Sridhar 2006; McKenzie 2009; Wyatt 1994; Zufryden 1996, 2000; cf. Reddy, Swaminathan, & Motley 1998 (for parallel findings involving Broadway shows). High concept: Wyatt 1994. Specific examples: Heitmueller 2006. High concept makes money: Wyatt 1994.

Exhibition. Word of mouth: De Silva 1998; cf. Liu 2006 (actually click of mouse). Positive feedback loop: Duan, Gu, & Whinston 2008. Information cascades: De Vany & Lee 2001; see also Hand 2001; cf. Maddison 2004. "A positive information cascade" Albert 1998, 252. Randomness: De Vany & Lee 2001.

Chapter 5—The Script: Does the Narrative's Nature Matter?

Movie guides that ignore writers: Bleiler 2004; Maltin 2007; Martin & Porter 2006.

Genres: Financial performance. Story type: De Silva 1998. Comedies, romances, sci-fi, fantasy, and horror films: Gemser, Leenders & Wijnberg 2008; Litman 1982; Litman & Kohl 1989; Simonton 2005b; Sochay 1994; Wyatt 1994. Irrelevant genres: Walls 2005b. Comedies: Lee 2006. Drama: Chang & Ki, 2005; Collins, Hand & Snell 2002; Litman & Kohl, 1989; Simonton, 2005b; Sochay, 1994; cf. Walls 2005b. Percentage of dramas: Simonton 2004d. Screens, first weekend, and gross: Simonton 2004c, 2004d; see also Chang & Ki 2005; Litman & Kohl 1989; Prag & Casavant 1994; Simonoff & Sparrow 2000; cf. Sochay 1994. Consumer preferences: Holbrook 1999; see also Anast 1967. Production costs and drama: Simonton 2005b.

Genres: Movie awards. All results in this section from Simonton 2005b; see also Simonton 2009a.

Genres: Critical evaluations. Positive association with drama: Simonton 2005b; see also Holbrook 1999; Simonton 2009a. Shakespeare's tragedies: Simonton 1986. Greek playwrights: Simonton 1983. Globe drama more predictive of Oscars: Pardoe & Simonton 2008. Musicals: Simonton 2005b.

Runtime. Average: Simonton 2004d, 2005b.

Runtime: Financial performance. Length and cost: Simonton 2005b, 2009a. Consumers and long films: Holbrook 1999. Screens, first weekend, and gross: Simonton 2005b.

Runtime: Movie awards. All from Simonton 2005b; see also Simonton 2009a.

Runtime: Critical evaluations. Again Simonton 2005b; see also Simonton 2009a.

MPAA ratings: Financial performance. Consumer preferences: Holbrook 1999. Ratings and box office: Chang & Ki 2005; Collins, Hand & Snell 2002; De Vany & Walls 2002; Medved 1992; Ravid 1999; Simonoff & Sparrow 2000; Simonton 2005b; 2009a; Sawhney & Eliasberg 1996; cf. Delmestri, Montanari, & Usai 2005; Litman & Ahn 1998; Terry, Butler, & De'Armond 2005; Walls 2005a. $12 million: Terry, Butler, & De'Armond 2005. Relative frequencies: Chang & Ki 2005; De Vany & Walls 1999; Wyatt 1994.

MPAA ratings: Movie awards. Main findings: Simonton 2005b; cf. Simonton 2009a.

MPAA ratings: Critical evaluations. Positive relation with R rating: Simonton 2005b; see also Holbrook 1999. No relation with R rating: Simonton 2009a.

Sex and violence: Financial performance. Sex doesn't sell (and other content): Cerridwen & Simonton 2009; see also Thompson and Yokota 2004. Sex and violence: Ravid & Basuroy 2004.

Sex and violence: Movie awards. Based on: Cerridwen & Simonton 2009.

Sex and violence: Critical evaluations. Based on: Cerridwen & Simonton 2009; see also Ravid & Basuroy 2004.

Sequels and remakes: Financial performance. Sequels: Basuroy, Chatterjee, & Ravid 2003; Chang & Ki 2005; Collins, Hand & Snell 2002; De Vany & Walls 1999; Litman & Kohl 1989; McKenzie 2009; Prag & Casavant 1994; Ravid 1999; Simonton 2005b, 2009a; Sawhney & Eliasberg 1996; Terry, Butler, & De'Armond 2005; Wyatt 1994; for rare exceptions see Litman 1982; Sochay 1994. Sequels cost more: Simonton 2005b, 2009a. Remakes: Simonton 2005b; cf. Simonton 2009a.

Sequels and remakes: Movie awards. Results: Simonton 2005b; cf. Simonton 2009a.

Sequels and remakes: Critical evaluations. Results: Simonton 2005b. Because of the small sample size, the results were not statistically significant for the Metacritic ratings, but I have since increased the sample size four-fold, thereby obtaining significant negative correlations, albeit not as strong as for the movie-guide ratings (see also Simonton 2009a).

True stories and biopics: Financial performance. Results: Simonton 2005b; see also Simonton 2009a.

True stories and biopics: Movie awards. Results: Simonton 2005b.

True stories and biopics: Critical evaluations. Results: Simonton 2005b, plus an unpublished replication and extension of the findings on a much larger sample using the same methods; cf. Simonton 2009a.

Adaptations. Frequency: Simonton 2005b.

Adaptations: Financial performance. Results: Simonton 2005b; but Chang & Ki (2005) found that adaptations were negatively correlated with number of screens regardless of original source; see also Simonton 2009a.

Adaptations: Movie awards. Results: Simonton 2005b; cf. Simonton 2009a.

Adaptations: Critical evaluations. Results: Simonton 2005b; cf. Simonton 2009a.

Unanswered questions. Table 5.1 original with this book. R^2s: Simonton 2005b; cf. Simonton 2009a.

Indirect content analyses. Plays: Simonton 1983; Simonton 1986. Novels: Harvey 1953 (quote on page 108). Short stories: Martindale et al. 1988. Opera: Simonton 2000. *Hamlet* vs. *The Merry Wives of Windsor*: Simonton 1986.

Direct content analyses. Protagonists: Beckwith 2007; later published as Beckwith 2009. Storylines: Eliashberg, Hui, & Zhang 2007.

Postscript: What about the writers? Results: Pritzker 2007; see also Pritzker & McGarva 2009. Literary masterpieces: Raskin 1936; Simonton 1975, 2007b. Individual creative freedom: Cattani & Ferriani 2007, 2008. Critical acclaim: Simonton 2005b. Budget and business: Simonton 2005b; cf. Simonton 2009a.

Chapter 6—The Auteur: Are Directors Experts or Artists?

Auteur theory: Blandford, Grant, & Hillier 2001, 16-18. Critical acclaim: Holbrook 1999. Best-picture honors: Simonton 2002, 2004c. AFI top-100: Allen & Lincoln 2004. Prior box-office success versus prior experience directing: Simonet, 1980; cf. Chang & Ki 2005. Null effect of star directors: Litman, 1982; Litman & Ahn, 1998; Sochay, 1994; cf. Chang & Ki 2005; Hadida 2009; Jansen 2005; Litman & Kohl 1989; Wyatt 1994. Vertical ties: Delmestri, Montanari, & Usai 2005. Production head's career course: Miller & Shamsie 2001.

Age and artistic achievement. 1835 study: Quételet 1968/1835. Subsequent investigations: Dennis 1966; Lehman 1953. General conclusions: Simonton 1988; cf. Lindauer 2003. Figure 6.1: from $p(t) = 1210(e^{-.04t} - e^{-.05t})$ [where $p(t)$ is creative productivity and t is career age], an equation adapted from Simonton 1984, 1997. Edison: Simonton 2004b. Peak in 30s: Lehman 1953. Classical composers: Simonton 1980, 1991. *Hamlet*: Simonton 1986. Expertise acquisition: Ericsson 1996; see also Ericsson, Charness, Feltovich & Hoffman 2006. Learning curve: Ohlsson 1992. Swan-song phenomenon: Simonton 1989; see also Lindauer 2003.

Film polls. Main study: Lehman 1941. Artists, scientists, and scholars: Dennis 1966; cf. Lindauer 2003.

Movie awards. Direction predicts best picture: Kaplan 2006; Pardoe & Simonton 2008; Simonton 2002. Correlation of .70 calculated from database collected for Simonton 2004c, 2004d, 2005b.

Critical evaluations. Main study: Zickar & Slaughter 1999.

Creative life cycles. Main study: Galenson & Kotin 2005. Figure 6.2 original with this book. Modern painters: Galenson 2001. Artists in general: Galenson 2005. Economists: Weisberg & Galenson 2005. Criticisms of Galenson's theory: Simonton 2007b.

Concluding comments. Theoretical model: Simonton 1997. Poets vs. novelists: Simonton 1975, 1989, 2007b. Auteur list: http://en.wikipedia.org/wiki/List_of_auteurs.

Chapter 7—The Stars: Sexism in Cinema?

Income. Female cast and crew proportions and production costs: Cerridwen & Simonton 2009. Women reveal more of bodies: Greenberg, Siemicki, Dorfman, Heeter, Stanley, Soderman, & Linsangan 1993. Top 12 in 2003: E! Online 2003. Actors hired to increase gross: Chisholm 2004. Blockbusters: Beckwith 2007; later published as Beckwith 2009. Sequels: Chisholm 2004. Films 1956-1988: Wallace, Seigerman, & Holbrook 1993. Films 1915-1939: Lehman 1941. Films 1957, 1983 vs. the 1930s: Levy 1989. For parallel gender differences for writers: Bielby & Bielby 1992, 1996.

Origins. 129 movie stars: Levy 1989. Women writers: Simonton 1992.

Progressions. Male dominance: Cerridwen & Simonton 2009. Abbreviated careers: Levy 1989. 23-27 vs. 30-34: Lehman 1941. Best performances: Lehman 1941. Double jeopardy: Lincoln & Allen 2004. Oscar ages: Markson & Taylor 1993. Oscar nominees and Emmy winners: Gilberg & Hines 2000. Controlling for age career onset: Lincoln 2004, 2007. 2003 Oscar ceremony: Lincoln & Allen 2004.

Award-winning films. Main study: Levy 1990. More famous men than women: Murray 2003.

Money-making movies. Main study: Bazzini, McIntosh, Smith, Cook, & Harris 1997. Beauty and goodness: Smith, McIntosh, & Bazzini 1999.

Critical acclaim. Oscars: Simonton 2002. Follow-up: Simonton 2004a.

Best picture honors. Main study: Simonton 2004a. Best picture: Beckwith 2007; later published as Beckwith 2009. Oscars and money: Deuchert, Adjamah, & Pauly 2005.

Conclusions. Trend in effect: Simonton 2004a (Figure 7.1 adapted from Figure 1).

Chapter 8—Music: Is Silence Golden?

The case for music. Mood, emotion, or arousal: Ellis & Simons2005; Pfaus, Myronuk, & Jacobs 1986. Cognitive understanding: Boltz 2001, 2004; Bullerjahn & Güldenring 1994; Vitouch 2001. Temporal structures: Cohen 2001, 2002; Rosar 1994. Visual perception: Iwamiya 1994; Thompson, Russo, & Sinclair 1994; see also Lipscomb & Kendall 1994; Marshall & Cohen 1988.

The case against music. Oscar films: Simonton 2002; see also Simonton 2004a, 2009a. Creative clusters: Simonton 2004d. Multiple criteria: Simonton 2005a; see also Simonton 2009a.

Two follow-up studies. Cluster reliabilities: Simonton 2004d.

Inclusive sample (with animated and foreign-language films). Tables 8.1 and 8.2 adapted from Simonton 2007c.

Exclusive sample (without animated and foreign-language films). Table 8.3 adapted from Simonton 2007c.

Cinema composers. Career landmarks: Simonton 1997. Classical composers: Simonton 1991. Two studies: Simonton 2007a. For the record, the author of these studies, namely me, actually likes to listen to "new music" by "modern classical" composers. But it has become an acquired taste. Even classical music radio stations seldom feature recent compositions.

Popular soundtrack composers. Table 8.4 adapted from Table 1 in Simonton 2007a. Multiple regression results: Table 2 in Simonton 2007a. One-hit wonders: Kozbelt 2008.

Oscar-honored composers. Table 8.5 adapted from Table 4 in Simonton 2007a. Additional results: Table 5 in Simonton 2007a.

Chapter 9—Razzies: Is Bad the Opposite of Good?

Negative versus positive assessments: Cacioppo, Gardner, & Berntson 1997. Negative bigger than positive: Baumeister, Bratslavsky, Finkenauer,

& Vohs 2001. Negative more complex: Rozin & Royzman 2001. "Happy families are all alike": Tolstoy 1875-1877/1917, 1)

Four big questions. Main study: Simonton 2007d.

Four big answers. Main study: Simonton 2007d. Tables 9.1-9.5 adapted from Tables 1.5.

The good, the bad and the ugly. "Hailed as the worst movie": Maltin 2007, 1071.

Chapter 10—Epilogue: The Science of Cinema

What don't we know? For reviews of the issues: Eliashberg, Elberse & Leenders 2006; Hadida 2008; Simonton 2009b. Additional discussion on comparing best-picture films: Ginsburgh & Weyers 2006. For study of sleepers: Simonton 2009c. Table 10.1 original in this book. It would be rousing a hornet's nest to mention that there have been extremely few studies of the psychological traits associated with those who contribute to the cinematic product: cf. Domino 1974; Pagel, Kwiatkowski, & Broyles 1999.

References

Acheson, K., & Maule, C. J. (1994). Understanding Hollywood's organization and continuing success. *Journal of Cultural Economics*, 18, 271–300.

Adler, M. (1985). Stardom and talent. *American Economic Review*, 75, 208–212.

Ainslie, A., Drèze, X., & Zufryden, F. (2005). Modeling movie life cycles and market share. *Marketing Science*, 24, 508–517.

Albert, S. (1998). Movie stars and the distribution of financially successful films in the motion picture industry. *Journal of Cultural Economics*, 22, 249–270.

Allen, P. A., & Lincoln, A. E. (2004). Critical discourse and the cultural consecration of American films. *Social Forces*, 82, 871–894.

American Film Institute. (2000). *AFI's 100 years ... 100 movies: America's greatest movies*. [DVD]. Los Angeles: American Film Institute.

Anast, P. (1967). Differential movie appeals as correlates of attendance. *Journalism Quarterly*, 44, 86–90.

Arnheim, R. (1957). *Film as art*. Berkeley: University of California Press.

Austin, B. (1983). Critics' and consumers' evaluation of motion pictures: A longitudinal test of the taste culture and elite hypotheses. *Journal of Popular Film and Television*, 10, 157–167.

Baker, W. E., & Faulkner, R. R. (1991). Role as resource in the Hollywood film industry. *American Journal of Sociology*, 97, 279–309.

Bakker, G. (2005). The decline and fall of the European film industry: Sunk costs, market size, and market structure, 1890–1927. *Economic History Review*, 58, 310–351.

Barrett, E. (Ed.). (1876). *The Carlyle anthology*. New York: Holt.

Basuroy, S., Chatterjee, S., & Ravid, S. A. (2003). How critical are critical reviews? The box office effects of film critics, star power, and budgets. *Journal of Marketing*, 67, 103–117.

Baumann, S. (2001). Intellectualization and art world development: Film in the United States. *American Sociological Review*, 66, 404–426.

Baumeister, R. R., Bratslavsky, E., Finkenauer, C., & Vohs, K. D. (2001). Bad is stronger than good. *Review of General Psychology*, 5, 323–370.

Bazzini, D. G., McIntosh, W. D., Smith, S. M., Cook, S., & Harris, C. (1997). The aging women in popular film: Underrepresented, unattractive, unfriendly, and unintelligent. *Sex Roles*, 36, 531–543.

Beckwith, D. C. (2007). *Personal values of protagonists in best pictures and block-busters: 1996–2005.* Unpublished doctoral dissertation, Saybrook Graduate School and Research Center.

Beckwith, D. C. (2009). Values of protagonists in best pictures and blockbusters: Implications for marketing. *Psychology and Marketing*, 26, 445–469.

Bennett, K. L., & Bennett, J. M. (1998). And the winner is: A statistical analysis of the best actor and actress Academy Awards. *Stats*, 23, 10–17.

Bielby, W. T., & Bielby, D. D. (1992). Cumulative versus continuous disadvantage in an unstructured labor market: Gender differences in the careers of television writers. *Work and Occupations*, 19, 366–386.

Bielby, D. D., & Bielby, W. T. (1996). Women and men in film: Gender inequality among writers in a culture industry. *Gender and Society*, 10, 248–270.

Blandford, S., Grant, B. K., & Hillier, J. (2001). *The film studies dictionary*. New York: Oxford University Press.

Bleiler, D. (Ed.). (2004). *TLA film and video guide: The discerning film lover's guide 2005*. New York: St. Martin's/Griffin.

Boltz, M. G. (2001). Musical soundtracks as a schematic influence on the cognitive processing of filmed events. *Music Perception*, 18, 427–454.

Boltz, M. G. (2004). The cognitive processing of film and musical soundtracks. *Memory & Cognition*, 32, 1194–1205.

Boor, M. (1990). Reliability of ratings of movies by professional movie critics. *Psychological Reports*, 67, 243–257.

Boor, M. (1992). Relationships among ratings of motion pictures by viewers and six professional movie critics. *Psychological Reports*, 70, 1011–1021.

Boyle, M., & Chiou, L. (2009). Broadway productions and the value of a Tony award. *Journal of Cultural Economics*, 33, 49–68.

Bullerjahn, C. & Güldenring, M. (1994). An empirical investigation of effects of film music using qualitative content analysis. *Psychomusicology*, 13, 99–118.

Canterbery, E. R., & Marvasti, A. (2001). The U.S. motion pictures industry: An empirical approach. *Review of Industrial Organization*, 19, 81–98.

Cacioppo, J. T., Gardner, W. L., & Berntson, G. G. (1997). Beyond bipolar conceptualizations and measures: The case of attitudes and evaluative space. *Personality and Social Psychology Review*, 1, 3–25.

Cattani, G., & Ferriani, S. (2007). A relational perspective on individual creative performance: Social networks and cinematic achievements in the Hollywood film industry, Working Paper, Stern School of Business, New York University.

Cattani, G., & Ferriani, S. (2008). A core/periphery perspective on individual creative performance: Social networks and cinematic achievements in the Hollywood film industry. *Organization Science*, 19, 824–844.

Cerridwen, A., & Simonton, D. K. (2009). Sex doesn't sell – nor impress: Content, box office, critics, and awards in mainstream cinema. *Psychology of Aesthetics, Creativity, and the Arts*, 3, 200–210.

Chang, B.-H., & Ki, E.-J. (2005). Devising a practical model for predicting theatrical movie success: Focusing on the experience good property. *Journal of Media Economics*, 18, 247–269.

Chisholm, D. C. (2004). Two-part share contracts, risk, and the life cycle of stars: Some empirical results from motion picture contracts. *Journal of Cultural Economics*, 28, 37–56.

Chung, K. H., & Cox, R. A. K. (1994). A stochastic model of superstardom: An application of the Yule distribution. *Review of Economics and Statistics*, 76, 771–775.

Cohen, A. J. (2001). Music as a source of emotion in film. In P. Juslin & J. Sloboda (Eds.), *Music and emotion: Theory and research* (pp. 249–272). New York: Oxford University Press.

Cohen, A. J. (2002). Music cognition and the cognitive psychology of film structure. *Canadian Psychology*, 43, 215–232.

Collins, A., & Hand, C. (2006). Vote clustering in tournaments: What can Oscar tell us? *Creativity Research Journal*, 18, 427–434.

Collins, A., Hand, C., & Snell, M. C. (2002). What makes a blockbuster? Economic analysis of film success in the United Kingdom. *Managerial and Decision Economics*, 23, 343–354.

Craddock, J. (Ed.). (2008). *VideoHound's golden movie retriever 2008*. New York: Gale.

d'Astous, A., & Touil, N. (1999). Consumer evaluations of movies on the basis of critics' judgments. *Psychology & Marketing*, 16, 677–694.

De Silva, I. (1998). Consumer selection of motion pictures. In B. R. Litman (Ed.), *The motion picture mega-industry* (pp. 144–171). Boston: Allyn and Bacon.

De Vany, A. (2004). *Hollywood economics*. London and New York: Routledge.

De Vany, A., & Lee, C. (2001). Quality signals in information cascades and the dynamics of the distribution of motion picture box office revenues. *Journal of Economic Dynamics & Control*, 25, 593–614.

De Vany, A., & Walls, W. D. (1997). The market for motion pictures: Rank, revenue, and survival. *Economic Inquiry*, 35, 783–798.

De Vany, A., & Walls, W. D. (1999). Uncertainty in the movie industry: Does star power reduce the terror of the box office? *Journal of Cultural Economics*, 23, 285–318.

De Vany, A., & Walls, W. D. (2002). Does Hollywood make too many R-rated movies? Risk, stochastic dominance, and the illusion of expectation. *Journal of Business*, 75, 425–451.

De Vany, A., & Walls, W. D. (2004). Motion picture profit, the stable Paretian hypothesis, and the curse of the superstar. *Journal of Economic Dynamics and Control*, 28, 1035–1057.

Delmestri, G., Montanari, F., & Usai, A. (2005). Reputation and strength of ties in predicting commercial success and artistic merit of independents in the Italian feature film industry. *Journal of Management Studies*, 42, 975–1002.

Dennis, W. (1966). Creative productivity between the ages of 20 and 80 years. *Journal of Gerontology*, 21, 1–8.

Desai, K. K., & Basuroy, S. (2005). Interactive influence of genre familiarity, star power, and critics' reviews in the cultural goods industry: The case of motion pictures. *Psychology and Marketing*, 22, 203–223.

Deuchert, E., Adjamah, K., & Pauly, F. (2005). For Oscar glory or Oscar money? Academy Awards and movie success. *Journal of Cultural Economics*, 29, 159–176.

Dodds, J. C., & Holbrook, M. B. (1988). What's an Oscar worth? An empirical estimation of the effect of nominations and awards on movie distribution and revenues. In B. A. Austin (Ed.), *Current research on film: Audiences, economics and law* (Vol. 4, pp. 72–88). Norwood, NJ: Ablex Publishing.

Domino, G. (1974). Assessment of cinematographic creativity. *Journal of Personality and Social Psychology, 30*, 150–154.

Duan, W., Gu, B., & Whinston, A. B. (2008). The dynamics of online word-of-mouth and product sales–An empirical investigation of the movie industry. *Journal of Retailing, 84*, 233–242.

E! Online. http://www.eonline.com/Features/Features/Salaries/index2.html. Accessed on March 26, 2003.

Elberse, A., & Eliashberg, J. (2003). Demand and supply dynamics for sequentially released products in international markets: The case of motion pictures. *Marketing Science, 22*, 329–354.

Eliashberg, J., Elberse, A., & Leenders, M. A. A. M. (2006). The motion picture industry: Critical issues in practice, current research, and new research directions. *Marketing Science, 25*, 638–631.

Eliashberg, J., & Shugan, S. M. (1997). Film critics: Influencers or predictors? *Journal of Marketing, 61*, 68–78.

Eliashberg, J., Hui, S. K., & Zhang, Z. J. (2007). From storyline to box office: A new approach for green-lighting movie scripts. *Management Science, 53*, 881–893.

Ellis, R. J., & Simons, R. F. (2005). The impact of music on subjective and physiological indices of emotion while viewing films. *Psychomusicology, 19*, 15–40.

Ericsson, K. A. (1996). The acquisition of expert performance: An introduction to some of the issues. In K. A. Ericsson (Ed.), *The road to expert performance: Empirical evidence from the arts and sciences, sports, and games* (pp. 1–50). Mahwah, NJ: Erlbaum.

Ericsson, K. A., Charness, N., Feltovich, P. J., & Hoffman, R. R. (Eds.). (2006). *The Cambridge handbook of expertise and expert performance.* New York: Cambridge University Press.

Faulkner, R. R., & Anderson, A. B. (1987). Short-term projects and emergent careers: Evidence from Hollywood. *American Journal of Sociology, 92*, 879–909.

Ferriani, S., Corrado, R., & Boschetti, C. (2005). Organizational learning under organizational impermanence: Collaborative ties in film project firms. *Journal of Management and Governance, 9*, 257–285.

Frey, B. S. (2006). Giving and receiving awards. *Perspectives on Psychological Science, 1*, 377–388.

Galenson, D. W. (2001). *Painting outside the lines: Patterns of creativity in modern art.* Cambridge, MA: Harvard University Press.

Galenson, D. W. (2005). *Old masters and young geniuses: The two life cycles of artistic creativity.* Princeton, NJ: Princeton University Press.

Galenson, D. W., & Kotin, J. (2005). Filming images or filming reality: the life cycles of movie directors from D. W. Griffith to Federico Fellini. Working Paper 11486, National Bureau of Economic Research, accessed from http://papers.nber.org/papers/, January 23, 2006.

Gemser, G., Leenders, M. A. A. M., & Wijnberg, N. M. (2008). Why some awards are more effective signals of quality than others: A study of movie awards. *Journal of Management, 34*, 25–54.

Gilberg, M., & Hines, T. (2000). Male entertainment award winners are older than female winners. *Psychological Reports, 86*, 175–178.

Ginsburgh, V. (2003). Awards, success and aesthetic quality in the arts. *Journal of Economic Perspectives, 17*, 99–111.

Ginsburgh, V., & Weyers, S. A. (1999). On the perceived quality of movies. *Journal of Cultural Economics*, 23, 269–283.

Ginsburgh, V., & Weyers, S. A. (2006). Comparing artistic values: The example of movies. *Empirical Studies of the Arts*, 24, 163–175.

Greenberg, B. S., Siemicki, M., Dorfman, S., et al. (1993). Sex content in R-rated films viewed by adolescents. In B. S. Greenberg, J. D. Brown & N. Buerkel-Rothfuss (Eds.), *Media, sex and the adolescent* (pp. 45–58). Cresshill, NJ: Hampton Press.

Hadida, A. L. (2008). Motion picture performance: A review and research agenda. *International Journal of Management Reviews*, 11, 297–335.

Hadida, A. L. (2009). Commercial success and artistic recognition of motion picture projects. *Journal of Cultural Economics*, DOI: 10.1007/s10824-009-9109-z

Hand, C. (2001). Increasing returns to information: Further evidence from the UK film market. *Applied Economics Letters*, 8, 419–421.

Harvey, J. (1953). The content characteristics of best-selling novels. *Public Opinion Quarterly*, 17, 91–114.

Heitmueller, K. (2006, July 11). Rewind: Sometimes 'high concept' is just plain old awful. Retrieved March 15, 2008 from http://www.mtv.com/movies/news/articles/1535928/story.jhtml.

Hennig-Thurau, T., Houston, M. B., & Sridhar, S. (2006). Can good marketing carry a bad product? Evidence from the motion picture industry. *Marketing Letters*, 17, 205–219.

Hirschman, E. C, & Pieros, A., Jr. (1985). Relationships among indicators of success in Broadway plays and motion pictures. *Journal of Cultural Economics*, 9, 35–63.

Holbrook, M. B. (1999). Popular appeal versus expert judgments of motion pictures. *Journal of Consumer Research*, 26, 144–155.

Holbrook, M. B. (2005). The role of ordinary evaluations in the market for popular culture: Do consumers have "good taste"? *Marketing Letters*, 16, 75–86.

Holbrook, M. B., & Addis, M. (2008). Art versus commerce in the movie industry: A two-path model of motion-picture success. *Journal of Cultural Economics*, 32, 87–107.

Holbrook, M. B., & Schindler, R. M. (1994). Age, sex, and attitude toward the past as predictors of consumers' aesthetic tastes for cultural products. *Journal of Marketing Research*, 31, 412–422.

Holden, A. (1993). *Behind the Oscar: The secret history of the Academy Awards.* New York: Simon & Schuster.

Hsu, G. (2006). Evaluative schemas and the attention of critics in the US film industry. *Industrial and Corporate Change*, 15, 467–496.

Internet Movie Database (n.d.). Accessed from http://www.imdb.com

Ilies, R., Gerhardt, M. W., & Le, H. (2004). Individual differences in leadership emergence: Integrating meta-analytic findings and behavioral genetics estimates. *International Journal of Selection and Assessment*, 12, 207–219.

Iwamiya, S. (1994). Interactions between auditory and visual processing when listening to music in an audio-visual context: I. Matching II. Audio quality. *Psychomusicology*, 13, 133–154.

Jansen, C. (2005). The performance of German motion pictures, profits and subsidies: Some empirical evidence. *Journal of Cultural Economics*, 29, 191–212.

Jayakar, K. P., & Waterman, D. (2000). The economics of American theatrical movie exports: An empirical analysis. *Journal of Media Economics*, 13, 153–169.

Jedidi, K., Krider, R. E., & Weinberg, C. B. (1998). Clustering at the movies. *Marketing Letters*, 9, 393–405.

Kaplan, D. (2006). And the Oscar goes to ... a logistic regression model for predicting Academy Award results. *Journal of Applied Economics and Policy*, 25, 23–41.

Kindem, G. (1982). Hollywood's movie star system: A historical overview. In G. Kindem (Ed.), *The American movie industry: The business of motion pictures* (pp. 79–94). Carbondale, IL: Southern Illinois University Press.

Kozbelt, A. (2008). One-hit wonders in classical music: Evidence and (partial) explanations for an early career peak. *Creativity Research Journal*, 20, 179–195.

Krider, R. E., Li, T., Liu, Y., & Weinberg, C. B. (2005). The lead-lag puzzle of demand and distribution: A graphical method applied to movies. *Marketing Science*, 24, 635–645.

Krider, R. E., & Weinberg, C. B. (1998). Competitive dynamics and the introduction of new products: The motion picture timing game. *Journal of Marketing Research*, 35, 1–15.

Lampel, J., & Shamsie, J. (2000). Critical push: Strategies for creating momentum in the motion picture industry. *Journal of Management*, 26, 233–257.

Lee, F. L. F. (2006). Cultural discount and cross-culture predictability: Examining the box office performance of American movies in Hong Kong. *Journal of Media Economics*, 19, 259–278.

Lehman, H. C. (1941). The chronological ages of some recipients of large annual incomes. *Social Forces*, 20, 196–206.

Lehman, H. C. (1953). *Age and achievement.* Princeton, NJ: Princeton University Press.

Levin, A. M., Levin, I. P., & Heath, C. E. (1997). Movie stars and authors as brand names: Measuring brand equity in experiential products. *Advances in Consumer Research*, 24, 175–181.

Levy, E. (1989). The democratic elite: America's movie stars. *Qualitative Sociology*, 12, 29–54.

Levy, E. (1990). Stage, sex, and suffering: Images of women in American films. *Empirical Studies of the Arts*, 8, 53–76.

Lincoln, A. E. (2004). Sex and experience in the Academy Award nomination process. *Psychological Reports*, 95, 589–592.

Lincoln, A. E. (2007). Cultural honors and career events: Re-conceptualizing prizes in the field of cultural production. *Cultural Trends*, 16, 3–15.

Lincoln, A. E., & Allen, M. P. (2004). Double jeopardy in Hollywood: Age and gender in the careers of film actors, 1926–1999. *Sociological Forum*, 19, 611–631.

Lindauer, M. S. (2003). *Aging, creativity, and art: A positive perspective on late-life development.* New York: Kluwer Academic/Plenum Publishers.

Linton, J. M., & Petrovich, J. A. (1988). The application of the consumer information acquisition approach to movie selection: An exploratory study. *Current Research in Film*, 4, 24–45.

Lipscomb, S. D., & Kendall, R. A. (1994). Perceptual judgement of the relationship between musical and visual components in film. *Psychomusicology*, 13, 60–98.

Litman, B. R. (1983). Predicting success of theatrical movies: An empirical study. *Journal of Popular Culture*, 16, 159–175.

Litman, B. R., & Ahn, H. (1998). Predicting financial success of motion pictures: The early '90s experience. In B. R. Litman (Ed.), *The motion picture mega-industry* (pp. 172–197). Boston: Allyn and Bacon.

Litman, B. R., & Kohl, L. S. (1989). Predicting financial success of motion pictures: The '80s experience. *Journal of Media Economics*, 2, 35–50.

Liu, Y. (2006). Word of mouth for movies: Its dynamics and impact on box office revenue. *Journal of Marketing*, 70, 74–89.

McKenzie, J. (2009). Revealed word-of-mouth demand and adaptive supply: Survival of motion pictures at the Australian box office. *Journal of Cultural Economics*, 33, 279–299.

Murray, C. (2003). *Human accomplishment: The pursuit of excellence in the arts and sciences, 800 B.C. to 1950*. New York: HarperCollins.

Maddison, D. (2004). Increasing returns to information and the survival of Broadway theatre productions. *Applied Economics Letters*, 11 (10), 1350–4851.

Maltin, L. (Ed.). (2007). *Leonard Maltin's 2008 movie & video guide*. New York: Signet.

Markson, E. W., & Taylor, C. A. (1993). Real versus reel world: Older women and the Academy Awards. *Women and Therapy*, 14, 157–172.

Marshall, S. K., & Cohen, A. J. (1988). Effects of musical soundtracks on attitudes toward animated geometric figures. *Music Perception*, 6, 95–112.

Martin, M., & Porter, M. (2006). *Video movie guide 2007*. New York: Ballantine.

Martindale, C., Brewer, W. F., Helson, R., et al. (1988). Structure, theme, style, and reader response in Hungarian and American short stories. In C. Martindale (Ed.), *Psychological approaches to the study of literary narratives* (pp. 267–289). Hamburg: Buske.

Marvasti, A., & Canterbery, E. R. (2005). Cultural and other barriers to motion pictures trade. *Economic Inquiry*, 43, 39–54.

Medved, M. (1992). *Hollywood vs. America: Popular culture and the war on traditional values* (1st ed). New York: HarperCollins.

Meyer, G. J., Finn, S. E., Eyde, L. D., et al. (2001). Psychological testing and psychological assessment: A review of evidence and issues. *American Psychologist*, 56, 128–165.

Miller, D., & Shamsie, J. (2001). Learning across the life cycle: Experimentation and performance among the Hollywood studio heads. *Strategic Management Journal*, 22, 725–745.

Muünsterberg, H. (1916). *The photoplay: A psychological study*. New York: Appleton.

Neelamegham, R., & Chintagunta, P. (1999). A Bayesian model to forecast new product performance in domestic and international markets. *Marketing Science*, 18, 115–136.

Nelson, R. A., Donihue, M. R., Waldman, D. M., & Wheaton, C. (2001). What's an Oscar worth? *Economic Inquiry*, 39, 1–16.

Ohlsson, S. (1992). The learning curve for writing books: Evidence from Professor Asimov. *Psychological Science*, 3, 380–382.

Pagel, J. F., Kwiatkowski, C., & Broyles, K E. (1999). Dream use in film making. *Dreaming*, 9, 247–256.

Pardoe, I. (2005). Just how predictable are the Oscars? *Chance*, 18, 32–39.

Pardoe, I., & Simonton, D. K. (2008). Applying discrete choice models to predict Academy Award winners. *Journal of the Royal Statistical Society: Series A (Statistics in Society)*, 171, 375–394.

Peary, D. (1993). *Alternate Oscars: One critic's defiant choices for best picture, actor, and actress from 1927 to the present*. New York: Delta.

Pfaus, J. G., Myronuk, L. D., & Jacobs, W. J. (1986). Soundtrack contents and depicted sexual violence. *Archives of Sexual Behavior*, 15, 231–237.

Plucker, J. A., Holden, J., & Neustadter, D. (2008). The criterion problem and creativity in film: Psychometric characteristics of various measures. *Psychology of Aesthetics, Creativity, and the Arts*, 2, 190–196.

Plucker, J. A., Kaufman, J. C., Temple, J. S., & Qian, M. (2009). Do experts and novices evaluate movies the same way? *Psychology and Marketing*, 26, 470–478.

Pokorny, M., & Sedgwick, J. (2001). Stardom and the profitability of film making: Warner Bros. in the 1930s. *Journal of Cultural Economics*, 25, 157–184.

Prag, J., & Casavant, J. (1994). An empirical study of the determinants of revenues and marketing expenditures in the motion picture industry. *Journal of Cultural Economics*, 18, 217–235.

Pritzker, S. R. (2007, August). Characteristics of eminent screenwriters. In S. R. Pritzker (Chair), *Creativity and the movies*. Symposium conducted at the meeting of the American Psychological Association, San Francisco, CA.

Pritzker, S. R., & McGarva, D. J. (2009). Characteristics of eminent screenwriters: Who *are* those guys? In S. B. Kaufman & J. C. Kaufman (Eds.), *The psychology of creative writing* (pp. 57–59). New York: Cambridge University Press.

Quételet, A. (1968). *A treatise on man and the development of his faculties*. New York: Franklin. (Reprint of 1842 Edinburgh translation of 1835 French original)

Radas, S., & Shugan, S. M. (1998). Seasonal marketing and timing new product introductions. *Journal of Marketing Research*, 35, 296–315.

Raskin, E. A. (1936). Comparison of scientific and literary ability: A biographical study of eminent scientists and men of letters of the nineteenth century. *Journal of Abnormal and Social Psychology*, 31, 20–35.

Ravid, S. A. (1999). Information, blockbusters, and stars: A study of the film industry. *Journal of Business*, 72, 463–492.

Ravid, S. A., & Basuroy, S. (2004). Managerial objectives, the R-rating puzzle, and the production of violent films. *Journal of Business*, 77, S155–S192.

Reddy, S. K., Swaminathan, V., & Motley, C. M. (1998). Exploring the determinants of Broadway show success. *Journal of Marketing Research*, 35, 370–383.

Reinstein, D. A., & Snyder, C. M. (2005). Influence of expert reviews on consumer demand for experience goods: A case study of movie critics. *Journal of Industrial Economics*, 53, 27–51.

Rosar, W. H. (1994). Film music and Heinz Werner's theory of physiognomic perception. *Psychomusicology*, 13, 154–165.

Rosen, S. (1981). The economics of superstars. *American Economic Review*, 71, 845–858.

Rozin, P. & Royzman, E. B. (2001). Negativity bias, negativity dominance, and contagion. *Personality and Social Psychology Review*, 5, 296–320.

Sawhney, M. S., & Eliasberg, J. (1996). A parsimonious model for forecasting gross box-office revenues of motion pictures. *Marketing Science*, 15, 113–131.

Sedgwick, J., & Pokorny, M. (1999). Movie stars and the distribution of financially successful films in the motion picture industry. *Journal of Cultural Economics*, 23, 319–323.

Simonet, T. S. (1980). *Regression analysis of prior experience of key production personnel as predictors of revenues from high-grossing motion pictures in American release*. New York: Arno Press.

Simonoff, J., & Sparrow, I. (2000). Predicting movie grosses: Winners and losers, blockbusters and sleepers. *Chance*, 13 (3), 15–24.

Simonton, D. K. (1975). Age and literary creativity: A cross-cultural and transhistorical survey. *Journal of Cross-Cultural Psychology*, 6, 259–277.

Simonton, D. K. (1980). Thematic fame, melodic originality, and musical zeitgeist: A biographical and transhistorical content analysis. *Journal of Personality and Social Psychology*, 38, 972–983.

Simonton, D. K. (1983). Dramatic greatness and content: A quantitative study of eighty-one Athenian and Shakespearean plays. *Empirical Studies of the Arts*, 1, 109–123.

Simonton, D. K. (1984). Creative productivity and age: A mathematical model based on a two-step cognitive process. *Developmental Review*, 4, 77–111.

Simonton, D. K. (1986). Popularity, content, and context in 37 Shakespeare plays. *Poetics*, 15, 493–510.

Simonton, D. K. (1988). Age and outstanding achievement: What do we know after a century of research? *Psychological Bulletin*, 104, 251–267.

Simonton, D. K. (1989). The swan-song phenomenon: Last-works effects for 172 classical composers. *Psychology and Aging*, 4, 42–47.

Simonton, D. K. (1991). Emergence and realization of genius: The lives and works of 120 classical composers. *Journal of Personality and Social Psychology*, 61, 829–840.

Simonton, D. K. (1992). Gender and genius in Japan: Feminine eminence in masculine culture. *Sex Roles*, 27, 101–119.

Simonton, D. K. (1997). Creative productivity: A predictive and explanatory model of career trajectories and landmarks. *Psychological Review*, 104, 66–89.

Simonton, D. K. (2000). The music or the words? Or, how important is the libretto for an opera's aesthetic success? *Empirical Studies of the Arts*, 18, 105–118.

Simonton, D. K. (2002). Collaborative aesthetics in the feature film: Cinematic components predicting the differential impact of 2,323 Oscar-nominated movies. *Empirical Studies of the Arts*, 20, 115–125.

Simonton, D. K. (2004a). The "Best Actress" paradox: Outstanding feature films versus exceptional performances by women. *Sex Roles*, 50, 781–795.

Simonton, D. K. (2004b). *Creativity in science: Chance, logic, genius, and zeitgeist.* Cambridge, England: Cambridge University Press.

Simonton, D. K. (2004c). Film awards as indicators of cinematic creativity and achievement: A quantitative comparison of the Oscars and six alternatives. *Creativity Research Journal*, 16, 163–172.

Simonton, D. K. (2004d). Group artistic creativity: Creative clusters and cinematic success in 1,327 feature films. *Journal of Applied Social Psychology*, 34, 1494–1520.

Simonton, D. K. (2005a). Cinematic creativity and production budgets: Does money make the movie? *Journal of Creative Behavior*, 39, 1–15.

Simonton, D. K. (2005b). Film as art versus film as business: Differential correlates of screenplay characteristics. *Empirical Studies of the Arts*, 23, 93–117.

Simonton, D. K. (2007a). Cinema composers: Career trajectories for creative productivity in film music. *Psychology of Aesthetics, Creativity, and the Arts*, 1, 160–169.

Simonton, D. K. (2007b). Creative life cycles in literature: Poets versus novelists or conceptualists versus experimentalists? *Psychology of Aesthetics, Creativity, and the Arts*, 1, 133–139.

Simonton, D. K. (2007c). Film music: Are award-winning scores and songs heard in successful motion pictures? *Psychology of Aesthetics, Creativity, and the Arts*, 1, 53–60.

Simonton, D. K. (2007d). Is bad art the opposite of good art? Positive versus negative cinematic assessments of 877 feature films. *Empirical Studies of the Arts*, 25, 143–161.

Simonton, D. K. (2009a). Cinematic success, aesthetics, and economics: An exploratory recursive model. *Psychology of Creativity, Aesthetics, and the Arts*, 3, 128–138.

Simonton, D. K. (2009b). Cinematic success criteria and their predictors: The art and business of the film industry. *Psychology and Marketing*, 26, 400–420.

Simonton, D. K. (2009c). Controversial and volatile flicks: Contemporary consensus and temporal stability in film critic assessments. *Creativity Research Journal*, 21, 311–318.

Smith, S. M., McIntosh, W. D., & Bazzini, D. G. (1999). Are the beautiful good in Hollywood? An investigation of the beauty-and-goodness stereotype on film. *Basic and Applied Social Psychology*, 21, 69–80.

Smith, S. P., & Smith, V. K. (1986). Successful movies: A preliminary empirical analysis. *Applied Economics*, 18, 501–507.

Sochay, S. (1994). Predicting the performance of motion pictures. *Journal of Media Economics*, 7, 1–20.

Sommers, P. M. (1983–1984). Reel analysis. *Journal of Recreational Mathematics*, 16, 161–166.

Taylor, R. A. (1974). Television movie audiences and movie awards: A statistical study. *Journal of Broadcasting*, 18, 181–186.

Terry, N., Butler, M., & De'Armond, D. (2005). Determinants of domestic box office performance in the motion picture industry. *Southwestern Economic Review*, 32, 137–148.

Thompson, K. M., & Yokota, F. (2004). Violence, sex, and profanity in films: Correlation of movie ratings with content. *Medscape General Medicine*, 6(3), 3–54.

Thompson, W. F., Russo, F. A., & Sinclair, D. (1994). Effects of underscoring on the perception of closure in filmed events. *Psychomusicology*, 13, 9–27.

Tolstoy, L. (1917). *Anna Karenin* (Vol. 1, C. Garnett, Trans.). New York: Collier. (Original work published 1875–1877)

Trump, D. (1987). *Trump: The art of the deal*. New York: Random House.

Vitouch, O. (2001). When your ear sets the stage: Musical context effects in film perception. *Psychology of Music*, 29, 70–83.

Vogel, H. L. (1998). *Entertainment industry economics: A guide for financial analysis*. New York: Cambridge University Press.

Wainer, H. (1976). Estimating coefficients in linear models: It don't make no nevermind. *Psychological Bulletin*, 83, 213–217.

Walker, J. (Ed.). (2004). *Halliwell's film & video guide 2005*. New York: HarperCollins.

Wallace, W. T., Seigerman, A., & Holbrook, M. B. (1993). The role of actors and actresses in the success of films: How much is a movie star worth? *Journal of Cultural Economics*, 17, 1–27.

Walls, W. D. (2005a). Modelling heavy tails and skewness in film returns. *Applied Financial Economics*, 15, 1181–1188.

Walls, W. D. (2005b). Modeling movie success when "Nobody knows anything": Conditional stable-distribution analysis of film returns. *Journal of Cultural Economics*, 29, 177–190.

Wanderer, J. J. (1970). In defense of popular taste: Film ratings among professionals and lay audiences. *American Journal of Sociology*, 76, 262–272.

Waterman, D. (2005). *Hollywood's road to riches*. Cambridge, MA: Harvard University Press.

Weisberg, B. A., & Galenson, D. W. (2005). Creative careers: The life cycles of Nobel laureates in economics. Working Paper 11799, National Bureau of Economic Research, accessed from http://papers.nber.org/papers/, August 29, 2006.

Wiley, M., & Bona, D. (1993). *Inside Oscar: The unofficial history of the Academy Awards* (C. MacColl, Ed.). New York: Ballantine Books.

Wyatt, J. (1994). *High concept: Movies and marketing in Hollywood.* Austin, TX: University of Texas Press.

Zickar, M. J, & Slaughter, J. E. (1999). Examining creative performance over time using hierarchical linear modeling: An illustration using film directors. *Human Performance, 12,* 211–230.

Zufryden, F. S. (1996). Linking advertising to box office performance of new film releases: A marketing planning model. *Journal of Advertising Research, 36,* 29–41.

Zufryden, F. S. (2000). New film website promotion and box-office performance. *Journal of Advertising Research, 40,* 55–64.

Index